T0277173

OOPS!

OOPS!

The Worst Blunders of All Time

From Pandora's Box to Putin's War

David P. Barash

Skyhorse Publishing

In honor of Asa Jay Barash, who definitely is not an oops.

Skyhorse Publishing books may be purchased in bulk at special discounts for sales promotion, corporate gifts, fund-raising, or educational purposes. Special editions can also be created to specifications. For details, contact the Special Sales Department, Skyhorse Publishing, 307 West 36th Street, 11th Floor, New York, NY 10018 or info@skyhorsepublishing.com.

Skyhorse® and Skyhorse Publishing® are registered trademarks of Skyhorse Publishing, Inc.®, a Delaware corporation.

Visit our website at www.skyhorsepublishing.com.

10 9 8 7 6 5 4 3 2 1

Library of Congress Cataloging-in-Publication Data is available on file.

Cover design by Kai Texel
Cover images from Getty Images
All images contained within are public domain, from Wikimedia Commons.

Print ISBN: 978-1-5107-7635-7
Ebook ISBN: 978-1-5107-7661-6

Printed in the United States of America

Contents

Getting Started

We all make mistakes and nearly everyone likes to learn about them—especially when they've been made by someone else! Here you will encounter some of the most notable blunders, from the silly to the consequential, mythical to real, ancient history to current events. My hope is that these tales provide the pleasure of *Schadenfreude* along with some other, more reputable pleasures, too.

"Oops" is one of the first things that many toddlers say, and for good reason. They make a lot of mistakes, although no more than the rest of us. It has also become an internet meme, an apologetic subject line when someone realizes they have made a text or email error. This book, however, goes beyond private oops (oopses?) and looks instead at times when relatively big things have gone wrong and couldn't be called back.

It includes well-known blunders, from the iconic—Pandora opening that troublesome box, Eve taking her ill-advised bite—to great historical mistakes such as Napoleon's invasion of Russia in 1812, as well as some less monumental but nonetheless exemplary errors, such as the "Curse of the Bambino," when the Boston Red Sox sold Babe Ruth—at the time, primarily a pitcher—to the New York Yankees. (Red Sox fans still fume at the memory, while Yankee fans smirk.)

We'll also explore recent blunders that have had serious consequences, such as the tragically misguided use of thalidomide as a treatment for "morning sickness," while showcasing lesser-known but nonetheless important cases in history, such as how English General "Gentleman Johnny" Burgoyne made a string of unforced errors during the American Revolutionary War. They led to his disastrous defeat at the Battle of Saratoga, which then led to France committing itself to the American cause, and which in turn made that battle the war's turning point—and rendered Burgoyne's blunders especially consequential.

We'll visit the whimsical and the tragic, the former represented by, for example, "Wrong Way Corrigan," an early twentieth century aviator who was supposed to be flying nonstop from New York to California, but ended up in Ireland (most likely on purpose). The tragic is exemplified (but alas, not exhausted) by George W. Bush's disastrous invasion of Iraq and such medical missteps as lobotomy. Pointing out these and other mistakes will be an idiosyncratic journey, based on my own preferences and inclinations. This is necessarily true even in a book of nonfiction, because no writer can avoid putting their own spin on even the most scrupulous narration. But such writerly bias is particularly prominent in this book, perhaps because a work devoted to mistakes cannot help absorbing something of its subject matter. Selection bias is also unavoidable given that some of you, dear readers, will feel outraged that your own pet peeve was not included, or that others that made the cut don't deserve being labelled a mistake at all. Amazingly, at least to me, there are people who seriously believe that Donald Trump's handling of the COVID pandemic was a laudable example of presidential leadership during a public health crisis.[i] And even some who maintain that it wasn't a crisis or even that it never existed. Alternative facts, anyone?

Whatever else it is, this book is an exercise in Monday morning quarterbacking and 20/20 hindsight. Thus, we'll "backstrapolate": looking in the rearview mirror at mistakes made by others, as distinct from the extrapolation that everyone does in real time when they try to anticipate the future impact of something. However you look at it, no one is immune to errors. So, it's time for us "oopsers" to do less self-flagellation, an easing-up made easier by appreciating the colossal seriousness of some monumental mistakes that others have made, while also chuckling on occasion at the foolish blunders of others. Especially important others. They put their pants on one leg at a time, and they screw up all the time.

In 1987, Senator Lloyd Bentsen immodestly said, "I don't make many mistakes," and then added a dose of humility: "but when I do, it's a real doozy." Mr. Rogers used to reassure his young audience by singing, "Everyone makes mistakes, so why can't you. . . ?" Readers will find themselves not only informed but also reassured, all the more because you will encounter some doozies, made or alleged to have been made by others—many of which were really important, compared to which our own quotidian blunders are consolingly trivial.

This is neither an advice book nor a series of cautionary tales. It's an easy read, but also an informative one. It should also give rise to some useful take-home messages. Ideally, we should all benefit from our mistakes, making lemonade out of lemons. So, let's also follow Eleanor Roosevelt's advice and, "Learn from the mistakes of others. You cannot live long enough to make them all yourself." Indeed, learning from others' oops is generally easier than engaging in painful self-reflection, which is why it is often considered wise—sometimes even mandatory—to do a post-mortem on events and to debrief observers on how to avoid identified blunders in the future. In this way, an

---

[i] There is a Neapolitan saying that even a cockroach is beautiful in the eyes of its mother. Is this true of cult leaders in the eyes of their followers?

oops can become a learning opportunity. The epilogue briefly considers this process, which, for better or worse, must be left to each reader.

The third decade of the twenty-first century has been more than challenging. Part of my goal in writing *OOPS!* is not to downplay today's serious problems, but to provide an antidote to some of the dark sides of contemporary life. My hope is that *OOPS!* will give readers a temporary respite at a time when many might be tired of doom-scrolling and are ready for a restorative break, to look back and even smile on occasion at various milestones in our collective history of blunders. It is designed to be interesting, informative, somewhat thought-provoking, and also entertaining—sometimes darkly so. Hence, there is no consistent tone throughout. One stance, namely being something of a wise-ass, is suitable when describing "fat-finger trades" or Willie Shoemaker's premature celebratory stand-up, while a different attitude is called for when it comes to the Tuskegee Experiment or the Ukraine War. Given the subject matter of this book, such inconsistency is itself called for. If, as Ralph Waldo Emerson wrote, "A foolish consistency is the hobgoblin of little minds," we may reasonably conclude that the subjects herein are of little minds indeed, because they are foolishly consistent when it comes to making all sorts of mistakes.

Without descending into linguistic fussiness, it warrants mention that a "mistake" can be taken in several ways. Pretty much any war of choice is a mistake insofar as it is a crime against humanity. If initiated for plunder, glory, or territorial expansion, with disregard of its human or environmental costs, it is morally indefensible and a crime against humanity. But in the sense employed here, it is not necessarily a mistake unless it turns out to work against the goals and expectations of those making such a bad decision. For example, Adolf Hitler's invasion of the Soviet Union was a heinous act with despicable consequences (the death of millions, on both sides). What made it a "mistake," however—and thus worthy of inclusion in this book—is that it turned out to be a blunder from the perpetrator's perspective: it contributed greatly to Hitler losing World War II and his life. Donald Trump's various immoral and illegal acts have violated decency as well as the law, but what will enroll them in the annals of oops for our purposes is if and when he is held to account for these actions. (As of this writing, in mid-2023, he has been indicted on multiple counts of at least one felony crime, with others likely to follow.)

OOPS! is not intended for specialists, although I can foresee it appealing to anyone interested in human frailty. (Who isn't?) In some places, it is an "unwinding" book: appropriate for people who cherish the opportunity to, well, unwind, after a hard day at work—or, often as difficult if not more so, supervising children at home. It can be read straight through or opened at any point, when the mood strikes, because of its internal stand-alone structure. It also offers variety, not only in tone and subject matter, but also in the length of each entry.

Throughout, some serious contemporary problems such as Trump's monumental COVID blundering and Vladimir Putin's Ukraine War, will be seriously addressed. In others, the overriding tone will be puckish, especially when exploring events in the more distant past that were tragic for participants at the time, but are now blessedly in the rearview mirror. Regardless of tone, the frequent wise-guy commentary, and the unavoidable authorial subjectivity, please be assured that the factual material you are about to encounter is accurate. Okay, enough explanation, excuses, and equivocation. Let's really get started.

Enjoy!

Chapter

1

Iconic Myths

Many of the best-known stories involve mistakes and their consequences. We'll start with some notable ones from the Western tradition, which have no discernible basis in fact, but have nonetheless achieved significant cultural status.

1.1. The Apple of Their Eyes

Let's start at the beginning, with perhaps the biggest oops of all: Adam and Eve and that damned apple. (The serpent, too.) All three Abrahamic religions take this story seriously, although only Christianity holds that this

Adam and Eve making their Big Mistake (painting by Lucas Cranach the Elder, 1526).

early screw-up was responsible for the fall of humanity, along with the literal fall of the serpent. Two narratives are found in the Hebrew Bible; we'll deal only with the better-known second one in which God created Adam out of dust, ensconced him in the Garden of Eden, and said he could munch on whatever struck his fancy, but that he must not eat of the Tree of Knowledge of Good and Evil. Eve was then generated out of one of Adam's ribs and was presumably given the same injunction. But a nasty serpent showed up and disreputably told Eve that God really wouldn't punish her if she ate of that tree's fruit—more likely a fig than an apple—whereupon her "eyes would be opened," and she'd know good from evil, thus becoming "like God." The offer was so enticing that Eve took a bite. Then she proceeded to convince weak-willed Adam to do the same.

God was pissed.

He punished the serpent, decreeing that henceforth it must slither on its belly;[i] the fall of "man" thereby caused the literal falling down of that corrupt creature. Even the seemingly innocent ground suffered, forced to grow thistles and briars. But God's greatest wrath fell upon Adam and Eve, who had already lost their purity and innocence, having gained by their disobedient munching the wrong kind of knowledge: that they should be ashamed of their nakedness. God interrogated Adam, who blamed Eve, saving some implied blame for God himself; since after all, Adam didn't create that temptress, Eve, did he? Eve, in turn, blamed the serpent, who had no one to pin the blame on. There is, incidentally, no evidence implicating Satan directly. The serpent seems to have been a private contractor.

God cursed Adam with a life of hard labor, ending with death ("In the sweat of thy face shalt thou eat bread, till thou return unto the ground; for out of it wast thou taken: for dust thou art, and unto dust shalt thou return"). Eve was damned with painful childbirth and being forever subordinate to her husband. Moreover, both were banished from Eden so they wouldn't eat from another tree that would have given them eternal life. Cherubim with

---

[i] This was especially unfortunate because it deprived modern herpetologists the opportunity to see how the accursed creature had previously moved, perhaps uniquely by hopping on its tail like a pogo stick.

flaming swords were set to guard the Edenic gates, lest the two miscreants try to sneak back in. They didn't. And we, their descendants, have been stuck with the consequences of their screw-up ever since.

The Hebrew Bible contains many other examples of errors, some of them quite costly. There is, for example, Lot's wife looking back at Sodom when she wasn't supposed to do so; as a result, she was turned into a pillar of salt. There is also the Pharaoh's huge mistake in not letting the Israelites go, which brought about a sequence of water turning to blood, of frogs, lice, flies, livestock pestilence, boils, hail, locusts, darkness, and the killing of firstborn children. Then, Pharaoh oopsed by deciding to pursue the Israelites as they fled from bondage across the Red Sea, which parted for Moses and the good guys but then roared back and drowned Pharaoh and his pursuing chariot army. But the Israelites weren't immune to their own blunders. There are many cases in which they later disobeyed God and were punished as a result. (Indeed, Moses spent much of his time, especially in Numbers and Deuteronomy, interceding with God on their behalf—not always with success.)

1.2. Pandora's Problematic Pandemonium

The ancient Greeks had their own early blunderer: Pandora. According to Hesiod's poem *Works and Days*—written around 700 BCE—Pandora was the first woman, created by Hephaestus at the command of an angry Zeus in order to punish humanity for having accepted fire from Prometheus. She was designed as "an evil thing for men, as the price for fire." Pandora was made uniquely alluring, as well as insatiably curious, and was offered as a wife to Epimetheus, brother of Prometheus. Epimetheus had been warned by his brother to refuse any gift from the vengeful gods, but Pandora was so lovely that he couldn't resist (first mistake). As Hesiod misogynistically puts it, Pandora embodied "the deadly race and tribe of women who live amongst mortal men to their great trouble." (It's at least possible, but unlikely, that Hesiod's "their" refers to women's trouble and not to men's.)

Pandora had been given a jar, subsequently mistranslated (it appears, by the sixteenth-century humanist, Erasmus) as a box. She was told to keep it closed. Being curious, she couldn't resist opening it (second and most iconic mistake) whereupon all the world's evils, a.k.a. the seven deadly sins—Wrath, Gluttony, Greed, Envy, Sloth, Pride, and Lust— that had, unknown to Pandora, been put inside, flew out, to vex and burden the world ever since. Although it is widely thought that these sins are derived from the bible, in fact the whole troublesome array comes from Hesiod's poem

Pandora trying to close that box (based on a work by F. S. Church, nineteenth century).

depicting Pandora's actions.[ii] Appalled at her blunder, Pandora hastened to close the box/jar, keeping one more thing inside: hope.

It's worth noting that Hesiod's "hope" (ἐλπίς in ancient Greek) could also be translated as "expectation of good" or as "expectation of bad," and even as "deceptive expectation," the choice reflecting one's optimistic or pessimistic worldview.

It is certainly tempting to see hope remaining behind as comforting, insofar as it is therefore available to us. Or was Pandora's quick action a third mistake, because it kept hope forever trapped inside and thus unavailable? Finally, there is an even more dispiriting possibility. In *Human, All too Human*, Friedrich Nietzsche argued that hope is the cruelest sensation of all, because

> Man thinks the world of this treasure. It is at his service; he reaches for it when he fancies it. For he does not know that the jar which Pandora brought was the jar of evils, and he takes the remaining evil for the greatest worldly good—it is hope, for Zeus did not want man to throw his life away, no matter how much the other evils might torment him, but rather to go on letting himself be tormented anew. To that end, he gives man hope. In truth, it is the most evil of evils because it prolongs man's torment.[1]

Is the afterlife of hope, then, a fourth mistake, committed by the rest of us, something we are stuck with and that merely leads us on with false promises? Later in his poem, Hesiod comes down on the pessimistic side, arguing that hope is downright evil, not because it prolongs our torment, à la Nietzsche, but because it fills humanity with false expectations, making us lazy and less industrious.

[ii] Worth asking: Is it merely a coincidence that both of the primary bringers of trouble—Eve and Pandora—are depicted as women?

However you see it, Pandora, like Eve, is widely represented as nude, hence sexually alluring as well as a misogynistic representation of how our blundering species went from ease, plenitude, and happy innocence to our current fallen state.

1.3. A Horse, a Horse, Their City for a Horse

Just as Epimetheus couldn't resist Pandora, the Trojans couldn't resist a certain now-infamous horse, actually a huge wooden equine statue, built by the Greeks after ten years unsuccessfully besieging Troy. But those tricky Greeks were merely pretending to give up and sail home, having left their oversized "gift" outside the city gates while announcing that it was an offering for the goddess Athena, or, according to some accounts, a talisman of divine protection. Either way, the grateful, deluded Trojans were eager to bring the horse into their city, unaware that it was packed with Greek warriors including the famously cunning Odysseus (who had dreamed up the whole enterprise). A lethal oops.

A certain troublesome horse being dragged into Troy (painting by Giovanni Domenico Tiepolo, 1760).

Not all the Trojans were taken in, however. The priest, Laocoön, anticipated the plot and tried to warn his compatriots, famously announcing,
according to Virgil, "Beware of Greeks bearing gifts." But two sea serpents—
probably sent by Poseidon or perhaps Athena (who, wily herself, was especially fond of "wily Odysseus")—emerged and strangled Laocoön and
his two sons, whereupon the supposed wise men of Troy concluded that
Laocoön's warning was bogus. The soothsayer of Troy, Cassandra, also
prophesied woe, but there was a catch: it seems that Apollo had earlier promised her the gift of prophecy if she would have sex with him. She accepted
his gift but then, after it was bestowed, she reneged on her part of the deal,
whereupon Apollo—prohibited, like all gods, from taking back what he
had granted—added the punishment that, although Cassandra's prophecies
would indeed be correct, they wouldn't be believed.

The bottom line is that the people of Troy made one of the greatest
mistakes of all time: they brought in the horse, whereupon that night the
Greek warriors exited its innards and opened the city gates. In rushed the
Greek armies and Troy was looted and razed, its inhabitants massacred.
Although no single oops in imagined ancient Greek history compares
with the Trojan Horse, events surrounding the Trojan War offer some
other notable cases. Ten years earlier, the Greek commanding general,
Agamemnon, had been about to sail for Troy to bring back Helen, wife of
Ag's brother Menelaus. But Agamemnon angered Artemis by killing one of
her sacred deer, so the goddess arranged for unfavorable winds to keep the
Greek invasion fleet from setting sail. Artemis announced that she wouldn't
relent until Agamemnon agreed to sacrifice his daughter, Iphigenia, in
propitiation. He did so, the winds turned favorable, but when Agamemnon
returned home, he was murdered by Iphigenia's infuriated mother, his wife
Clytemnestra (aided, perhaps, by her lover Aegisthus).

Even before Agamemnon's error and setting the stage for the whole
fiasco was the ill-fated romantic rendezvous between Paris and Helen. Paris,
one of the innumerable children of Troy's King Priam, had the hots for
Helen, purportedly the world's loveliest woman, the face that launched a
thousand ships and all that. She was also—a minor inconvenience—already

married to Menelaus, king of Sparta and Agamemnon's less notable brother. In fairness to the lust-besotted Paris, he had been promised Helen by Aphrodite, goddess of beauty and sexual attraction, so perhaps he had no choice, being led by his cock-sure certainty that he was entitled to her. Also, Helen warrants some responsibility: although it seems unlikely that "no means no" was a policy operative in ancient Greece, there is no evidence that she was coerced to run away with pretty-boy Paris. Helen was a big girl and not just a beautiful one, so she was not innocent . . . in any sense of the word.

While besieging Troy, in an effort to retrieve Helen (an expedition whose payoff hardly seems worth all the death and destruction it generated), Agamemnon made yet another renowned mistake. A young woman named Chryseis had been captured by Achilles and given to Agamemnon as a prize of war. It turned out that Chryseis's father was a priest of Apollo, and, when Agamemnon refused to return her, Apollo was incensed and visited a devastating plague upon the Greeks, who eventually prevailed upon Agamemnon to return Chryseis. The Greek commander reluctantly agreed but to salve his pride insisted on taking Briseis, another "war bride" whom he fancied, from Achilles, who in turn was infuriated at the assault on his honor. This, in turn, precipitated the famous anger of Achilles, so prominent throughout *The Iliad*.

Achilles proceeded to sulk in his tent, refusing to fight, which also turned out to be a big, fat oops. His absence not only caused great battle losses for the Greeks, but induced them to persuade Achilles's dear friend (and possible lover), Patroclus, to fight in his stead. Achilles objected but eventually agreed to lend Patroclus his armor, which turned out to be yet another big mistake: in the ensuing battle, Patroclus was killed by the Trojan hero, Hector, who may have thought he was Achilles, Troy's bane. The death of Patroclus so upset Achilles that he returned to the fray and killed Hector. So, Agamemnon lost prestige by initially refusing to return Chryseis, which caused his army to lose men to a devastating plague; Achilles lost his friend/lover; and Hector lost his life, as did, eventually, Achilles, Agamemnon, and most of the Trojans . . . excepting Aeneas, who escaped and went on to found Rome.

OOPS!

The blunders continued: On his way home after the Trojan War, Odysseus taunted the cyclops, Polyphemus, after putting out the latter's one eye. Polyphemus was a son of the sea god, Poseidon, whose enmity from then on produced an array of disastrous storms that kept blowing Odysseus and his crew off course. One time, the crew thought that a bag that had been given to Odysseus by Aeolus, god of the wind, contained a treasure that Odysseus planned to hog for himself (which, they assumed, was why he never opened it)—but it contained a collection of ill winds, which the god had caught in the bag to be kept closed for the voyagers' benefit. Having been let out (shades of Pandora's oops), those winds proceeded to push them around the Mediterranean, delaying return to Ithaca by another five years. It seems that Odysseus's crew just couldn't resist making mistakes: once, having been warned not to touch sacred cattle belonging to the sun god, Helios, they slaughtered them nonetheless; okay, they were hungry. But as a result, their ship was splintered by a lightning bolt and only Odysseus survived to tell the tale.

Greek mythology presents its descendants with an especially wide array of "screw-oops," mostly committed by mortals in defiance of the gods. For example, Arachne brags about her skill in weaving and is turned into a spider by Athena. Sisyphus was an incorrigible trickster, eventually cursed for his effrontery by being condemned to eternally roll a great rock up a steep hill, only to have it roll back down again. While hunting, the Theban hero, Actaeon, happened to see the chaste goddess, Artemis, while she was bathing naked, whereupon she turned him into a stag that was torn to pieces by his own hunting dogs. Prometheus had the gall to give fire to human beings, for which he was chained to a mountain in the Caucasus and condemned to have his abdomen ripped open and his liver torn out every day by a great eagle, only to have it grow back each night whereupon he continued to serve as a bird feeder the next day.

Tantalus stole ambrosia from the gods and also tried to feed one of his dismembered children to the Olympians—ill-considered actions for which he was condemned to be eternally hungry and thirsty, with "tantalizing" food and drink withdrawing just out of reach when he tried to grab it.

Midas was a wealthy, incorrigibly avaricious king in Asia Minor, who was owed a favor by the god Dionysus. Midas wished that everything he touched would be turned to gold, whereupon his wish was granted, and Midas was initially delighted as he strutted about his palace transmuting objects into his favorite substance. But he soon recognized his oops when whatever he tried to eat or drink also turned to gold.

There was also a pair of high-altitude flops, Greek fly-boys who literally got carried away with their aerial exploits and didn't live to tell the tale. (Fortunately, someone else did.) The first fumbling and falling flyer was Phaethon, son of the sun god, Helios, or, in some accounts, Apollo. In any event, Phaethon found himself regularly teased and bullied by his contemporaries, who refused to believe that his father was a god. Phaethon asked his mother, an ocean nymph, whether his dad really was divine. She confirmed his paternity, and suggested that Phaethon talk to the old man about it. Phaethon begged his dad to help him prove that he really was the sun's son, by somehow linking him to the sun itself for everyone to see. Helios (or Apollo) agreed to help, and to prove his paternity he agreed to grant Phaethon whatever the young man asked. Like a teenager without a license who pleaded to drive the car, Phaethon asked to be allowed to drive his father's chariot of the sun in its daily journey across the sky, "Just for one day, dad. What could possibly go wrong?" Helios, or Apollo, was convinced it was a bad idea and as his son soon discovered, father knows best. But a promise is a promise, and Helios consented. Young Phaethon, who didn't even have a learner's permit, was totally unable to control the feisty and powerful horses that pulled the chariot of the sun, which veered too close to Earth and began to catch it on fire. Zeus wasn't pleased, and to save his favorite planet, he did his usual thing: he hurled a thunderbolt at Phaethon, who crashed, but at least the Earth didn't burn.

Our other flying fool was Icarus, son of Daedalus, who was no fool. Daddy Daedalus was the world's greatest engineer and construction maven. He designed the plan for the magnificent Minoan Palace of Knossis. When he sculpted a statue, it had to be tied down because it was so lifelike that it would otherwise walk away. Daedalus also had a major role in one of the most unsavory sexual episodes of Greek mythology. King Minos of Crete had asked the god Poseidon for a spectacularly beautiful bull as a sign of his favor, promising that he'd return the beast to Poseidon by sacrificing it. (Minos had the Greeks' greatest sea fleet at the time, so a good relationship with the ocean god was a big deal.) But Minos reneged on his promise—evidently, the beauty of the beast was also a big deal, one that was about to get even bigger. Infuriated by Minos's betrayal, Poseidon arranged for the king's wife, Pasifae, to go completely nuts over this bull, burning with passion to have sex with it; that's right, sex with a bull. Not as crazy as you might think: this bull was uniquely handsome. But this particular bull wouldn't oblige. Maybe its recalcitrance was also part of Poseidon's revenge.

In any event, so it was that an unbearably frustrated Pasifae called upon Daedalus, who fashioned a wooden statue of a sexy cow. With Pasifae inside and suitably contorted, the bull performed perfectly and Pasifae was perfectly satisfied. Sure enough, she became perfectly pregnant and gave birth to a grotesquely imperfect bull-human hybrid, the Minotaur. For some reason, King Minos wasn't especially proud of his stepson, so he, too, commissioned Daedalus, this time to design a labyrinth within which to stash his wife's shame—and shortly, to also stash his enemies as well as unfortunate people regularly sent to Crete as tribute to the local hegemon, knowing that the monstrous creature would do them in. No bull.

Minos and Daedalus soon had a falling out when Daedalus advised Minos's 100 percent human daughter, Princess Ariadne, to endow her visiting boyfriend Theseus with a ball of string, which, when unraveled, allowed Theseus to find his way out after killing the aforementioned Mino-taur. Minos was seriously irked and stuck Daedalus and his son, Icarus, in the labyrinth: the prison-designer imprisoned in his creation. Daedalus, however, was a clever fellow. According to Ovid, in his *Metamorphoses*, Daedalus reasoned that "'He [Minos] may thwart our escape by land or sea but the sky is surely open to us: we will go that way: Minos rules everything but he does not rule the heavens.'"[2] True enough, but Daedalus was soon to discover that he, Daedalus, did not rule his son.

Daedalus giving Icarus a push (engraving by A.G.L. Desnoyers, date unknown).

Daddy Daedalus fashioned enormous wings out of feathers (in some versions, branches) held together with wax, and he and his son took to the air. Free at last! Clever Dad had warned Icarus not to fly too close to the sun or the wax would melt, or too close to the ocean lest the wings get soggy and stop working. But Icarus, being young and super-psyched at his aerial freedom, violated his father's precepts and ascended too near the sun. The wax holding his wings together melted and he fell into the sea and drowned.

In both stories, sons have brief, lethally cogent reasons to regret disobeying dear old dad, which should be a cautionary tale for everyone, but isn't. More useful, on the other hand, has been employing the sad fates of both Phaethon and Icarus as warnings about the oops of solar over-reach.

1.4. I Dream of Genie ... and Wish I Hadn't Opened That Damned Bottle

In yet another iconic oops from a different culture, let's turn to a famous story from the *Arabian Nights*. A poor Arab fisherman would regularly cast his net four times each day, but never more. One day, he repeatedly cast his net but with disappointing results: first he pulled up a dead donkey, then a

Fisherman confronted by an unfriendly Genie (painting by René Bull, 1898).

pitcher filled with dirt, and then pieces of broken pottery. The fourth time, however, he was overjoyed to find a copper bottle in his net, capped with the seal of Solomon. He figured he could sell it for a lot of money, but was curious about what was inside and so—you guessed it—he opened it (channeling Pandora). Out came a torrent of smoke that condensed into a malign genie, "as big as a mountain," who offered the terrified fisherman a reward: he could choose how the genie would kill him, whereupon our fisher-friend realized that he made a big boo-boo indeed. It turned out that Mr. Genie had been nursing a grudge against humankind ever since being encased in that container by Solomon himself some centuries ago.

The genie told the aghast fisherman that for the first century of his bottled-up, undersea imprisonment, he had sworn to reward whoever liberated him with great wealth. But no one came. The second century, he swore to grant three wishes to his liberator—again to no avail. After that, the genie became enraged and vowed to grant his liberator only the choice of how to be killed. Fortunately the condemned man was a quick-thinker; it just wasn't possible, he claimed, for such an immense creature to have been contained in such a small bottle. Eager to show off his potent genie-hood—but evidently not very bright—the genie obliged by transforming back into smoke and re-entering his former prison, at which point the fisherman promptly re-stoppered the bottle. After telling each other a number of stories, interspersed with the genie's pleas for release and promises to aid the fisherman in return, the fisherman finally relented and let out the genie once again. The genie kept his word and they all lived happily ever after, giving an unusually happy ending to a pair of classic blunders: first, the fisherman's mistake in opening the bottle and letting out the genie, and then the genie's mistake in letting himself be talked into going back in.

As we'll see, most of the time when someone uncorks a comparable bottle—whether in fiction or reality—the genie can't be put back.

Chapter

2

Famous Fiction

The previous cases are all fiction, or, at most, renowned narratives embroidering upon real events. The material in this chapter, by contrast, will involve fiction qua fiction. Their prominence speaks to the abiding human interest in stories about mistakes.

2.1. Bloody Bluebeard's Bad News Basement

Bluebeard has become a cultural meme and a most unpleasant one. It has an ancient history, reflected in various folk tales from distant lands, but the version most familiar to Westerners comes from medieval France. It speaks of a wealthy and powerful man who may or may not have had a blue beard. No matter. He evidently was fond of murdering his wives (to whom he seems never to have extended any personal fondness) by chopping off their heads and then hanging their corpses on the walls of his secret basement chamber. Before conclusively ending each of his marriages, he would announce that he had to go out of town, giving his bride a ring of keys, and inviting each woman to enter any room they wish, to enjoy whatever treasures and delights were therein stored. But under no circumstance—get it? as in never, ever— were they to use the smallest key, by which they would gain admittance to a particular locked chamber in the basement. You, dear reader, can guess what happened. Each time.

Yet another case of pinning the tale on a disobedient damsel.

Our story begins with Mr. Bluebeard, notoriously ugly but extraordinarily wealthy, who uses the allure of the latter to convince beautiful country girls to ignore the former. In a particularly widespread version of the tale, our anti-hero is already considered a bit suspect because each of his wives seems to mysteriously disappear, soon replaced by new ones. Mr. Beard visits a neighbor and promptly asks to marry one of his daughters, each of whom is terrified. But he wows them with a sumptuous banquet and the youngest daughter is won over. Accordingly, she becomes mistress of his great household, but they don't quite live happily ever after.

Mr. Beard soon announces that he must make a solo trip, but before leaving, he gives his bride the usual rigmarole: here's a ring of keys and you may use them to open all of the doors in the palace . . . except for the smallest key, which leads to a room in the cellar. Déjà vu. Keep out of that one, he tells her, "but if you happen to open it, you may expect my just anger and resentment." Oscar Wilde once announced "I can resist anything except temptation," and the same applies to Mrs. Bluebeard as it had to her predecessors. She unlocks the door, enters the forbidden room, and finds the floor awash in blood, with the corpses of her husband's previous wives hanging by hooks on the walls. Horrified, she leaves immediately, relocking the door, but in her panic she had dropped the key onto the floor, leaving it stained with blood. Channeling Lady Macbeth and her hands, our heroine tries desperately to wash the key clean, but to no avail, so when Bluebeard returns and demands to look at the keys, the jig is up.

Bluebeard and one of his wives (engraving by Gustave Doré, 1862).

But there is a happy ending (at least for Mrs. B): Just as the evil fellow is about to chop off her head, her brothers arrive and dispatch him instead. The newly widowed but very much alive Mrs. B eventually marries a Prince Charming, who doesn't appear to have a ring full of keys, an axe, a bloody, secret chamber, or a slew of murder victims in his past. Compared with her former hubby, he is charming indeed.

There's an obvious reason to see Mrs. B as the oopser, and she is, twice over: for opening the forbidden door and for agreeing to marry the creep in the first place. Bluebeard's prior wives all made the same two mistakes, and of course, Bluebeard himself made some big ones. No surprise that there is a Freudian take on this tale, in which the key is a penis, the room a womb, and the keyhole a vagina, while blood on the key represents loss of virginity. More often, the story of Bluebeard and his victims is seen as a cautionary misogynistic tale, warning people—women in particular—to do what they're told. A more relevant take-home message is a warning to women who find themselves in relationships in which their lover or husband initially seems desirable and benevolent, only to discover that an abusive Bluebeard lurks underneath.

2.2. To Do or Not to Do? (Will's Advice: Not!)

William Shakespeare's plays, especially his tragedies, are marinated in mistakes by the principle characters, including excessive credulousness, plain old-fashioned foolishness, hot-headedness, general weakness of character, or overweening ambition. King Lear immediately starts off his own play with an egregious oops in Act 1, Scene 1, foolishly dividing his kingdom among his daughters, two of whom he lethally misjudges as reliably committed to him while banishing Cordelia, his only truly loving child. The result is the death of both Lear and Cordelia, and many others to boot. In the same play, another main character, Gloucester, foolishly disparages his out-of-wedlock son, Edmund, after which the (literal and figurative) bastard—motivated by outsized greed and ambition along with anger at his father—turns on his half-brother Edgar, who credulously accepts Edmund's lies. Their father,

King Lear, wrongfully angry at Cordelia (print by Richard Earlom, 1792).

Gloucester, like Lear, also mistakes the character of his children, believing his bad son, Edmund, and turning against his good one, Edgar. As if these oops aren't enough, there are more galore: Both of Lear's nasty daughters fall for the same bad bastard, Edmund, and each kills the other. Cordelia, the good one, tries to help her father by invading Lear's former domain with a French army, but fails, is captured, and eventually killed. Cornwall, the husband of one of Lear's no-good daughters, shows excessive cruelty when he blinds Gloucester and is killed as a result.

Macbeth's initial and ultimately lethal blunder is overconfidence, after being told by a trio of witches that he'll become king. He also succumbs to the murderous ambition of Lady M, which she cleverly combines with appeals to his manly man vanity. (Or perhaps his anxiety.) In any event, after murdering King Duncan to speed up the prophecy and then having become

MACBETH.

Toil and trouble;
Fire burns and cauldron bubble!

Macbeth meeting the Three Witches (anonymous lithograph, 1825).

king, Macbeth commits one oops after another, killing anyone he considers a threat to his crown, thereby increasing the number of outraged subjects who in fact become threats to his crown. Macbeth's final oops is foolishly mistaking the witches' announcement that he's safe until Burnham Wood comes to Dunsinane Castle, and, moreover, that no man born of woman can kill him. Both happen. And of course, Lady Macbeth felt remorse for her role in the murder of King Duncan. "Will these hands ne'er be clean?" Answer: Ne'er. Another big mistake that can't be undone. Or washed away.

Othello believes Iago's lies that Desdemona has been cheating, so he kills his innocent wife. Credulousness plus an unhealthy dose of violent sexual jealousy. In his final speech, Othello begs his listeners to speak of him "as one that lov'd not wisely but too well." Not wisely indeed. Iago, too, makes more than his share of mistakes, not least his entire evil plan, acting upon nothing but what Samuel Coleridge called "motiveless malignity." Then there's the famously dithering Hamlet, who finally acts, thinking he's stabbing his murderous uncle, Claudius, but instead killing the elderly

Othello after killing Desdemona (painting by Alexandre-Marie Colin, 1825).

bumbler, Polonius, who had made his own oops by hiding behind an arras. This Polonius assault causes genuine trouble for the melancholy Dane, who compounds the blunder by angrily dismissing Ophelia, his true love. Not to be outdone, Shakespeare's history plays are a continuing chronicle of people thinking, incorrectly, that they can literally get away with murder. In pretty much all cases, they can't.

Hamlet, immediately after his Polonius assault (print by Eugène Delacroix, 1835).

2.3. Mary Shelley Writes about a Frankly Scary Oops

It was a dark and stormy night. Really. A group of creative, unconventional young adults—eighteen-year-old Mary Shelley, her husband, Percy Bysshe Shelley, Lord Byron, his sometime lover and Mary's stepsister, Claire Clairmont, and physician John Polidori—were stuck because of terrible weather in a rented house on Lake Geneva. They agreed to write ghost stories, whereupon young Mary came up with a beaut. First oops, committed by nearly everyone, is referring to the eponymous monster as Frankenstein, whereas in fact "Frankenstein" is Dr. Victor Frankenstein, who created the creature. Another widespread reader's oops is thinking

Frankenstein's monster, portrayed by Boris Karloff (from *The Bride of Frankenstein*, Universal Studios, NBCUniversal, 1935).

that the monster is a hulking, grunting idiot, an error generated by the many dramatizations of Shelley's story, not least via Lon Cheney's portrayal.[i] In Mrs. Shelley's original version, hulking he is, but hardly grunting: the monster quickly learns English and soon speaks eloquently and with philosophical panache.

But the blunders inherent in the novel are overwhelmingly those of Victor Frankenstein, starting with creating the creature in the first place. Looking back on his enormous oops and its terrible consequences, Victor urges his readers to "Learn from me . . . by my example, how dangerous is the acquirement of knowledge and how much happier that man is who believes his native town to be the world, than he who aspires to become greater than his nature will allow."[1] In short, hubris is a big no-no.

When Victor F sees his creation, he is immediately repelled, not only at what he had done, but at the physical appearance of his creation. He had tried to make the creature handsome, but it turns out deformed and hideous to see: "I had worked hard for nearly two years, for the sole purpose

---

[i] Don't confuse Lon with Dick.

of infusing life into an inanimate body. For this I had deprived myself of rest and health. I had desired it with an ardour that far exceeded moderation; but now that I had finished, the beauty of the dream vanished, and breathless horror and disgust filled my heart."[2]

He is shocked, shocked at what he had wrought:

How can I describe my emotions at this catastrophe, or how delineate the wretch whom with such infinite pains and care I had endeavoured to form? His limbs were in proportion, and I had selected his features as beautiful. Beautiful! Great god, His yellow skin scarcely covered the work of muscle and arteries beneath; his hair was of a lustrous black, and flowing; his teeth of a pearly whiteness; but these luxuriances only formed a more horrid contrast with his watery eyes, that seemed almost of the same colour as the dun white sockets in which they were set, his shriveled complexion, and straight black lips.

I beheld the wretch—the miserable monster whom I had created. . . . No mortal could support the horror of that countenance. A mummy again endued with animation could not be so hideous as that wretch. I had gazed on him while unfinished; he was ugly then, but when those muscles and joints were rendered capable of motion, it became a thing such as even Dante could not have conceived.[3]

Victor's horror at his creation may have been unavoidable, but a strategic white lie ("Hi there, aren't you cute!") would have served everybody well, although the story would have been much less compelling and likely not included in the present book. Instead, his rejection of the "wretch" (a.k.a. "fiend," "monster," etc.) is yet another monstrous oops, causing Mr. Monster to leave in a huff and attempt to make it on his own. What could go wrong? As the creature recounts:

I knew that I possessed no money, no friends, no kind of property. I was, besides, endowed with a figure hideously deformed and loathsome; I was not even of the same nature as man. I was more agile than they and could subsist upon coarser diet; I bore the extremes of heat and cold with less injury to my frame; my stature far exceeded theirs. When I looked around I saw and heard of none like me. Was I, then, a monster, a blot upon the earth, from which all men fled and whom all men disowned? . . .

Accursed creator! Why did you form a monster so hideous that even *you* turned from me in disgust? God, in pity, made man beautiful and alluring, after his own image; but my form is a filthy type of yours, more horrid even from the very resemblance. Satan had his companions, fellow devils, to admire and encourage him, but I am solitary and abhorred.[4]

In his anger and despair, our miserable monster offers to go far away and not bother anyone again if Dr. Frank would go further and make him a mate. The scientist initially agrees, then changes his mind and destroys the prospective bride, thereby consigning his creation to a life of solitary bachelorhood, on top of his intolerable isolation from all of humankind. Another big oops. As the creature puts it, "the fallen angel becomes a malignant devil. Yet even that enemy of God and man had friends and associates in his desolation; I am alone."[5] The infuriated "fiend" fiendishly announces that he will be with Victor on the latter's wedding night. Having been denied his own connubial bliss, the "wretch" kills Victor's bride, along with many others, thereby compounding the consequences of Victor's blunders, who devotes the rest of his life to hunting and, if possible, destroying the manifestation of all of his mistakes. He dies instead, or rather, first.

Toward the story's end, the sad and sorry monster confesses to a ship captain that his crimes were themselves major mistakes, and have only made him more miserable.

Let that be a lesson to us all.

Chapter 3

A Multiplicity of Major, Myopic Military Mistakes

From here we move from fiction to fact, and a heavy dose of death. There is a famous observation, widely attributed to the French diplomat, Talleyrand, that executing one of the Bourbon dukes during the French Revolution was "worse than a crime; it was a mistake." We don't know for sure who said this but it applies to all the oops presented in this chapter, and to many others as well.

3.1. The Silliness in Sicily

The bloody and brutal Peloponnesian War between Athens and Sparta had been grinding on inconclusively for many years. But by 416 BCE there was an uneasy truce, more like a prolonged Cold War known as the Peace of Nicias (we'll hear more of Nicias shortly). Word soon arrived in Athens that Segesta, a small Athenian-allied city in Sicily, was seeking help in a war with another Sicilian city, this one allied with Sparta. In order to encourage Athenian support, the Segestans promised that they would defray costs for an Athenian naval expedition. They deceived the Athenian ambassadors, making it seem that Segesta was wealthier than it was by showing part of their gold and silver cache and claiming that there was "more where that came from."

When the Segestan representatives arrived in Athens and made their request, the Athenian Assembly was tempted to acquiesce, but held back for several reasons: Sicily was far away, such an enterprise would likely cause war with Syracuse, the most powerful city-state on Sicily, and—worse yet—it risked provoking renewed war with Sparta. On the other hand, Syracuse was closely allied with Corinth, long the greatest commercial rival of Athens, so giving the Syracusans a black eye was an appealing prospect. The decision was stalemated.

Enter Alcibiades, a rising young Athenian aristocrat and aspiring war-leader who was ambitious, charismatic, vain, and a brilliant orator. Three years earlier, and even though Athens and Sparta were officially enjoying the Peace of Nicias, he had attempted to orchestrate a league of anti-Spartan city-states located on the Peloponnese, the oddly shaped Greek peninsula where Sparta was located. The effort failed, but Alcibiades bounced back, becoming a general and leader of the political faction eager for renewed war with Sparta. Alcibiades pushed so strongly for a Sicilian military expedition that it was eventually approved—and proved to be the beginning of Athens's undoing. Fifteen years previously, shortly before the great plague of Athens (around 430 BCE), its finest leader, Pericles, had observed in his renowned funeral oration, "What I fear is not the enemy's strength, but our own mistakes."[1] Cue the Sicilian expedition.

At the time, there was a highly regarded politician and general named Nicias who had fought for a decade against Sparta, earning a reputation as a cautious but effective military leader. He also didn't like Alcibiades. More a "dove" than a "hawk," Nicias had negotiated the peace with Sparta that bore his name, and—to no one's surprise—was strongly opposed to a new military undertaking to Sicily, being concerned that it might fail, and that it risked renewing the Peloponnesian War, in which he had fought and which he had worked so hard to end. Nicias criticized Alcibiades as too young and too fond of his own personal advancement. Trying to undercut Alcibiades's persuasiveness, Nicias pointed to the strength and wealth of Syracuse, emphasizing how massive and costly a successful invasion would have to be, even if Sparta were to stay out of the ensuing fray.

But Nicias's efforts backfired, becoming the biggest oops of his previously successful life. Thus, instead of dousing Athenian enthusiasm, his warnings ended up convincing the assembly to approve an even larger expedition so as to guarantee success. Thanks to Nicias's misreading of the Athenian military mood, the Athenian Armada was expanded from sixty ships to 140, with associated men, horses, and supplies. It set sail with three generals put in charge: Alcibiades (the war hawk), Nicias (the skeptic), and Lamachus (neither pro nor con; probably included to provide a calming and balancing influence). But a whole lot was to go wrong.

The next oops occurred before the expedition even reached Sicily. The Athenians had expected to pick up allies along the south coast of Italy, but no such luck. They were regularly turned down, eventually realizing that they would have to conquer Sicily by themselves. Then the Athenians learned, belatedly, that the Segestans didn't have anything like the wealth they had claimed, so they couldn't underwrite the war. Athens and its citizens would also have to pay for it by themselves. Nicias suggested that the expedition should therefore give up its attempt and return to Athens, after briefly showing the flag around various Sicilian ports. But Alcibiades and the war party won out. Again.

Then came more bad news: the fleet got word from Athens that Alcibiades, the leader most responsible for the whole enterprise, the most dynamic of the generals, and the one the troops most eagerly followed, was to be arrested and brought back to be tried for his life. It turns out that just before the expedition sailed, someone had defaced sacred statues of the god Hermes, and Alcibiades was accused of the capital crime. He agreed to go back, but instead snuck away and hightailed it to . . . Sparta!

This defection turned out to be doubly costly to Athens. Not only was Alcibiades (despite his drawbacks) a capable and popular general, but, having been sentenced to death *in absentia* back in Athens, he retaliated—and sought to endear himself to his new Spartan hosts—by disclosing Athens's military plans to his home city's sworn enemy. He also used his knowledge of Athenian geostrategic weaknesses to advise the Spartans how to initiate an effective land blockade of Athens, which was duly done, and which turned out to be devastatingly effective.

When they finally landed in Sicily, the Athenian invaders found that the Syracusans were initially a bit slow preparing their defenses, in part because some within the city had argued that advance notice of the Athenian invasion was fake news. (Denying reality, to one's detriment, has a long pedigree.) But once it got organized, Syracuse was far more effective militarily than had been anticipated. The initial Athenian assaults were successful enough, however, so that the city was effectively besieged. But Syracusan forces were about to be reinforced by a large Spartan expedition, for which our old friend Alcibiades was responsible. He had agitated the Spartan leadership by claiming that if the Athenians were victorious in Sicily, their next move would be against Sparta itself.

Before the Spartans arrived to buttress the Syracusans, Athenian reinforcements appeared, and things looked better for their side. The seesawing continued yet again, when a Spartan convoy landed, bringing among other military force, a large cavalry contingent; the Athenians had almost no horses. The fighting went on, with Athenian losses especially heavy, and when the general Lamachus was killed in battle, this left tired, ill, and unenthusiastic Nicias in sole command. He sent a desperate message to Athens, requesting that the expedition be recalled or that, alternatively, Athens send massive reinforcements.

Athenian navy off the coast of Sicily (anonymous engraving, nineteenth century).

But yet again, Nicias was misjudging his Athenian colleagues, assuming once more that they were militarily cautious, like himself. His ploy failed in much the same way as his earlier effort: instead of ordering a strategic retreat, the assembly opted to double down, succumbing to the fallacy of sunken costs, sometimes called the Gambler's Fallacy, in which individuals often insist on investing more if they have already spent a lot in the past. A rational, and far better, tactic is to spend based on the likely return on what that *present* investment is likely to generate. (Americans fell prey to this fallacy during the Vietnam War, when it was argued that we've gone so far, we can't stop now, or else the people and treasure already lost will have been sacrificed in vain. As a result, yet more lives and treasure were sacrificed ... also in vain.)

By approving more ships and soldiers, Athens continued to throw good money, good men, good horses, and good ships after bad, while the war went worse yet. Even after the additional expedition landed in Sicily, the Athenian situation continued to deteriorate until finally, Nicias was about to get his way at last and take his depleted army and navy back home. He hadn't reckoned, however, on an eclipse of the moon. (Most of us don't.) Nicias was very superstitious, and he interpreted a lunar eclipse as a bad omen. He consulted soothsayers, who advised waiting several weeks before high-tailing it back to Athens. And so, the Athenians dithered and delayed, further ceding the initiative to the combined forces of Syracuse and Sparta.

The besiegers found themselves besieged and soon the Athenian expedition was wiped out, pretty much to the last man. Nicias surrendered and was executed. The failed Sicily expedition was a devastating blow to Athens, which lost something like forty thousand men and two hundred warships, thereby depleting both its military manpower and its once invincible navy. At least as bad, news of the disaster induced many of Athens's allies, eager to be on the winning side, to desert it and align themselves with Sparta. Persia also joined in against Athens, whose Delian League began to fall apart.

According to Thucydides, in his *History of the Peloponnesian War*, no one in contemporary Greece was surprised that, after this disastrous campaign (lasting from 415–413 BCE), Athens eventually fell to Sparta. For them, the Sicilian Campaign was indeed the beginning of the end. What was remarkable was that the Athenians somehow managed to hold out and continue fighting for another ten years. Also remarkable was the extent to which Athens had blundered, having been duped—or duped themselves—about so many things: the nonexistent wealth of their importunate ally in Sicily; the failed prospect of recruiting additional allies en route; their anticipated ability to overwhelm Syracuse; their stubborn confidence that the war could be won if they just sent additional expeditions into the Sicilian meatgrinder; and their failure to anticipate Spartan intervention. Then there was Nicias's twice repeated, counterproductive misreading of Athenian eagerness for war along with his own indecisiveness in the field, combined with his superstitiousness. But the greatest Athenian oops was letting themselves be bamboozled by Alcibiades in the first place.

This fellow was a piece of work. His flexible allegiance had been such that after enthusiastically beating the drum for the ultimately catastrophic campaign in Sicily, and after defecting to Sparta, he then left abruptly (having worn out his welcome there, even without defacing any holy statues) to join the anti-Greek Persian Empire and *then*, astonishingly, was re-invited to Athens where he was given another generalship, before eventually dying under disputed conditions back in the Persian Empire.

In his book, *The Lives of the Noble Greeks and Romans*, Plutarch described Alcibiades as "the least scrupulous and most entirely careless of human beings"—by which he meant ethically indifferent, not sloppy— while according to Aristophanes, in his comedy, *Frogs*, Athens "yearns for him, and hates him too, but ever wants him back." A man of extraordinary charm, ability, a sociopath, narcissist, and a master of treachery, Alcibiades made a career of causing others to err, although the Sicily campaign also showcased the Athenian capacity for oops, even without his unique contribution.

3.2. Teutonic Triumph in the Teutoburg

Jumping ahead two centuries, the Greeks had descended while the Romans ascended. The year was 217 BCE during the Second Punic War with Carthage, and Rome was about to fall prey to one of the most notable ambushes in history. Making the proverbial long (and fascinating) story short, after famously crossing the Alps, Hannibal lured a Roman army to attack what they thought was a small Carthaginian force at Lake Trasimene, whereupon Hannibal descended upon them from a forest where the bulk of the Carthaginian army had been hiding. The surprised Roman legions were either cut down immediately or forced into the lake where they were promptly massacred or drowned in their heavy armor. An entire Roman army was lost, and the city of Rome thrust (temporarily) into panic mode.

For all its magnificent military successes, Roman forces periodically endured some of history's most momentous disasters, which is unsurprising given that the Pax Romana lasted a long time, during which Pax was only part of what happened. Nonetheless, being so thoroughly outwitted by Hannibal at Lake Trasimene was among the great oops of all time.

Sometimes military disasters occur simply because battles tend to be "zero-sum games" in which there is a winner and a loser. Other times, however, losing comes from a blunder that is easy to recognize . . . in retrospect. Among these, the Battle of Teutoburg Forest is especially infamous, once again for the defeat that Rome suffered, this time two centuries after their shellacking by Hannibal at Lake Trasimene.

The condensed account is as follows. It was 9 CE, two centuries after the end of the Punic Wars against Carthage, which Rome eventually won. Augustus Caesar was emperor and there was about to be another ambush, one that once again (from the Roman perspective) could have and should have been avoided. An alliance of Germanic tribes ambushed and destroyed three entire Roman Legions, roughly twenty thousand men. Varus was the commanding Roman general of what Roman historians subsequently called the Varian Disaster—which gives away the outcome. Varus had been lethally deceived by his top assistant, Arminius, and therein lies a tale of treachery if you are Roman, or of brilliant strategizing if you are a Germanic "barbarian," and of a big-time blunder if you are reading this book.

Arminius's father was a Germanic king who had been defeated by Roman forces, whereupon the young Arminius was sent to Rome as a hostage to ensure his father's good behavior. This was common practice at the time. Armenius was a capable student who rose within Roman ranks and reached the level of "equestrian," an aristocratic class ranking just below that of senator. As part of his education, Arminius learned perfect Latin, earned the trust of the Roman leadership, and familiarized himself with Roman battle tactics, all the while intending to chastise Rome for its harsh treatment of "Germania" and its people. Just twenty-five years old, he was sent from Rome to provide General Varus with an insider's knowledge on how to put down a revolt of the Germanic tribes. Insider indeed: unknown to Varus, Arminius began plotting with local leaders to unite the feuding locals against the Romans.

In the autumn of 9 CE, Varus was obliged to send eight of his eleven legions to put down a distant Germanic rebellion, whereupon Arminius sensed his opportunity. He gave a false report to Varus about a nearby rebellion in northern Germania, persuading him to divert his remaining three legions along with three cavalry detachments and six legionary cohorts, which had been heading to winter quarters, in order to suppress this nonexistent rebellion. It would be, Arminius confidently stated, the Roman equivalent of a cakewalk. The night before the column departed, Varus had been told by Arminius's own father-in-law to beware of Arminius, but Varus ignored the warning, thinking that it simply sprang from a personal feud between the two men. To Varus, Arminius was a reliable and subservient vassal. Moreover, Varus's gullibility was further revealed when he followed his young "advisor's" directions and took a supposed short cut that involved marching along a narrow road through a dense forest. It was just what Arminius needed to spring his trap.

Once the Romans were deep within the woods, turning back was almost impossible, in part because of the difficulty of reversing direction on so restricted a path, and because their line was stretched out something like ten miles, with the troops and their interspersed camp followers struggling with gloom and mud. Arminius then left Varus's side, saying that he was going to arouse some Germanic tribes to reinforce the Romans. And arouse them he did, to fight, but hardly on their side. The Romans, not expecting any armed resistance, were not marching in battle formation. After all, they had a local guide, and the rebels were supposedly some distance off. The legionary line was not only thin and constrained by dense forest on both sides as well as perilously long, but to make matters worse, the over-confident Varus neglected to send scouting parties ahead.

Battle of Teutoburg Forest (painting by Otto Albert Koch, 1909).

Unable to maneuver, retreat, or advance, the Roman army was suddenly set upon, front, back, and from all sides. Roman forces, unable to form a battle line, were annihilated after a one-sided three-day fight. Varus fell on his sword, following what turned out to be one of the most devastating defeats suffered by Rome and one of ancient Germany's most celebrated victories. The Battle of Teutoburg Forest also marked the end of what had been Rome's triumphant expansion in central Europe. Never again did Rome conquer the people east of the Rhine, although not for want of trying.

Arminius sent the severed head of Varus to another Germanic king, hoping to establish an alliance, but the recipient refused the offer and sent it on to Rome, for burial, after which the two early German leaders led their forces against each other in a war for local supremacy that nobody won. Even after Rome's depleted forces were reconstituted, the numbers XVII, XVIII, and XIX—the labels of the legions that had been slaughtered—became the equivalent of today's unlucky number thirteen and were never used again to identify a Roman legion. (Any similarity to the policy of many modern sports teams, which retire the number of a revered star, is more than a bit misplaced.)

According to the historian Suetonius, when Augustus, the Roman Emperor, learned of the massive defeat, he banged his head against the walls of his palace, shouting, "Give me back my legions."

3.3. Yankee Doodle Gets a Favor from Gentleman Johnny

Historians generally see the Battle of Saratoga as the tipping point of the Revolutionary War. Although this battle was won fair and square by the American rebels, it was tipped in turn by several preceding redcoat oops. In 1777, Gentleman Johnny Burgoyne, so labelled for his fondness for the perks of high society, descended with a formidable army from British-held Canada into upstate New York, intending to come down the Hudson River and meet up with General William Howe, who was to be leading another English army up from New York City.

The plan, not a bad one, was to cut off the revolutionaries operating out of the American northeast from their southern and western confreres. Confident that the operation would be relatively easy, and true to his reputation, Gen. Gentleman Johnny traveled in style, having assembled a huge convoy with all the appropriate accoutrements, such as elaborate clothing, fancy carved furniture, elegant dinnerware, and a selection of fine wines. As a result, his army traveled slowly and wasn't especially maneuverable.

General Burgoyne, "redcoat" in his red coat, surrendering after the Battle of Saratoga (painting by John Trumbull, between 1822 and 1832).

After taking Fort Ticonderoga on Lake Champlain, Gentleman Johnny could have sailed a bit north and then proceeded down the Hudson River to Albany, as originally planned, where he expected to meet General Howe's forces coming north. But he decided instead to go directly south, plunging into the dense northern forest—with all his stuff in tow. Not a good decision: hacking his way through a wilderness considerably more challenging than anything encountered in Merry Olde England turned out to be exhausting. It also consumed time as well as supplies and was made more painful by American guerilla raiders who burned bridges and felled trees along their route, making forward progress even more difficult and deadly.

It was a diminished and exhausted English army that finally emerged at the Hudson River just north of Saratoga. The next blunder was that General Howe wasn't coming north after all. He had decided to embark from New York City and to go south instead, taking the rebel capital of Philadelphia. Apparently liking it there, Howe stayed, which led Benjamin Franklin, in Paris, to quip that Howe had intended to take Philadelphia, but instead,

Philadelphia took him. The English side of the war was being run at the time by George Germain, Secretary of State for America, back in London. For some reason, Germain never bothered to convey Gentleman Johnny's expectation to Howe, or Howe's alternative decision to him. The right hand didn't know what the left was doing, and vice versa, because the guy in the middle—on the other side of the Atlantic—didn't tell either one.

The result was that after several firefights, Gentleman Johnny—his army bedraggled from its ordeal in the forest primeval, bogged down with too much stuff, and fighting without Howe's anticipated contingent—eventually surrendered to the Americans, having lost about six thousand men (and, one can assume, most of his fine china), while the rebels got a greatly needed morale boost. Far more important is that the outcome convinced the French government that those rag-tag colonials had a realistic chance of beating the hated British after all, whereupon they agreed to aid the American cause with guns, manpower, and much needed naval forces. The latter was to be crucial at the war's concluding Battle of Yorktown.

The British blunders tend to be underplayed in subsequent US accounts of the events leading up to the successful Battle of Saratoga, probably because a series of oops on the other side engenders less patriotic panache than does focusing on the victorious fighting spirit of the hometown patriots. Also little mentioned: the real American hero of the Saratoga campaign wasn't the US commanding general, Horatio Gates, whose reports back to the Continental Congress gave himself most of the credit, but rather, Benedict Arnold, who at the time was an extraordinarily courageous, imaginative, successful, and altogether patriotic American officer. Not getting the credit he deserved went a long way toward embittering the proud and ambitious Arnold, who eventually and infamously sought to betray the American cause by handing West Point—which he later commanded, having been seriously injured several times in battle on the Continental side—over to the British. When his intended treason was revealed, Arnold escaped to the British lines, where he was commissioned a Brigadier General and led a regiment composed of royalist Americans.

And Gentleman Johnny? After ceremoniously handing over his sword while wearing one of those snazzy uniforms he had so carefully carted down from Canada and somehow kept clean and pressed, he returned shame-facedly to England, where he was never again given a field command, but wrote a few well-regarded plays.

Although the Yanks made their share, the English (and not only Gentleman Johnny) clearly out-oopsed them. For example, the English plan of concentrating on the American south-east might have succeeded—at least in retaining Florida, Georgia, and the Carolinas—had not Gen. Charles Cornwallis, who led the ill-advised English southern strategy, disobeyed orders and strutted off to Virginia instead. There, he found himself trapped by a French fleet at a place called Yorktown. Recall that this French involve-ment had itself been stimulated by the earlier outcome of the Battle of Sara-toga, courtesy of Gentleman Johnny.

In matters military, there are always enough errors to go around. The Battle of Trenton, earlier than Saratoga in the Revolutionary War, was also an important triumph and morale booster for the beleaguered Continental Army. Under General George Washington, American troops really did cross the Delaware River, as memorialized—albeit inaccurately—in the most famous painting of the Revolutionary War. Once across they attacked a large contingent of Hessian mercenaries who were caught unawares. As it happens, the Hessian commander, Colonel Johann Rall, had received a note from a loyalist spy, warning that Washington was about to surprise him, but Rall was playing cards at the time and put the note in his pocket, unread. It was later discovered when the colonel's tunic was unbuttoned to minister to fatal gunshot wounds incurred during the battle.

When it comes to the Revolutionary War, purists insist on pointing out that the most famous battle, Bunker Hill, was fought at Breed's Hill. That's where, in an effort to conserve scarce ammunition, a Continental commander is said to have yelled to his men, "Don't fire until you see the whites of their eyes." As it happened, their cannons almost didn't get to fire at all. Here's what happened. The outnumbered Continentals were expecting an assault by the Redcoats, so they hastily built fortifications, including a quickly constructed wall behind which they placed their meager stock of artillery. But just before the battle, they realized that in their haste, they had forgotten to make muzzle slits through which the cannons could shoot! But sure enough, Yankee ingenuity came to the rescue: they made the requisite openings by a tactical maneuver never seen before or since in the annals of warfare. They backed up the cannons and fired point-blank at the wall, making the requisite openings.

3.4. Agony at Agincourt

The Battle of Agincourt is probably the most famous and improbable English military victory of all time, when a greatly outnumbered army on foot defeated a huge French force, including the cream of its mounted aristocrat cavalry-men. But it wasn't merely because of those renowned doughty English longbowmen. Something else, less renowned, helped immensely: the French committed a monstrous oops, charging across a muddy field, where their heavy armored cavalry slipped, bogged down, and were slaughtered, mostly by English arrows shot from a distance.

An English army, led by Henry V, had been marching across northern France in 1415, trying to make it to English-held Calais. They were hungry, suffering from dysentery and heavy battle casualties when their way was blocked by a numerically superior French army, which needed only to stall the English until they collapsed on their own. But the French chose to gallop across a sloppy, soggy, marshy mess, right into English arrows. The French losses were in the thousands, including the most renowned of their military aristocracy, while the English, led by Henry V, may have lost as few as one hundred. The result was England's greatest ever military victory.

Another such English victory once again resulted in large part from an oops by its opponent, this time Spain. By 1588, Spain overshadowed England on the world stage and was at the height of its power, controlling the Netherlands as well as huge territories in the Western Hemisphere. King Philip II assembled his fabled Armada, which sailed for England, causing panic in that island nation. The Armada was a huge fleet—130 ships—that sailed from Lisbon with the plan of escorting an army from Flanders to invade England, overthrow the Protestant Queen Elizabeth I, and set a Catholic on the throne.

The Spanish Armada under attack by English fireships (painting by Philip James de Loutherbourg, 1796).

Well known in retrospect is that the Armada was devastated by a fortuitous storm (fortuitous, that is, for England). Lesser-known, however, is how Spanish blunders played a big role. For starters, the commander of the Armada, Alonso Pérez de Guzmán y de Zúñiga-Soto-mayor, 7th Duke of Medina Sidonia, was an aristocrat with no prior naval combat experience who had been ordered to rendezvous with the proposed invading army and transport it across the English Channel. Large as it was, the Spanish naval force was technically outclassed by their English Navy counterparts,[i] which were at the forefront of a naval revolution that would soon have them "rule the waves." The English had lighter, stronger, faster ships, as well as more accurate, more powerful,

---

[i] The phrase Royal Navy came into use nearly a century later, in 1660, following the restoration of the English monarchy under Charles II.

and quicker-loading cannon, manned by more experienced and competent crews. One Spanish captain foresaw the likely forthcoming disaster when he wrote, "We are sailing against England in the confident hope of a miracle."[2] Not a reliable battle plan.

Medina Sidonia nonetheless had a golden opportunity to defeat the English navy early in the invasion campaign. The Armada had been passing the Cornwall coast just when the Brits were re-supplying their ships in Plymouth Harbor, where they would have been trapped and vulnerable to attack—which is precisely what Medina Sidonia's officers urged. But the duke was under strict orders from Philip II to proceed directly to its appointed rendezvous with the invading Spanish army off the European mainland. Soon, it was the Armada that found itself essentially trapped off Calais, in a tightly-packed defensive formation. But unlike the Spanish shortly before, the English didn't hesitate to press their advantage. They sent eight flaming fire ships toward the anchored galleons, which did little damage themselves, but disrupted the Spanish fleet, which scattered in its haste to avoid being set ablaze and exploded by their own on-board munitions. In the succeeding Battle of Gravelines, the English were able to take on the disordered and separated ships of the Armada, and deal them a crushing defeat.

The surviving Spanish vessels were less nimble than their English counterparts and could only sail with the wind at their back. Strong south-westerly winds (subsequently labeled the "Protestant wind" by the Brits), along with pursuing warships, forced the remains of the once-mighty Armada to return to Spain by escaping north along the east coast of Britain and then south via the Scottish and Irish coasts. It was then that the renowned storm, in reality several of them, made things even worse. Less than two-thirds of the initial Armada limped back to Spain, never having embarked that planned invasion force, never mind actually attacking England itself.

King Philip II later rebuilt his fleet and dispatched two more Armadas in the 1590s, both of which were again devastated by storms. Historians note that he has also been called Philip the Prudent. Really.

3.5. Even Bonaparte Made Boo-Boos

It might seem churlish to include Napoleon in a catalog of blunders and blunderers; after all, at one point he had conquered almost all of Europe. But, channeling Mr. Rogers once again, "Everyone makes mistakes . . ." even Monsieur Bonaparte. And he did eventually come to a bad end. Furthermore, illuminating some of his errors italicizes their importance and ubiquity.

Before Bonaparte's blunders, there was the case of Louis XVI, who, when it became evident even to this rather slow-witted monarch that the French people had developed a different view of the divine right of kings, tried to make a run for it, but stumbled. The French Revolution was a pivotal event in world history and many Americans know that a pivot of *that* pivot occurred with the guillotining of Lackluster Louis. Fewer know that a pivot of that pivot of the pivotal French Revolution occurred when Louis attempted to escape Paris but was captured with his wife, Marie, and brought back in disgrace. And fewer yet know of the many oops on the king's part that resulted in this failure, including his decision to run away with his family in a large, relatively ponderous but suitably comfy coach, fit for a king but not for a quick getaway, instead of going in two smaller, lighter, faster, and less luxurious ones, as had originally been planned. But Louis, channeling Gentleman Johnny, insisted on traveling in style. The overloaded royal coach broke down and ended up traveling more slowly than a local citizen who recognized him on route and rode ahead to warn the restive French "sans culottes" at the next stop. Upon being unceremoniously returned, Louis was accused of treasonously planning to rendezvous with an Austrian army and invade his own country—which he probably was. Marie Antoinette was Austrian, which made her distrusted among "her" subjects. Louis's oops caused him and Queen Marie to lose most of the regard he had still retained in France, and, soon thereafter, his and his wife's heads.

Louis XVI being brought to the guillotine (anonymous engraving, late eighteenth century).

Napoleon's successes are well known, His oops, not so much. Best known of Bonaparte's blunders was invading Russia in 1812, whereupon he "succeeded" in occupying Moscow, where he wasted five weeks (while the notoriously brutal Russian winter began to arrive), expecting Czar Alexander to surrender. No such luck. Napoleon's accomplishment was more like a fly successfully invading the flypaper. When the *Grande Armée* finally started to withdraw to central Europe on October 19, the soldiers were still wearing their summer uniforms.

The Russian retreat from Moscow had been a strategic one, engineered by the wily general Mikhail Illarionovich Golenishchev-Kutuzov, who reasoned that by abandoning Moscow, he would impose a pyrrhic victory on Napoleon. This is exactly what happened, and, as winter was setting in, the French emperor ended up deserting his *Grande Armée*, which, in ignominious retreat and harassed by Russian partisans and the devastatingly cold Russian winter, was pretty much wiped out, losing something like five hundred thousand men. (Hitler was to make a similar error, although he didn't quite get to Moscow.)

Napoleon retreating from Russia (painting by Alfred Wierusz-Kowalski, unknown date).

Napoleon also made some less widely known mistakes, such as his earlier invasion of Egypt, from which he again ran away, abandoning his Egyptian Expeditionary Army years before he was to do the same in Russia. This failed endeavor also brought about the second anti-France coalition, which combined Austria, England, Russia, and Turkey. Then there was Napoleon's invasion of the Iberian Peninsula, yet another serious mistake, which led to the Peninsular War that induced the first usage of "guerilla" (Spanish for "little war") warfare, although its cost wasn't little, since it eventually tied up nearly three hundred thousand French soldiers and was described as a years-long "bleeding ulcer" in the body of Napoleon's military ambitions. This Napoleonic oops also provided a steppingstone for a mid-ranking English military leader named Arthur Wellesley, later known to history as the Duke of Wellington and the architect of Napoleon's subsequent final discomfiture at Waterloo.

Another of Napoleon's ill-fated endeavors was his disastrous effort to undo Haiti's slave revolution, and—least widely known of his major errors and thus especially worth noting—his rejection of the 1813 Frankfurt

Proposal from Austrian foreign minister, Metternich. This came late in the game when Bonaparte's fortunes were low (he had just lost the Battle of Leipzig) and about to go lower. Had he agreed, Napoleon could have remained emperor of France, which would have kept its pre-war "natural borders," plus Belgium, Savoy, and the Rhineland, all of which had been conquered earlier during the French Revolutionary wars.

History records that he should have taken Metternich's generous proposal. Later, after the combined armies of the Sixth Coalition battered their way into France, Napoleon tried to reopen negotiations, seeking the same terms, but was met with the chilling British response to German soldiers who, during World War I, kept fighting and only sought to surrender at the last minute: "Too late, chum." He had missed his chance and ended up abdicating in 1814. A year later came Waterloo and the second and final of Bonaparte's banishments.

3.6. Half a League, Half a League, Half a League Oopsward

The Light Brigade charged. Shortly afterward, Alfred, Lord Tennyson famously noted that "someone had blundered." That notable, blundering charge happened as part of the Battle of Balaclava in 1854, during the Crimean War when the Brits, French, and Turks were allied against the Russians, who had just captured some Turkish artillery. It would have been good generalship for Lord Raglan, the British commander, to send his light cavalry to swoop in and prevent the Russians from removing those guns; nineteenth century light cavalry was designed for just this sort of engagement. But instead, the Light Brigade was ordered to make a hopeless frontal assault against a *different*, well-positioned Russian artillery battery at the far end of a long, open valley that afforded the czar's troops an excellent defensive fire-field. As it happened, Raglan's instructions hadn't been clearly expressed and when the brigade commander—astonished at the ridiculous and sure-to-be disastrous order—asked for clarification, the military courier vaguely gestured with his arm. And so "into the valley of death rode the six hundred."

Charge of the Light Brigade (painting by William Simpson, 1855).

The Charge wasn't the only oops involved. Tennyson himself oopsed about it: mortality within the Light Brigade—107 out of 676—was unacceptably high, but not nearly what Tennyson had thought when he wrote his poem, and even after the truth was apparent, he published it anyhow, because it was so effective. In the movie *The Man Who Shot Liberty Valance*, a journalist confronted with a dilemma between fact and fiction observes: "When the legend becomes fact, print the legend." Popular memory regarding this genuine blunder has been fixed by Tennyson's stirring patriotic poem, an interesting example of how literary brilliance can overwhelm historical reality.[ii]

3.7. A Selective Peek at Some Civil War Slip-Ups

The American Civil War has been sliced, diced, turned inside out and upside down, looked at from every angle, argued about, re-enacted, and, in summary,

[ii] Another notable example concerns England's King Richard III, masterfully portrayed in Shakespeare's play as an irredeemably murderous tyrant—and widely considered so, as a result—whereas historians paint a far more supportive picture.

minutely examined by professional historians and amateurs *ad infinitum* and *ad nauseam*. So, we'll do it again, this time briefly and selectively. First, a quick disclaimer: It is said that history is written by the winners, but it ain't necessarily so. It's written by those who write about it, which means the losers if they hold a grudge and keep stubbornly spreading their version of what happened. Serbs lost the Battle of the Field of Blackbirds in 1389, but can't let it go. The USSR became the UFFR (the Union of Fewer and Fewer Republics) beginning in 1990, and some die-hards—notably one Vladimir Putin—haven't been able to get over the loss.

This is especially true of the American Civil War, about which southern partisans have been particularly voluble, leaving the rest of us with a lot of myths: Ulysses S. Grant was a drunkard and a butcher; Robert E. Lee was a brilliant leader of men, a saintly gentleman who never made a mistake; the South shoulda, coulda, woulda won if only they didn't have fewer soldiers and insufficient material resources (this, at least, is true, as it is for most losing sides); and the rebels were fighting for states' rights in the face of federal over-reach, and for their superior, godly, and blessedly genteel civilization. Most pernicious: southern secession was a noble "lost cause" that had nothing to do with preserving the cruel and barbaric enslavement of human beings.

Following is a brief catalog of some things that went wrong in the Civil War, mostly inept generalship. But first, let's note that American military history—like military history worldwide—is filled with arguments based on twenty/twenty hindsight, such as the atomic bombings of Hiroshima and Nagasaki, the Vietnam War (justification for the war itself as well as how it was fought), and ditto for the US wars in Iraq, Afghanistan, and pretty much everywhere. But when it comes to ingredients for disputing the past, the Civil War is so firmly baked that it takes the cake, especially why it occurred and how it played out.

At one point during World War I, it was said that the British constituted an army of lions commanded by donkeys. Half a century earlier and especially in the first years of the Civil War, this was true of the Union forces. Initially, they were under the overall command of George McClellan, who gave caution a bad name. He was a persistent oopser, not so much over what he did but what he didn't: always over-estimating Lee's forces and refusing to pursue his opponent when doing so likely could have ended the war years earlier had he only acted with, not daring, but just good generalship, which is often defined as taking advantage of the other side when you have, well, an advantage.

In his book, *Lincoln and His Generals*, historian T. Harry Williams characterized McClellan to a T:

> He was a fine organizer and trainer of troops; and his men, sensing that he identified with them, idolized him. In preparing for battle he was confident and energetic, but as he approached the field of operations he became slow and timid. He magnified every obstacle; in particular, the size of the enemy army increased in his mind the closer he got to it. In battle he tended to interpret sights and sounds in his front as unfavorable to him; he hesitated to throw in his whole force at the supreme moment; and he withdrew when bolder men would have attacked.[3]

McClellan's reputation was already in tatters, following multiple blunders in the Peninsula Campaign earlier in the year and having been accused of a "criminal tardiness" in responding to a call for reinforcements from another Union general—which was especially ironic given that McClellan had a pattern of repeatedly pleading for reinforcements when in fact he didn't need them. As a result, a majority of Lincoln's cabinet had drawn up a formal "remonstrance" urging that "at this time, it is not safe to entrust to Major General McClellan the command of any of the armies of the United States."[4] No matter. Before it was formally sent, the cabinet's opinion became irrelevant when Lincoln announced that he had appointed McClellan head of the large combined Union Army in the East. It was a bad decision on the president's part, and as a result, Lincoln deserves part of the discredit subsequently heaped on McClellan. An important role of the commander-in-chief is to put high quality people in charge, and in this regard, Abe honestly goofed. But the immediate battlefield blunders were all McClellan's.

The most egregious occurred on September 18, 1862, immediately after the Battle of Antietam, the bloodiest in US history up to that time.

Lee's Confederates had pushed into Maryland, hoping to deliver a victory sufficient to induce Britain and possibly France to recognize the Confederacy and maybe get the Union to negotiate a peace on the South's terms. McClellan as usual was tardy in engaging Lee, maintaining that the Confederate force was much too strong for his army to confront. At one point he telegraphed to Lincoln that the "gigantic rebel army before us . . . amounting to not less than 120,000 men . . . are numerically superior to ours by at least twenty-five per cent."[5] Not for the first time, McClellan greatly exaggerated his opponent's strength, whether because of bad intelligence (defined however you wish) or excessive caution, we'll probably never know. But reality at the time was almost precisely the other way around.

In addition, a few days earlier, McClellan had a piece of luck about which commanding generals can only dream. A Union soldier had found a lengthy communication, signed by Robert E. Lee, and evidently dropped by a careless Confederate courier, which specified Lee's goals, the distribution and time-table of his four army columns, and the precise makeup of each. Crucially, it told McClellan that Lee was undertaking an extremely bold maneuver: dividing his already outnumbered forces, something that every military text-book cautions against. McClellan evidently knew what he had, because he exclaimed, "Here is a paper with which, if I cannot whip Bobbie Lee, I will be willing to go home."[6] He promptly proceeded to blow it, dithering away the next eighteen hours before doing anything to make use of this precious information. This gave Lee—who had been warned by a Confederate spy that the Union forces seemed for a change to be planning something—the opportunity to solidify his position. As noted, he had previously taken a big chance (Lee, unlike McClellan, was an aggressive risk-taker) and divided his army in the face of a superior force. He quickly drew it together before McClellan, cautious to a fault, acted. And as ever, it was too little and too late.

The two armies eventually fought at Antietam Creek, near Sharpsburg, Maryland, where Lee's army was greatly outnumbered by McClellan's. Worse for the rebs, Lee's army was extremely vulnerable, with its back up against the Potomac River and having lost one-quarter of its men in the Battle of Antietam the previous day. Many of his troops were exhausted after nearly two weeks of marching, while McClellan's were comparatively fresh. Moreover, 34,000 Union reinforcements had just augmented the Union side. Outnumbered almost three to one, Lee wisely ordered a retreat, but astonishingly, and despite being on the good side of that lopsided force imbalance, McClellan didn't pursue the Confederates. He insisted that Lee had nearly one hundred thousand troops under his command, plus an additional forty thousand after Stonewall Jackson arrived after capturing the Union garrison at Harper's Ferry. It doesn't take a military genius to figure that if Lee had such a force, he sure as hell wouldn't have retreated! (Maybe McClellan was projecting.) Meanwhile, McClellan was unaccountably pleased with his performance, thanking divine providence for his deliverance and convinced that a draw was the best he could have hoped for against so superior a foe.

Once reality became apparent—as it had been to most of the senior officers on both sides at the scene—President Lincoln and Chief General Henry Halleck vigorously urged McClellan to take it to Lee. They kept urging, but no dice. It took McClellan more than a month to get going into Virginia, by which time Lee was able to regroup, resupply, rest his army, and prepare his defenses. The Battle of Antietam therefore wasn't at all decisive, but it should have been. It did, however, have one important consequence: it caused the normally patient Lincoln to reach the end of his rope. He finally relieved McClellan from command of the Army of the Potomac. Like McClellan himself most of the time, that too was too late.

Tactically, the Battle of Antietam was a stalemate, and strategically it was something of a Union victory, despite McClellan having been out-generaled by Lee at every turn, because Lee had been the opposite of McClellan: too audacious. He returned to Virginia without a victory, which cooled any interest by the United Kingdom or France to side with the Confederacy. Nonetheless, Antietam (known in the South as the Battle of Sharpsburg) has to be reckoned the North's biggest lost opportunity of the war and McClellan's biggest failure. He had nearly three times Lee's forces and the extraordinary benefit of a complete read-out of Lee's battle plans and dispositions. Had Gen. McCautious done what any competent general would have been eager to do, the Confederate Army of Northern Virginia would almost certainly have been crushed, and the Confederate capital, Richmond, taken. But in any event—more like a non-event—the war lasted another two and a half years, during which there were many battles much bloodier than Antietam and many opportunities for many more costly mistakes, both of commission and of omission.

Abraham Lincoln and George McClellan, meeting after the Battle of Antietam (photo by Alexander Gardner, 1862).

OOPS!

Even Robert E. Lee made a big one, at a place called Gettysburg. Lee was a superb general, better than any on the Union side, but he wasn't a military Messiah; he, too, made mistakes. And at Gettysburg he made several. He first set the stage for Gettysburg, when he tried for a second time to invade the North, the first having led to the Battle of Antietam, which fell short of being a Confederate disaster only because of McClellan's ineptitude. By deciding to fight Northern troops in the North, he lost the benefit of doing battle on his own terrain. Moreover, Lee allowed the Union forces to choose the site of the battle, and in those days—as even now—attacking uphill was dangerous and often led to disaster. This problem was multiplied by the fact that the Union armies not only occupied the high ground of Round Top, Little Round Top, Cemetery Ridge, Cemetery Hill, and Culp's Hill but had also been able to set up effective defensive positions. Moreover, Lee had deprived himself of potentially crucial information when he sent Jeb Stuart[iii] on a prolonged cavalry raid and, as a result, was surprised to learn that a dangerously large contingent of Union troops had already crossed the Potomac and were able to establish themselves on the high ground. As a result, Lee's army offered battle on terrain chosen by the other side; moreover, there was nothing all that important about nearby Gettysburg. Lee would have been better off avoiding a confrontation under those conditions, but that was not his nature, on top of which he incorrectly assumed that other Union generals, such as George Meade who commanded his opposition, were as disastrously cautious as McClellan. So, Lee catastrophically and uncharacteristically under-estimated his enemy while at the same time overestimating his own troops, having developed an almost mystical conviction that they were literally the world's best soldiers, who could overcome any obstacle.

Up to July 1863, Lee had consistently succeeded despite being nearly always outnumbered, by a combination of choosing excellent terrain on which to fight and departing from conventional military wisdom to the point that he evidently had come to believe that he and his army of Northern Virginia were not governed by the usual wisdom of war. Especially important

---

[iii] So identified because of his given name, James Ewell Brown.

here was the old cliché that generals tend to re-fight the last war. More than a half-century after Napoleon's brilliant battlefield victories, military strategists often continued to follow some of his tactics, such as attempting flanking maneuvers whenever possible and—key when it came to the Battle of Gettysburg—a willingness to order charges over open ground against prepared defenses. Such tactics were often successful in Napoleon's day, largely because musketry at that time involved smooth-bore weapons, which were quite inaccurate except at close range, and, being flintlocks and even matchlocks, were slow to reload. But by the 1860s, most military long guns were rifled; that is, the muzzles had spiral groves that imparted a spin to the bullets, resulting in greater accuracy as well as longer range. Add it up and full-on infantry charges had become suicidal.

All of which sets the stage for what became the most famous single event in Civil War history: Pickett's Charge. It has grown to heroic, mythic stature, outpacing the reality that it was a full-on disaster. On the third and final day of the Battle of Gettysburg, Lee ordered that infantry under Maj. Gen. George G. Pickett—12,500 men in nine infantry brigades—assault the middle of the Union lines, in an effort to surmount and capture the aptly named Cemetery Ridge. This meant running for three-quarters of a mile on exposed terrain, subject to withering Union artillery and rifle fire. Knowing Lee's aggressiveness as a battlefield strategist, General Meade, commanding the Union defenders, expected just such an attack. The chargers were turned back with more than 50 percent casualties. Monday morning quarterbacks, attempting to figure out why Pickett's Charge was such a failure, have analyzed every contingency, at least in part in an effort to exonerate Lee, who, let's not forget, ordered the terrible thing. Asked how the disaster happened, years later, Pickett himself observed: "I've always thought the Yankees had something to do with it."[7] Tellingly, Pickett never forgave Lee for ordering the damned fool assault.

Gettysburg is often seen as the turning point of the Civil War, and whether or not that's a viable interpretation, the overall battle certainly turned on the generalship of Robert E. Lee, ending up not to his credit. In fact, Lee was severely criticized in the Confederate press, a judgment to which Lee himself concurred. He offered to resign, writing to Jefferson Davis, "No blame can be attached to the army for its failure to accomplish what was projected by me, nor should it be censured for the unreasonable expectations of the public—I am alone to blame, in perhaps expecting too much of its prowess and valor."[8] It would have been more accurate (and honest) had he said that he alone was to blame for failing to anticipate the lunacy of ordering a frontal assault against an entrenched, well-armed, and motivated opponent. And also, for failing to listen to the wise, contrary advice of his fellow officers. In any event, the Confederate armies limped back to Virginia and never again attempted to invade the North.

From here on, it was the North taking the war to the South, leading to the last of our big-time blundering battles, the lesser-known Battle of the Crater. In this case, the blunder was by the North. The battle itself turned on some inept and likely racist military leadership, although it wasn't especially consequential (except for those who died in it). In the early summer of 1864, Grant had failed to learn from Lee's blunder at Gettysburg and had stubbornly repeated the same oops when he had his army launch a doomed frontal assault across mostly open ground against fixed Confederate positions at the Battle of Cold Harbor. There is much truth in the adage that what we learn from history is that people don't learn from history. But after Cold Harbor and the loss of more than twelve thousand men, Grant finally did, so when his Army of the Potomac sought to take Petersburg, Virginia, a month later and encountered strong and well-prepared resistance from Lee's Army of Northern Virginia, he wasn't about to repeat his earlier folly. And so, by late July, the "siege of Petersburg" had stalemated into fixed lines of trench warfare, eerily presaging World War I.

As it happened, there were a number of Pennsylvania coal miners serving with the Union army and a novel tactic[iv] surfaced: dig a tunnel under no-man's-land, fill it with explosives, and detonate it so as to blow a hole in the rebel lines. This was done, with the business end packed with eight thousand pounds of gunpowder.

[iv] Novel, that is, during the Civil War. In the Middle Ages, besieging armies frequently tunneled under a city's walls, intending to detonate explosives that would breach the defenses. Sometimes the defenders would dig counter-tunnels, to blow up the attackers inside theirs. It isn't clear if this led to counter-counter-tunnels, and so on, *ad infinitum*.

After some false starts, it exploded with a huge blast that immediately killed nearly three hundred Confederate soldiers and caused great confusion. The Union plan had been for a division of "colored troops," commanded of course by a white officer, one Edward Ferrero, to lead the assault, with one brigade going to the left of the anticipated immense crater and the other to the right. The troops had trained for weeks and knew exactly what to do. But the day before the detonation, Gen. Meade changed the plan of attack, ordering that the Black soldiers not lead the assault, ostensibly because Meade worried that if it failed, he would be accused of needlessly sacrificing black lives, but more likely because he did not think the Black Americans were up to the job, and also quite possibly because if it succeeded, he didn't want them to get the credit. There were no last-minute white volunteers, so lots were drawn and the "winner" was a division led by one Brig. Gen. James Ledlie, who, in the event, didn't even bother to brief his men about the operation and spent it roaring drunk along with Ferrero, behind the ensuing battle lines.

No surprise: the Battle of the Crater was a disaster for the North. Ledlie's disorganized and untrained men had no idea what they were supposed to do and instead of going around the huge crater, they went into it. Meanwhile, the Confederate forces recovered from their shock and counter-attacked, firing rifles and artillery down into the crater in what was subsequently described as a "turkey shoot." With the plan clearly a fiasco and the battle lost, the Black American soldiers were then sent in. At that point, with rebel fire on both sides of the crater, Ferrero's men—without the drunken commander himself, of course—not unreasonably went into it as well, seeking protection. It was, in twenty-first-century parlance, a total cluster-fuck.

3.8. The Canonical, Comical Case of the Commune's Cannons

The Paris Commune (1871), a key and bloody event in modern European history, derived from a radical insurrection that immediately followed the Franco-Prussian War. Among its precipitating factors, all of which could easily have been avoided, was the French National Assembly's blockheaded demand that Parisians immediately pay their rents and debts, which had been forgiven during the devastating Prussian siege of Paris, combined with abruptly discontinuing the salaries of the populist National Guard, the members of which were therefore simultaneously stuck with both crushing payment obligations and no pay. Small wonder that the National Guard formed the core of the insurrection that gave rise to the Paris Commune. Most inflammatory, however, was the federal government's insistence on confiscating the four hundred cannons that had been purchased during the siege using voluntary subscriptions from the residents of Paris, and that were seen as symbolizing the city's patriotic commitment and honor. Yet another blunder, retrospectively hilarious, then ensued: elements of the French Army, which had been called in to dismantle the Commune, had been ordered to seize and remove the bulk of these cannons, but to do so during the night, in order to avoid roiling the citizenry. But someone forgot to arrange for horses to pull them away! So, when the morning dawned, the sorry Keystone Cops episode was revealed, whereupon insurrectionary violence soon followed, along with murderous suppression of the Paris Commune by the French Army.

Workers dragging National Guard cannon into position during the Paris Commune (anonymous illustration, 1870).

3.9. Gavrilo Princip "Succeeds" — in Starting World War I

World War I, "the war no one wanted," happened anyway. It was associated with a ton of blameworthy blunders, committed by pretty much everyone involved. Given that no one (or at least, hardly anyone) wanted it, virtually nobody who examines that debacle is surprised that it had many causes, each marinated in one mistake or another. Because it lasted considerably longer than the participants expected, even though God was with "us"— and both sides, of course, considered themselves "us"—we can all be assured that errors and failures abounded during the more than four years that the Great War dragged on. And given that a second and even more devastating world war began a mere two decades after that initial conflict ended (which, according to Woodrow Wilson, had been fought to end all wars), something went terribly wrong with the ending, too.

No war's causation has been more microscopically examined and historians are agreed that it was, as psychiatrists say, "over-determined." That is, there were many independent causes. The usual suspects include interlocking alliances, international distrust, and pressure to mobilize before your opponent did so, combined with the unyielding tyranny of pre-set mobilization schedules and a diverse set of national resentments: e.g., France's simmering anger at having lost Alsace and Lorraine to Germany as a result of the Franco-Prussian War; Germany's irritation that its meager colonial holdings neither compared with those of the other European powers nor reflected its national power; Austria-Hungary's anxiety about the state of its increasingly restive and rickety empire; a distinctly mediocre group of national leaders; and maybe even the fact that Europe hadn't had a major war since the Franco-Prussian in 1871 and thus many people didn't realize how truly awful full-scale hostilities would be.

The immediate precipitating factor, of course, was the assassination of the Austrian Archduke, Franz Ferdinand, in Sarajevo. This is well known. Less known are the multiple screw-ups that precipitated this precipitator. It was a world-shattering oops that only happened because of a bunch of immediately prior oops. Here is an abbreviated account.

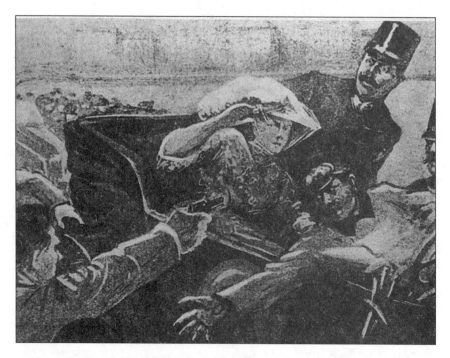

Assassination of Archduke Ferdinand (anonymous illustration, unknown date).

At the time, Serbia was a largely unwilling subordinate of the Austro-Hungarian Empire. A scruffy group of six Serbian nationalists had been armed and trained to kill the archduke, heir to the imperial throne, who was going to visit Sarajevo. The plot unfolded as a tragicomedy of errors. The touring car carrying the archduke and his wife, surrounded by his vehicular entourage, passed right by the first would-be assassin, who simply failed to throw his bomb. Ditto the second, who had both a bomb and a pistol.

The third managed to toss his explosive, which bounced off the arch-duke's car, rolled under a different vehicle and then blew up, wounding nearly two dozen people, but not touching the target. The bomber then swallowed a cyanide pill and jumped into the Miljacka River, but the cyanide was old and didn't work, and because of a hot, dry summer, the "river" was only five inches deep, so the blundering third assassin was captured alive.

But his story about having co-conspirators wasn't believed. The motorcade sped away nonetheless, passing the remaining three conspirators too rapidly for any of them to act.

The archduke's party eventually decided to go to the Sarajevo hospital to visit the victims of the bombing against the urging of his advisers, who worried that there might be more would-be assassins. En route, Ferdinand's driver took a wrong turn. When an officer riding in the royal car yelled to the driver to correct his error, the vehicle was barely moving, and just happened to be right in front of Gavrilo Princip, one of those three conspirators who hadn't been quick enough to fire his pistol earlier, and who by this time had despaired that the plot was totally ruined and had despondently wandered down a random side street where the archduke's car had no reason to be except for the wrong turn followed by the aborted effort to correct it. Thus began World War I, an international disaster that was itself begot by a bunch of blundering bunglers.

Meeting at Munich, with Neville Chamberlain at left, Mussolini center, and Hitler at right (anonymous photograph, 1938).

Now, its end. The Treaty of Versailles, which formalized that end, also involved an array of oops, followed by yet more, notably requiring Germany to pay unsustainable reparations and failing to resist subsequent German rearmament, along with the infamous appeasement of Hitler at Munich, itself one of the most renowned mistakes of the twentieth-century. As for the abundant blunders that befell all sides during the Great War itself, let us now examine the Schlieffen Plan, which was brilliantly designed and might have resulted in a German victory, if not for yet another array of oops, notably when the Kaiser's military command undercut the Plan itself.

German war-planners had long been obsessed with the nightmare scenario of simultaneously fighting a major two-front war, against France to the west and Russia to the east. The Schlieffen Plan had called for a lightning strike into northeastern France, outflanking the French army, capturing Paris, and quickly knocking France out of the war, thus freeing up German forces to go east and confront the Russian Army, which was seen as a greater threat, but whose mobilization was expected to take longer. It was further assumed (correctly, as it happened) that in the event of war, French armies would promptly attack German holdings in the southeast, seeking to retake Alsace and Lorraine.

The Schlieffen Plan counted, as well, on a widely promulgated French military doctrine that called for prompt offensive action, designed to carry any war to the enemy, an effort to learn a lesson from the disastrous Franco-Prussian War, which had been fought largely on French soil. Accordingly, the German high command planned that a smaller German army facing France's anticipated attack toward Alsace/Lorraine would strategically retreat, drawing in the expected French advance and thereby making those forces unavailable for the defense of Paris. But the German planners did not reckon on a key insight from another German, roughly a century earlier. In his classic treatise, *On War*, Carl von Clausewitz warned that the best-laid plans of military men often go astray in the "fog of war."

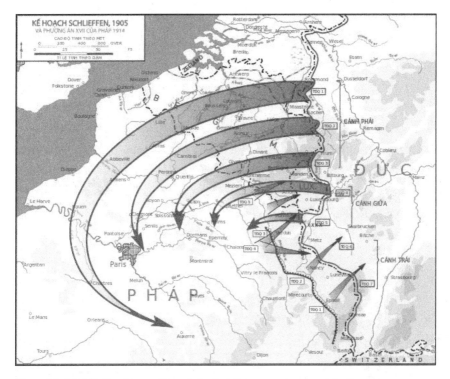

Map of the Schlieffen Plan, with anticipated German advances into France shown above and expected French counterattack shown below (anonymous, from 1914).

In 1914, that fog became initially manifest in a surprising way, which would not have surprised Clausewitz, but that ultimately upended the Schlieffen Plan. That second-string German army, initially designed as a decoy, found itself unexpectedly successful against its French counterpart, whereupon its commanders sought permission to pursue the retreating French into France. The overall German military leader, Helmuth von Moltke the Younger (one of whose failings was a peculiar inability to assert himself against his subordinates and even against his own better judgment), went along with this request. So, the southern German army advanced, French resistance stiffened once they were fighting on their own soil, and that confrontation quickly devolved into a stalemate.

As a result, instead of being lured into German territory, as originally planned by Count Alfred von Schlieffen—and therefore made unavailable for the crucial defense of the Parisian heart of France—the French were able to transfer substantial troops back north and ultimately stymie the key German push, via the "miracle of the Marne," which saved Paris, caused the Schlieffen Plan to fail, and may well have ultimately cost Germany the war.

Of course, the other side made its share of costly mistakes, too, not least being the stubborn insistence by the British Field Marshall Douglas Haig on sending waves of soldiers "over the top," to be mowed down by German machine guns. (The Germans did the same thing, although to a somewhat lesser extent.) Then there was Czar Nicholas, whose strategic inadequacies had earlier been displayed during the Russo-Japanese War. Russia had previously refrained from supporting fellow Slavs in Serbia when in 1908 the Austro-Hungarians had annexed the provinces of Bosnia and Herzegovina. This hadn't gone down well with the Russian public. And so, when the earlier annexer made yet further demands on Serbia, Nicholas worried that if he didn't stand up for "greater Serbia"—an oxymoron if ever there was one—he'd be risking his legitimacy. He even explained to an adviser that by going to war with Austria-Hungary, he'd unite the Russian people behind his leadership, "just like Napoleon had done in 1812,"[9] and as he had foolhardily expected would happen during the Russo-Japanese War. Instead, just as public anger over the conduct of the earlier war contributed greatly to the 1905 Russian uprising that almost succeeded in overthrowing the czar, his immense miscalculation on the eve of World War I resulted in Nicholas losing not only his legitimacy, but his life.

3.10. World War II and Thereafter: Oops Aplenty

There were many strategic blunders before and during World War II as well, not to mention a much larger number of tactical, battlefield ones. Number one—bridging tactical and strategic—was doubtless Hitler's decision to invade the USSR, following in the failed footsteps of Napoleon and consistent with the adage that the only thing we learn from history is that people don't learn from history. Hitler was so confident of swift victory that when German troops invaded the Soviet Union—Operation Barbarossa in June 1941—they were not even issued winter clothing. Tens of thousands froze to death during the ensuing winter. He and his High Command had believed that the Soviet Union would fall before the snows did.

"We have only to kick in the door," Hitler announced to his generals "and the whole rotten thing will come down."[10] The *Wehrmacht* indeed kicked in the Soviet door, but it was Germany, not the USSR, that came crashing down, more than anything because of this catastrophic invasion. The German army suffered 80 percent of its losses on its eastern front: Nearly 4.5 million soldiers, who amounted to 75 percent of the casualties suffered by the whole German army.

Yet another key oops of World War II was Stalin's refusal to accept repeated warnings that Hitler was planning his double-cross. (Germany and the Soviet Union had signed a non-aggression treaty, the Molotov-Ribbentrop Pact, two years previously.) Stalin was so stubborn in his denial that he ordered the execution of a Russian operative in Czechoslovakia who warned him that the German invasion, Operation Barbarossa, was imminent; the Soviet dictator concluded that his informant must be a British double agent, trying to sow discord between the USSR and Germany, in order to recruit the Soviets to the British side. After all, there is some legitimacy to the adage that the enemy of my enemy is my friend, so it was at least plausible that the Brits—desperately fighting for their survival, and, at the time, losing—might have wanted Stalin to ally with them and turn against Hitler, even though Churchill detested the Soviet leader. But the report was correct and as a result, the Soviets were disastrously unprepared to withstand the German invasion, even as the Germans were disastrously unprepared to make it succeed.

Other major, strategic World War II mistakes include Neville Chamberlain's appeasement of Hitler at Munich, Japan attacking Pearl Harbor in the expectation (more like a forlorn hope) that the shock would induce the United States to sue for an early peace, and another crucial unforced error by Hitler, namely declaring war on the United States within days of the Japanese attack, when he didn't have to do so. Moreover, with America suddenly committed to war with Japan, there was at the time relatively little stomach for a second front against Germany. American attitudes toward joining the war in Europe were decidedly mixed in any event, so FDR had been concerned that he didn't have enough public backing to go to war with Germany and thereby support the United Kingdom in its time of peril. Thanks to Hitler, that changed.

Big, strategic blunders are well known to military historians. Less renowned are the oops that overtake individual units. Among these, the World War II exploits of the *USS William D. Porter*, a Fletcher-class destroyer known to its crew as the "Willie-Dee," is in a class by itself. Yet, its tale of ignominy is little known. The night before it was supposed to leave port on its most important, and ultimately most notorious, mission, the Willie-Dee sideswiped its sister ship, which had been docked alongside, while backing up. The *Porter* wasn't damaged, but its anchor destroyed some of the other ship's railing and ripped apart some of its crucial on-deck equipment.

The Willie-Dee became part of a convoy in 1943 escorting President Franklin Roosevelt to the Teheran Conference where he was to meet with Churchill and Stalin. The day following its dockside collision, the *Porter* accidentally released a depth charge, which exploded (the safety had mistakenly not been set), causing the convoy to take evasive maneuvers because it was thought to be under U-boat attack. But it was merely the *Porter*, doing what turned out to be its thing. This nonfiction ship of fools subsequently experienced a boiler failure and had to drop out of line for a time, which, had it lasted longer, might have been a blessing for all concerned.

A few days later, in a firepower demonstration for the president, who was aboard the battleship *Iowa*, the destroyer followed instructions and took practice shots at the *Iowa*, which was to include launching torpedoes after their firing mechanisms had been disarmed. However, a crew member forgot to disarm one of those torpedoes, which, with its activated five-hundred-pound warhead, headed straight for the *Iowa* and the president, who was on deck in his wheelchair, eager to watch the show. There followed a bizarre series of communication failures, further complicated because the ships were under orders to maintain radio silence, so the *Porter*'s officers ran around in panic, shouting conflicting orders about what to do next. They tried sending flashing light signals—in the wrong direction, of course. Finally, they broke radio silence, just in time.

The American flagship finally understood its peril and maneuvered so that the torpedo missed, exploding in the battleship's wake. Worrying that perhaps this friendly fire incident was part of a German assassination attempt, the *Iowa* trained its main guns for a time on the hapless *Porter*. The crew was arrested and eventually put on trial, not as spies, but for being criminally incompetent. This was the first and only time in US history that the entire crew of a ship was arrested and tried. FDR intervened and requested—successfully—that they be spared legal punishment.

Later in the war, the Willie-Dee was assigned to winter duty in the Aleutian Islands, which was comparatively uneventful. Except that before leaving for its next assignment, it accidentally fired a five-inch shell that landed, but didn't detonate, in the front yard of the local commandant. The captain of the *USS William D. Porter* later made rear admiral.

The ill-fated USS *William D. Porter* sinking after a kamikaze attack off Okinawa in 1945 (anonymous photographer).

To some extent, every lost war is an oops, at least for the loser. This is especially true when the country that initiates a war ends up defeated, or at minimum, deflated. Germany and Austria-Hungary started World War I after Gavrilo Princip's matchless success in assassinating Archduke Ferdinand. Turkey later joined as well, on the wrong side. As a result of their defeats, all three countries lost their colonial possessions, which, in the case of Austria-Hungary and Turkey, meant breaking up their once-large empires. Germany didn't lose much in the way of overseas territory—because it didn't have much to begin with. But it was saddled with crippling and humiliating reparations, which, in turn, rebounded as an oops on the part of the victors, who just two decades later had to deal with the consequences of the draconian Treaty of Versailles.

Although some historians (and not just German and Austrian) claim that both sides share blame for World War I, there is no doubt about World War II. *They* really did start it. And there is no doubt who won and who lost. Or is there? At least in part because of post-war Allied generosity, motivated in no small measure by Cold War pressures on the United States to recruit its former foe as anti-communist allies, Germany and Japan recovered quickly and became wealthy world powers. One needn't be a cynic to question whether these "losers" ended up losing.

There are also, of course, many cases in which even a "victory" has been so costly as to be nearly a defeat, as with Napoleon's eventual occupation of Moscow, or the triumphs of Pyrrhus, a renowned Greek general who fought (for the most part successfully) against the early Roman Republic. His name is famous for "Pyrrhic victory," a term that derives from the costly victory his Greek army had won over the Romans at the Battle of Asculum. When he was congratulated for this success, Pyrrhus famously replied, "One more such victory and we are lost."

So, when it comes to warfare, losers have sometimes lost, but so have winners, while the real losers have been pretty much everyone, regardless of their affiliation, along with the natural environment. There is an African proverb that is painfully apt, both literally and metaphorically: when elephants fight, the grass gets trampled.

Miscommunication between elephants has often led to such fights. Many scholars believe, for example, that the Korean War, which began with the North's invasion of the South, was accidentally encouraged by a crucial mistake on the part of then-US Secretary of State Dean Acheson. In a speech to the National Press Club in January 1950, Acheson omitted South Korea from his description of the American "defensive security perimeter" in Asia. This evidently led the North Korean leadership to think that the United States would accept communist conquest of the South without risking war. (A similar mistake contributed to Saddam Hussein's ill-advised invasion of Kuwait in 1990. April Glaspie, the US ambassador to Iraq, stated that the United States "does not have an opinion" on Iraq's dispute with Kuwait.[11] Saddam interpreted this to mean that he would have a free hand, so Ms. Glaspie and Mr. Hussein, each in their own way, erred seriously.)

In any event, Acheson's earlier careless oops led to a corresponding oops of misinterpretation by the North's Kim Il Sung, whose country was eventually devastated by his misreading of the likely American response. In total, something like five million soldiers and civilians, mostly owing to intensive American bombing of the North, are believed to have died in what many in the United States now call the "Forgotten War."

The risk of being trampled by warring elephants is greatest when it comes to nuclear war. Although the Nuclear Age has not (yet) brought about the ultimate oops, assumptions about the deterrent effect of nukes have led to many painful errors. Here is just one example, again from the Korean War, which is forgotten at the risk of piling one blunder upon another. In 1950, early in that war, China was fourteen years from developing its own nuclear weapons, whereas the United States had dozens, perhaps hundreds, of atomic bombs. US military and civilian officials judged, moreover, that China's military was exhausted by decades of civil war and would not dare intervene against the world's sole nuclear superpower, even after MacArthur's forces succeeded in their surprise landing at Inchon and retook Seoul from the North Koreans. They were spectacularly wrong. In two ways.

OOPS!

For one, although Chinese Foreign Minister Zhou Enlai warned several times that if UN (i.e., US) troops approached the Yalu River, China would enter the war, MacArthur ignored Zhou's warnings, loudly proclaiming his intention to reach the Yalu, which forms the border between North Korea and Chinese Manchuria. The Chinese apparently feared that in his zeal, MacArthur wouldn't stop at the Yalu but would attempt to overthrow the newly established mainland Chinese government. Second, the assumption that the American arsenal would deter Mao & Co was entirely wrong. China sent more than three hundred thousand soldiers—alleged "volunteers"—south in a sudden move that totally surprised the allies, routing US and South Korean forces. British military historian Max Hastings noted that the disintegration of US and Republic of Korea forces at the time "resembled the collapse of the French in 1940 to the Nazis and the British at Singapore in 1942 to the Japanese."[12] Although rarely discussed in public, it was the worst military debacle suffered by the US military in the twentieth century. The resulting stalemate on the Korean peninsula divides it to this day, and has produced one of the world's most dangerous, unresolved standoffs.

Chinese "Volunteer" Army troops heading south, crossing the Amrok River during the Korean War (anonymous photographer, 1950).

The Bay of Pigs fiasco definitely warrants more gimlet-eyed recounting than it normally receives, as does the Vietnam War, known to the Vietnamese people as the American War. Ditto for the 2003 US-led invasion of Iraq, which, although conducted competently in its initial military phase, was orchestrated under false pretenses, followed by a stunningly obtuse occupation regime that stimulated a powerful Iraqi nationalistic backlash, inflamed murderous sectarian passions, and precipitated several additional disasters: a humanitarian catastrophe, for the Arab-speaking people of the Middle East, and a geopolitical one for the United States.

The Ukraine War will be taken up later, but for now, an account of military oops requires mention of some of the most hair-raising oops of all, the many cases of nuclear near-misses due to errors of communication, the pressure of international crises, human misjudgment, bad luck, and—most worrisome—false alarms, many of which were recognized as such literally at the last minute. Some of the high—rather, low—points of these near misses are taken up in section 5.3. We can be grateful that so far, human judgment (or luck) has been good enough to let us shake our heads at the oops of others.

Chapter

4

Medical Mix-ups

Much of what was thought in the past to be fact was later found to be fiction, and dangerous fiction at that. Sometimes the culprit was carelessness, sometimes plain old ignorance, and sometimes a stubborn insistence on following old ways that were tried, but alas, not at all true.

4.1. A Sense of Humors

There have been many mistaken medical ideas, often persisting for years, sometimes even centuries; e.g., Hippocrates's belief in the existence of four humors, corresponding to the ancient Greek belief in the four elements—earth, air, fire, and water. Black bile was somehow connected to earth, and therefore manifested cold and dry (isn't that obvious?). Blood was aligned with air, and therefore, for some reason, warm and moist. Yellow bile was associated with fire and thus, warm and dry. And phlegm corresponded to water, cold and moist. It was thought that each of these humors influenced its own personality types. Thus, black bile led to "melancholic" dispositions (highly sensitive, prone to depression and also artistic pursuits), yellow bile to choleric (intense, passionate, quick to anger), blood conduced to joyful, optimistic, friendly, and sociable, whereas those in whom phlegm predominates are especially inclined to be calm, hard-working, reasonable, and predisposed to compromise—in a word, phlegmatic.

The ancient Greek physician, Galen, working mostly in the second century AD, further refined these notions, emphasizing that troubled personalities resulted from imbalances in these underlying humors. As humorous as belief in humors appears today, it was immensely influential for literally thousands of years—from Hippocrates in the fifth century BCE to, in some cases, the middle of the twentieth century—and was reflected not only in what passed for medical practice, but also in literature and philosophy. Moreover, it represented perhaps the first serious efforts to connect body and mind, and in this sense was ancestral to psychology and psychiatry. In short, here is an extended oops that gave rise to important insights and eventually, empirical advances—and is, in this sense, analogous to the relationship of alchemy to chemistry. Although no direct harm clearly arose from the erroneous belief in humors, it is conceivable—maybe likely—that by hitching their wagon to a perspective so egregiously incorrect, physicians were inhibited from looking elsewhere for genuine explanations, and therefore, cures.

4.2. Brother, Can You Spare Some Blood?

Unlike the long-lived belief in humors, which at least followed Hippocrates's other persisting legacy ("Do no harm"), some other stubborn misjudgments were in fact hurtful. Prominent among them is "bleeding," a.k.a. "bloodletting," the deeply held notion that many medical problems, notably infections now known to be caused by pathogens, derived from an excess of certain fluids, notably blood. The practice of intentional bloodletting appears to have started in ancient Egypt and is thus about three thousand years old. It may have begun, oddly, via observations of hippos, which secrete "blood sweat," which is in fact neither blood nor sweat, but a natural sunscreen that protects the animals from sunburn. Maybe the ancient Egyptians reasoned that secreting blood somehow kept hippos healthy (and healthy they generally are), so they concluded that bloodletting would do the same for people.

Regardless of its origin, when the idea reached Greece, Hippocrates again contributed (not, in retrospect, to his credit), taking another cue from "natural" blood loss and arguing that just as menstruation served to purge women of their "bad humors," similar exsanguination would be beneficial to men as well. If it was so beneficial, one might question why men didn't menstruate, too, just as neither men nor women sweat blood—except metaphorically on occasion. But it appears that early medicine was an authoritarian discipline, in which devotion to orthodoxy and a hefty dose of hardening of the categories predominated. (Some argue that this is still the case.)

Belief in the curative power of bloodletting is the one major case in which the theory of humors had a directly detrimental effect on medical practice, because blood, being perhaps the least funny of those humors, was thought to be subject to over-production, or, as the ancients conceived it, "plethoras" of that humor. There were precise instrumental menus, specifying which veins or arteries were to be sliced open depending on the symptom to be treated. Blood was considered the key humor, and because it is the most charismatic and impressive of the humors, its extraction carried the aura of serious medical intervention, unlike its poorer and paler cousins, black bile, yellow bile, and phlegm. Making the process especially curative, the rules called for removing more blood in proportion to the severity of the sufferer's disease.

Remarkably, it was also considered particularly beneficial if the patient lost so much blood as to be on the verge of passing out. Through much of the nineteenth century, British medical orthodoxy called for bloodletting as treatment for essentially every malady known, from acne and asthma to typhoid and yaws. It was used in treating ailments that already involved dangerous amounts of blood loss, such as hemorrhaging after traumatic injury and as a prophylactic for hemophiliacs. It was frequently employed before amputations, with the amount of blood removed carefully calibrated to equal the amount present in the limb to be removed. Physicians regularly prescribed the procedure and were criticized if they didn't do so, analogous to modern patients who feel inadequately cared for when their doctor refuses to prescribe antibiotics for a viral infection. Hence, public demands plus the reigning orthodoxy of their own profession demanded that "there will be blood." Following doctor's orders, bloodletting was frequently carried out by "barber-surgeons." The red-and-white striped barber pole owes its colors to this history, the red standing for blood and the white, for bandages.

The death of George Washington (painting by Junius Brutus Stearns, 1853).

Bloodletting almost certainly contributed to the death of George Washington. The former president, having retired to his plantation, was evidently quite robust at age sixty-seven and spent a day riding his horse in December while it was snowing and the temperature below freezing. He later complained of a sore throat, followed by pulmonary distress; in retrospect, he probably had pneumonia. But Washington himself was a great believer in therapeutic bloodletting, and he urged his physician to take as much blood as possible; i.e., to do his best, which we now know was pretty bad. It is estimated that the Father of Our Country was "relieved" of about 40 percent of his blood. He died shortly thereafter.

(Incidentally, Hippocrates also strongly believed in eating ear wax.)

4.3. Good Riddance to Bad Medicine

Yet another erroneous belief was less a matter of physicians engaging in a hurtful, ostensibly therapeutic technique, such as bloodletting, than it involved a refusal to accept evidence that criticized their own daily behavior. An especially tragic and well-documented example comes from a traditional practice—or rather, absence of a practice—whereby physicians only rarely washed their hands. Of course, this was before Louis Pasteur, Robert Koch, and our modern understanding of how germs cause disease. Mortality and morbidity resulting from too much bloodletting and from not enough hand-washing qualify as "idiopathic," which translates to doctor-caused diseases.

Dr. Joseph Lister (1827–1912) observed that many deaths following surgery occurred as a result of infections and that, for example, compound fractures had much higher mortality rates than did simple fractures. Although many physicians resisted his insights, Lister demonstrated that antiseptic procedures reduced post-surgical mortality due to infection from 80 percent to nearly zero. Obstetrics suffered from the same problem as did surgery. Until the mid- to late-1800s, the major cause of mortality among post-partum women was doctors. Infections beginning in their reproductive tracts ("puerperal fever") caused these deaths, and those infections, followed typically by septic shock, were caused in turn by unhygienic vaginal exams, use of contaminated instruments, and the often germ-ridden hands of the physicians delivering babies. So-called "lying in" hospitals had become especially widespread in Europe, specializing in pregnant women, who not uncommonly found themselves lying in the blood and filth attributable to earlier patients—situations that were Petri dishes for lethal pathogens. Mortality rates typically hovered between 20 and 25 percent, occasionally skyrocketing to 100 percent in particular wards. The victims extended throughout society: the queen consort of Henry VII died of puerperal fever, as did way too many others. Henry VIII didn't behead all of his wives: Jane Seymour and Catherine Parr died of the same unnatural cause, as did Mary Wollstonecraft, who, ironically, wrote *Vindication of the Rights of Women* and who died roughly a week after giving birth to the aforementioned Mary Shelley.

Birth scene, with lurking threat of death pre-antibiotics (painting by Jean-Baptiste Carpeaux, 1870).

The nineteenth-century Hungarian physician Ignaz Semmelweis contended with the high death rates in maternity wards, comparable to Lister's pioneering work on post-surgical mortality. After being appointed to an obstetric division of the Vienna General Hospital in 1844, Semmelweis observed that the mortality rate from puerperal fever in one ward was eight times higher than in another, and that the high mortality ward was the one in which doctors attended their maternity patients without washing their hands immediately after performing autopsies on women who had died the day before. By contrast, the low mortality ward was the one in which midwives were trained. Midwives did not do autopsies. Semmelweis was also galvanized when a medical colleague died of septic infection after he accidentally cut his hand during a routine autopsy.

He noted, as well, that home births were associated with significantly fewer postpartum infections and lower death rates than occurred in maternity hospitals. After experimenting with various handwashing concoctions, Semmelweis ordered physicians to wash their hands with a primitive antiseptic solution (even though the scientific basis for such hygienic precaution was not known), and maternal mortality plummeted by 90 percent. Overwhelmingly, physicians were not pleased, valuing their traditional behavior and self-esteem over their patients' welfare[i] and seeing Semmelweis as rocking their fixed, procedural applecart, not to mention insulting their dignity by maintaining that they were dirty and therefore dangerous to their patients. Which of course they were.

A renowned physician of that time, one Charles Meigs, huffed that "physicians are gentlemen, and a gentleman's hands are always clean."[1] And according to Sir Frederick Treves, a prominent mid-nineteenth-century surgeon, "there was no object in being clean. Indeed, cleanliness was out of place. It was considered to be finicking and affected. An executioner might as well manicure his nails before chopping off a head."[2] The contempt, ridicule, and hatred directed at Semmelweis by his professional colleagues was

---

[i] It is worth speculating whether this response would have been different if the victims were men rather than women.

so intense, and Semmelweis so psychologically delicate, that he was hounded out of Vienna, after which he experienced some sort of emotional breakdown and was committed to a mental hospital, where he died.

The good news is that some medical oops are correctible. Puerperal fever is now extremely rare in modern, hygiene-conscious hospitals, although it is pretty much guaranteed to spike as back-alley, unsanitary abortions return to plague pregnant women in the United States following the dismantling of *Roe v. Wade*.

The bad news is that a study by Johns Hopkins University concluded that even now, medical errors—misdiagnoses, the administration of incorrect medicine, unanticipated drug interactions, nosocomial infections (those acquired in-hospital such as MRSA) and so forth—are the third leading cause of deaths in the United States. Oops lives on, even as some patients don't.

4.4. When Bad Drugs Happen to Good People

The United States has weathered a long history of paranoid conspiracy theories, many of them—at least in the past—claiming that for a variety of nefarious motives, and in a comparable variety of nefarious ways, the federal government has sought to poison its own citizens. (For readers of a certain age, paranoia over fluoridation comes to mind.) But in one case, it really did make such an attempt, and for some unfortunate victims, succeeded. The poisoning began with prohibition, which started in 1919, and was an oops in itself, a misguided effort to prevent people from consuming what prohibitionists considered a bad drug. Millions of Americans wanted to drink, however, and managed to do so illegally, by purchasing "urban moonshine," either directly from bootleggers or in the tens of thousands of speakeasies that popped up around the country. In addition, enterprising entrepreneurs as well as many thirsty, low-income citizens quickly discovered that inexpensive industrial alcohol—ethanol, used to produce many commercial products, from paints to perfume—could be consumed instead. The feds responded with a legal requirement that all alcohol, regardless of its intended use, be "denatured" by adding methanol, the lethal kissing-cousin of ethyl alcohol (ethanol), which is the active ingredient in alcoholic beverages.

Methanol causes blindness, psychotic delusions, and, in sufficient quantity, death. Bootleggers responded by distilling the dangerously denatured product, which removed most of the methanol; the "renatured" drink was only mildly toxic. The government, in turn, mandated ever more poison. Legislation in 1926 doubled the previous level of methanol, so that its toxicity couldn't be distilled away. Also legally required was the addition of benzene, noxious in taste and odor, which conveyed its own health hazards, notably cancer. None of this was designed to injure the public; rather it was part of a well-intentioned effort to get citizens to obey the law and keep demon rum at arm's length.

The increased methanol level was widely publicized by the government. In 1926, a government chemist explained to the *New York Times* that the heightened methanol content was instituted because "it gives a greater warning to the drinker that he is getting hold of something that he should leave alone."[3] The threat of dying would keep people from boozing. But many did, anyhow: an estimated ten thousand Americans drank the tainted cup and died.

Something analogous happened in the 1970s, when the United States sprayed a different poison, paraquat, on marijuana fields in Mexico. As with the methanol misadventure of the 1920s, paraquat doubtless deterred some people from smoking marijuana, but once again widespread suffering ensued, notably among the poor, who couldn't afford unadulterated liquor or unsprayed marijuana.

Methanol and paraquat are bad drugs, known to be bad; that was the idea. (They turned out to be bad ideas, too.) Now we turn to some drugs thought to be good, but that were bad, starting with thalidomide. It was developed and marketed in the 1950s to pregnant women, as both an anti-anxiety drug and a cure for severe morning sickness. It worked and was widely prescribed, especially in West Germany. At that time, new drugs were rarely tested in pregnant women[ii] and only later was it discovered that thalidomide caused numerous miscarriages, the death of roughly two thousand newborns,

---

[ii] Even today, drugs aren't tested on women as much as on men, the explanation (excuse?) being that women's physiology varies on a monthly basis, making interpretation of results more difficult.

and terrible birth defects (notably failure of limbs to develop normally) in ten thousand more, close to one-half in West Germany. The renowned bass-baritone Thomas Quasthoff, born in 1959, was a thalidomide baby. He stands 4'4," and has an enormous voice.

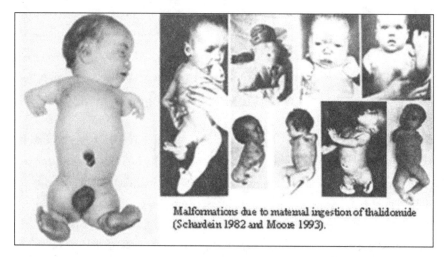

Malformations due to maternal ingestion of thalidomide (Schardein 1982 and Moore 1993).

Malformed newborns due to pregnant mothers' use of Thalidomide (anonymous photographers).

Thalidomide was eventually classified as a teratogen, a word derived from the Greek root meaning "monster," and that now includes alcohol, chlorobiphenyls, tegretol, and others, nearly all of them less teratogenic than thalidomide itself, which was finally taken off the market in 1961, and whose importation into the United States was severely restricted by on-the-ball watchdogs at the Food and Drug Administration (FDA). But by then, horrific damage had already been done, especially in Europe, and thalidomide became synonymous with any once-promising but disastrous medicine. Thalidomide remains in use, however, but under much more restricted conditions, as treatment for a limited range of conditions including leprosy, graft-host disease, and certain cancers such as multiple myeloma.

A positive outcome of the thalidomide blunder is that it inspired legislation that strengthened the powers of the FDA, such as requiring pharmaceutical companies to demonstrate the efficacy and especially the safety of new prescription drugs, and that any side effects be disclosed. Not surprisingly, Big Pharma was not pleased, but they didn't protest very loudly, having been chastened by the painful consequences of their eagerness to put profits over patient well-being. (The most painful of these anticipated consequences being the threat that public anger and patient boycotts would reduce their corporate bottom lines.)

Profit, not surprisingly, remains the Holy Grail of drug companies, as of pretty much all businesses. Researchers, on the other hand, are often motivated by scientific curiosity and zeal to promote the general welfare. Once the latter make a breakthrough, count on the former to take over, although researchers, too, aren't averse to join the profits bandwagon when possible. And so, we come to fun-fun with fen-phen.

In 1979, Dr. Michael Weintraub was a professor of clinical pharmacology at the University of Rochester. He was aware even in those far-off days that obesity was a significant health problem in the United States (one that has only gotten much worse in the intervening decades). Appetite suppressing drugs were well known in the 1960s, but had developed a bad reputation because they turned out to be habit-forming and also weren't especially effective. However, one drug, fenfluramine, had been approved by the FDA; it allegedly worked as an appetite suppressant by releasing large amounts of serotonin, a normal and necessary neurochemical, but one dangerous in excess. Another drug, phentermine, was a widely used stimulant.

It occurred to Dr. Weintraub that maybe the two combined would prove effective for weight-loss and that phentamine, which primarily releases norepinephrine, would balance the negative effects of fenfluramine's serotonin stimulation. It worked, up to a point at least, for weight loss. Not only did it help people shed some pounds but—the bane of dieting schemes— they were only able to keep it off so long as users continued taking the drugs. The special benefit of phentamine seemed to be that it kept patients cheerful, thus keeping them on the drugs that much longer. The moniker fen-phen was born, along with a new diet craze. The cover of *Time* magazine crowed about "The Hot New Diet Pill." *Reader's Digest* joined the bandwagon, and the public clamored for it. Many physicians obliged, setting up fen-phen prescription mills. Dr. Weintraub was appalled but couldn't stop this excessive over-embrace of his research, which had only been preliminary and had employed a small sample size.

Prescribing physicians were within their professional and legal rights, making use of an FDA policy that allows certain drugs to be used "off label"; that is, for purposes that differed from those for which the drug has been approved. Some doctors even devoted their entire practice to being, for all intents and purposes, fen-phen dispensaries. These fen-phen mills were at minimum somewhat unethical, since the average "doc-in-a-box" only rarely conducted careful medical examinations of their patients/clients and also weren't generally up to snuff when it came to careful clinical record-keeping. But hey, fenfluramine was approved for patient use and so was phentermine.

Here was a case, however, when the whole was a whole lot more dangerous than the sum of its parts. And although the FDA had approved fen and phen taken separately, it hadn't given a green light to combining the two. Wyeth-Ayerst Laboratories, which was already making a ton of money on the drugs, now requested FDA approval to market dexfenfluramine, a more potent form of fenfluramine, and Wyeth-Ayerst also requested that it be approved for indefinite use. At that time, diet drugs had only been approved for short-term consumption. Approval was duly granted, but only grudgingly and after a contentious debate in which several members of the committee expressed reservations. Dexfenfluramine had only been tested for use over a one-year period, not long term. Moreover, it was already known to hugely increase the risk of pulmonary hypertension, normally a blessedly rare but potentially fatal condition, in which lung capillaries become irretrievably hardened. But since the overall incidence of this untreatable condition was exceedingly low and by then obesity was increasingly recognized as a big-time public health threat, the drug combination squeaked over the bar.

Then things changed. In 1997, two years after fen-phen—by then, "dexfen-phen," rebranded Redux—was approved by the skin of its disappearing adipose tissue, physicians at the Mayo Clinic published a report in the *New England Journal of Medicine* showing that more than three months of the combo increased the risk of primary pulmonary hypertension (remember that?) by twenty-three times.[4] Two dozen women on the diet drug regime developed a serious heart valve abnormality that is normally quite rare and that can only be repaired via surgery. The regulatory roof was caving in. Five different medical centers independently reported that of nearly three hundred patients—mostly women—on the weight loss regime, a full third had damaged aortic valves. Almost immediately, by order of the FDA, fen-phen was fin-finished, but not before an estimated one to five million Americans had taken it.

As of 2005, alleged fen-phen victims had filed more than fifty thousand law suits for product liability. Google fen-phen and you're likely to come up with numerous ads from litigious trial lawyers, eager to represent victims. After all, Wyeth had designated $21.1 billion to meet the burgeoning demand, this time for compensation. Nothing approaching that amount was paid out, however; lawyers are also effective when it comes to derogating claims against their corporate clients. But at least fen-phen and its imitators are gone. In a sense, therefore, the system worked, for which we can be grateful, even though certain drug companies felt differently. As did those patients who were left broken-hearted in more ways than one.

When it comes to government blunders, greedy drug companies, unscrupulous physicians, and a tragically victimized public, neither methanol, paraquat, nor fen-phen hold a candle to America's opioid epidemic. This ongoing catastrophe is so well-known that it doesn't need much repetition here. Following is a bare-bones summary.

In 2020 alone, close to ninety-two thousand persons died from drug-involved overdose, roughly two-thirds due to opioids—whether illicit or prescription—including oxycodone and its longer-acting cousin, oxycontin, along with hydrocodone, codeine, and, increasingly, fentanyl. The number keeps rising. Opioids are narcotics and are important as pain relievers, although they can also induce euphoria, as well as addiction among vulnerable individuals. During the 1990s, the medical community came to recognize chronic pain as the "fifth vital sign," along with body temperature, pulse rate, respiratory rate, and blood pressure. Pain was seen as a syndrome, and a debilitating one at that, something that compassionate medicine needed to address. Opioids provided cheap and effective treatment and were increasingly prescribed for management of chronic pain. Between 1990 and 1999, the number of opioid prescriptions soared from 76 million to roughly 116 million, climbing dramatically ever since. In the twenty-first century, opioids are the most prescribed class of drugs in the country, used not only for pain relief but recreationally and as a result of addiction. At the same time, opioid prescriptions have favored increased potency such that by 2012, one third of drug users were getting prescriptions for medications more powerful—and more addictive—than morphine.

Following this "first wave" of opioid use, a second wave developed around 2010, notably involving substantial increases in heroin use, heroin being cheaper, more concentrated, and therefore an appealing transition for individuals already overusing medical opioids. At about the same time, a steeply increasing third wave resulted from synthetically produced opioids, notably black market fentanyl and its derivatives; these are generally even more potent than heroin.

Would anyone be surprised to learn that certain vulturine pharmaceutical companies and a number of money-hungry, unethical doctors surfed profitably on these waves? "Pill mills" proliferated, some of them seeing as many as fifty people per day and charging hundreds of dollars each for a brief "consult" and "examination" that often took mere minutes, after which either prescriptions or pills themselves were sold. As for the pharmaceutical companies, Perdue Pharma is the most infamous, although others have also been taking advantage of needy, desperate patients.

Numerous lawsuits were filed accusing Perdue (along with other companies) of aggressively marketing these dangerous drugs and willfully misleading claims of their safety, all the while essentially ignoring their potential for addiction and death. As a result, the Sackler family, owners of Perdue Pharma, reached a settlement paying $4.5 billion out of their personal holdings. In 2022, they were granted immunity from additional lawsuits in return for increasing their payment to $6 billion, still substantially less than the profits they had unethically made. (The Sackler family expressed "regret," but denied any "wrong-doing.")

The opioid epidemic is especially acute in the United States, where it has definite socio-economic components. It has been described as a disease of despair, especially pronounced in poor, rural areas where jobs have been low paying or non-existent, and the future, bleak. It has been exacerbated, as well, by the bizarrely unbalanced American health system, in which insurance is keyed to employment, and minimal or no coverage has reduced many chronic pain sufferers to accepting the cheapest possible treatment: a pill. Reliable data have been hard to come by on the number of opioid-related deaths, pills consumed, and even prescriptions written. And despite moralistic temptation to blame the victims for their ostensibly weak character, inability or refusal to look ahead at the consequences of their behavior, and the like, the reality is that there is plenty of blame to go around: blunders galore, oops aplenty, overwhelmingly by those—including criminal manufacturers and distributors—who have battened on human misery and profited mightily as purveyors of false hope, immiseration, and death.

As usual, the victims are those least responsible for their plight, and the least able to shoulder its consequences.

4.5. Better a Bottle in Front of Me Than a Frontal Lobotomy

Lobotomy (a.k.a. leucotomy) involves poking into a patient's brain and severing connections to and from the prefrontal lobes. It was pioneered and vigorously advertised (especially by those who profited by doing it) as a way to alleviate psychotic symptoms. Coincidentally—or not—it also served to control difficult mental patients. In Ken Kesey's novel, *One Flew Over the Cuckoo's Nest*, and the notable movie starring Jack Nicholson, the public was alerted to the immensity of psychiatric abuse encompassed by this devastating medical oops.

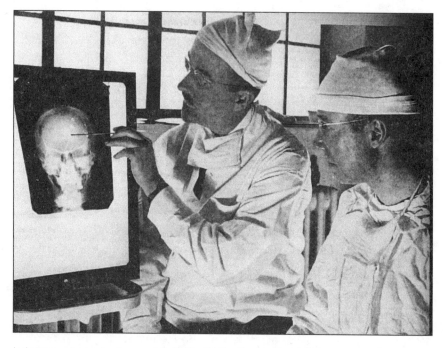

Lobotomy presurgical consult, with Dr. Walter Freeman at left (photograph by Harris A. Ewing, 1941).

Initially at least, practitioners weren't evil malefactors, even as, in retrospect, they evoke thoughts of the horrors of Nazi doctors who cruelly experimented on concentration camp victims in violation of all medical ethics. At the time (mostly beginning in the 1930s and continuing for several decades thereafter), the procedure seemed at least somewhat justified. A 1937 investigation reported that, at the time, 55 percent of US hospital beds were occupied by psychiatric patients, for whom no treatment was available. Psychoanalysis was useless when it came to helping psychotic individuals (it still is), and effective antipsychotic medications were decades in the future. Desperate physicians were attempting various "shock therapies," such as insulin overdoses, lengthy medicated sleep, ice baths, heat treatments, shock treatments, and the like. Lobotomy offered a window of hope for patients whose condition was otherwise considered hopeless. At least it offered results; alas, many of these results were disastrous.

In Kesey's novel, lobotomy is labelled "frontal-lobe castrations," described as a means of controlling unruly patients, and presented as Nurse Ratchet's ultimate triumph. When the now post-op and surgically modified McMurphy—previously flamboyant and over-the-top—is wheeled back to the psych ward on a gurney, his new condition is described by another inmate: "There's nothin' in the face. Just like one of those store dummies." Similarly, Sylvia Plath's semi-autobiographic 1963 novel, *The Bell Jar*, includes a scene in which the main character is hospitalized several times for suicidal depression, whereupon she is appalled by a lobotomized patient's "perpetual marble calm." Inducing that calm is often precisely the goal.

In his 1948 book, *Cybernetics*, famed mathematician Norbert Wiener wrote that "[P]refrontal lobotomy . . . has recently been having a certain vogue, probably not unconnected with the fact that it makes the custodial care of many patients easier. Let me remark in passing that killing them makes their custodial care still easier."[5] Rosemary Kennedy, sister of JFK, was lobotomized in 1941, which left her severely incapacitated and in need of in-hospital custodial care for the rest of her life.

Dr. Antonio Moniz, the father of lobotomy, was something of a self-promoter, with a blind spot for the downsides of his beloved baby. In 1937, he wrote that "the hypotheses underlying the procedure might be called into question; the surgical intervention might be considered very audacious; but such arguments occupy a secondary position because it can be affirmed now that these operations are not prejudicial to either physical or psychic life of the patient, and also that recovery or improvement may be obtained frequently in this way."[6] He asserted that undesirable outcomes were transitory and that 35 percent of his patients improved significantly, while an equal proportion were moderately improved, leaving the remaining 30 percent unchanged. Moniz reported no deaths and no post-op deterioration. What he didn't say is that his entire sample was just twenty people. Moreover, future data turned out to be significantly more worrying, but about these, Muniz was mum.

Walter Freeman, the lobotomist who so admired his patient's post-op docility, wasn't at all docile himself when it came to devising easy ways to do his work. When Dr. Moniz first developed the procedure as an effective clinical intervention (others had previously tried several largely unsuccessful variants), he started by injecting ethyl alcohol into the prefrontal cortex, to disrupt its functioning. Then he moved to using a kind of rotating blade. Dr. Freeman was an enthusiastic acolyte, who apparently began as an honest evangelist for lobotomies. Both of Dr. Moniz's techniques required drilling into the patient's skull, and thus had to be performed by a trained neurosurgeon in a traditional operating room. Dr. Freeman was concerned that most psychiatric hospitals did not have surgical suites and, moreover, that psychiatrists lacked surgical training. So, he looked for ways to simplify the procedure in order to make lobotomies more widely available. He settled on an ice pick and a "transorbital" approach; i.e. through the eye sockets. If this sounds both primitive and barbaric, that's what it was.

The lobotomist lifts the patient's upper eyelid and inserts the pick (endowed with either of two more respectable monikers, leucotome or orbitoclast) beneath the retracted eyelid, just along the edge of the eye socket, essentially where the upper edge of the nose meets the forehead, aiming up toward the top of the skull. Next, bang with a hammer, pounding the business end of the pick parallel to the bridge of the nose and a full two inches into the frontal lobes of the brain. Then, pivot the pick to scythe the brain connections on the opposite side of the patient's head. After returning the instrument to its initial position, smash it in another inch or so for good measure and pivot around once more, slicing upward, inward, and outward. The process wasn't so much like using a sledge hammer to kill a fly; it was more like the now-infamous US Army officer's account of the fate of South Vietnam's Ben Tre during the Vietnam War's Tet offensive: "We had to destroy the village in order to save it."[7]

What this new, revised procedure offered in simplicity—it could be performed by non-surgeon psychiatrists in mental hospitals that lacked standard surgical facilities—it made up for in brutality. Lobotomy became an "in office" technique that could essentially be mass produced. And it was. By 1951, nearly nineteen thousand people had been lobotomized in the United States alone. Before the procedure was terminated in the United States—the last one having been performed by Dr. Freeman in 1967, and resulting in the death of the patient—more than forty thousand people had been lobotomized in this country, the majority being women. The Scandinavian countries conducted more lobotomies per capita than any others, while in Japan the procedure was especially likely to be conducted *on children*. Remarkably, lobotomies continued up to the late 1970s, and, inexplicably, into the 1980s in France. Despite its deplorable history of misusing psychiatry for political repression, the Soviet Union banned lobotomies in 1950, a year after Moniz was awarded the Nobel Prize for Physiology or Medicine,[iii] and just as it was gaining steam in the United States.

Now that lobotomies are defunct, stabbed in the skull by the ice pick of history and tossed in a bin with other medical waste, what can we conclude about who benefitted and who blundered? It can certainly be argued that neither Moniz nor Freeman were mistake-prone failures. If nothing else, they achieved temporary fame and large incomes, even though their reputations are rather sullied today (perhaps unfairly). The patients? They had little or no choice but to go along. Their psychoses often wouldn't have allowed them "informed consent," something that is *de rigueur* these days, but an ethical requirement that didn't exist during the first half of the twentieth century. And the likes of McMurphy, for all his pre-lobotomy volubility, couldn't testify after the fact as to whether it made them feel better or worse. To some extent, many of them weren't feeling or thinking very much at all following their experience. Was post-lobotomy innocence a kind of bliss? Or were they locked into a perpetually boring "marble calm?" What about patients' families? Some clearly were relieved to be spared the stress of coping with a troublesome relative, who indeed became, in most cases, easier to manage. Others were shocked, shocked by an irreversible outcome for their loved-ones that they had not expected . . . or so they claimed. But did the real-life avatars of Nurse Ratchet feel any remorse?

[iii] The Nobel Committee has been petitioned repeatedly to rescind Moniz's prize, decrying it as an inexcusable scientific and ethical miscarriage, but the organization has thus far stuck to its ice picks.

4.6. Public Health Overdosing

Dear reader, please don't despair! There have been many positive outcomes of modern medicine, with the greatest health benefits coming not from wonder drugs—pain-killing and otherwise—nor new surgical techniques, but from advances in public hygiene. A close second has been antibiotics, which have saved millions of lives. However, these benefits are themselves at risk and already in decline, because of antibiotic over-use. Thus, anti-biotics are ineffective against viruses, yet are often demanded by patients not suffering from bacterial disease. In many developing countries such as India and much of Africa and Latin America, they can be obtained without a prescription. Moreover, patients often stop taking even correctly prescribed antibiotics as soon as disease symptoms disappear, rather than continuing each medicine for its full recommended course. Stopping too soon sets the stage for the evolution of drug resistance among pathogens. This is because instead of being wiped out as they would be if patients adequately persevered in their antibiotic use, some microbes can often survive long enough that resistant forms can multiply, and this gener-ates unintended artificial selection for drug-resistant pathogens. As a result, yesterday's "miracle drugs" lose their miraculousness. This leaves modern medicine helpless against dangerous invaders, back to the years before antibiotics were developed. On top of this, unused antibiotics are often discarded, finding their way into waste-water and from there into the more general bacterial environment, where their low-level persistence provides a perfect biochemical stew for the unintended evolution of yet more drug-resistant germs.

Compounding this is the widespread use of antibiotics in the meat and dairy industry. In pursuit of profits and indifferent to public health, "big ag" indiscriminately feeds antibiotics to even healthy chickens, pigs, sheep, goats, and especially cattle in order to increase their growth and productivity. The result has been artificial selection, once again and in large part unnecessarily, for yet more ineffectiveness of important drugs when they are really needed. The evolutionary biology in all of these cases is relatively straight-forward, even as evolution itself is often denied by livestock farmers[iv] whose liveli-hoods are threatened when susceptible "bugs" are killed off, leaving drug resistant survivors. Overuse of antibiotics is a kind of unintended unilateral disarmament.

Because of these accumulated errors, entire categories of former "wonder drugs" no longer work, and numbers of potentially deadly micro-organisms that used to succumb to antibiotic treatments are now becoming danger-ously resistant to them. This includes, but isn't limited to *Clostridoides diffi-cile, Candida auris*, methicillin resistant *Staphylococcus aureus* (MRSA), and *Streptococcus pneumoniae*, as well as those causing tuberculosis, gonorrhea, and certain forms of salmonella.

4.7. COVID-19: Invincible Ignorance, Egregious Egos, and Playing Politics While the Pandemic Burned (Nero Redux)

Toward the end of Donald Trump's presidency, a detailed study by Harvard's T. H. Chan School of Public Health concluded that "ineffective national poli-cies and responses, especially as compared to those of other wealthy nations or compared to the intricate preparation and planning by previous admin-istrations of both parties, have been driving the terrible toll of COVID-19 and its inequities in the U.S."[8] In other words, it's clear, even in a sober and carefully worded university report, that we—notably President Trump and his camp followers—really screwed up. There is one exception, for which the Trump Administration deserves some credit: they helped to sponsor a scien-tific surge to develop vaccines for the disease. Unfortunately, this success was overshadowed by such derogation of biomedical science generally and of the seriousness of the pandemic itself that many people became anti-vaxxers, seeing their stance as somehow a statement of support for Mr. Trump, even

---

[iv] Many of these farmers rue the fact that they find themselves obliged to use ever-larger doses of insecticides and herbicides, something that they have brought about, and that serve as textbook cases of evolution in action.

though he gave himself many pats on the back for vaccine development during his presidency, a claim that—as we'll see—is largely unjustified.

As the pandemic raged, errors were repeatedly made, often the same ones over and over, and the American people suffered because of them. Although the virus continued making things difficult during the Biden Administration, mostly because of the emergence of a string of variants, Trump's blunders started us off on a lethally wrong foot. Not only was the virus given a tragic head start, but Trump *et al.* set the stage for politicizing the pandemic, which has made it harder yet to win this public health battle.

It didn't have to be this way. Here is a brief account of the main miscues.

- Right off the bat, the administration dropped the ball, refusing to acknowledge that COVID was serious, and, as a result, delaying any serious national response. As the pandemic spread, the administration's response was never as serious and effective as it should have been. By contrast, when confronted with the first US cases of H1N1—which was much less troublesome— President Barack Obama declared a public health emergency two weeks after the first cases were reported in California. It took Trump more than seven weeks after Washington State reported the first COVID cases to do this. Trump simply made things up, trying to duck any notion that things were bad and getting worse, and that—heaven forbid—he might have any responsibility for the national welfare. After all, acknowledging trouble was, for him, equivalent to acknowledging personal weakness; better that the country itself should be weakened.

Trump and his cronies became obsessed with managing not the pandemic, but public opinion, minimizing the seriousness of the problem rather than the problem itself. So, he proclaimed that "99 percent" of COVID cases are "totally harmless," although the World Health Organization (WHO) pointed out that roughly 15 percent of cases are likely to be "severe," and 5 percent, "critical." In October 2022, the House Select Subcommittee

on the Coronavirus Crisis released the results of their two-year investigation in which they interviewed former Trump Administration officials. Its
report paints a damning portrait of how the Centers for Disease Control
and Prevention (CDC) was muzzled and manipulated into keeping the
American public in the dark: "After a February 25, 2020, CDC telebriefing
'angered' President Trump, the White House wrested control of coronavirus
communications away from CDC and mandated on February 26 that all
media requests related to the pandemic be approved by the Office of the Vice
President prior to release." Furthermore, "Trump Administration officials
blocked CDC from conducting telebriefings on critical, emerging public
health issues for three months and restricted scientists from participating
in interviews—at a time that coincided with a rapid explosion in coronavirus cases."⁹ The goal was clear: to convey only positive news, to downplay
the risks, and to manipulate public opinion so as to keep the American
people from realizing what a mess the Administration had made, and were
continuing to make.

But even as the president kept up his happy talk, he confided to the
Washington Post's Bob Woodward that the disease had the potential to be
truly catastrophic. Trump went further and described any criticism of his
handling of the pandemic "a hoax," while many of his true believers followed
his lead and went further, derogating the pandemic itself as "fake news"
made up by scientists, doctors, victims, news organizations, and Democrats to make their hero "look bad." Because this remarkably large cohort of
Trumpian true believers became convinced that COVID itself was a myth,
it led to the spectacle of people dying of a disease that, with their last breath,
they claimed didn't exist.

- As evidence mounted and became undeniable, Trump
  compared COVID to the common cold or seasonal flu and
  continued to use his loud public megaphone to send mixed
  messages and sow doubt about COVID's seriousness and toll:
  "Within a couple days it [the pandemic] is going to be down
  to close to zero," followed by a breezy, "It will go away." Even in

the worst case, "What happens is, you get better" after being a little bit sick. "That's what happens: You get better. . . . You get better and then you're immune." And children are "virtually immune" right from the get-go. It is sobering, or should be for those who saw Trump as some sort of medical messiah, that there is a positive correlation between 2020 voter preference for Trump in congressional districts and the rates of infection and COVID deaths: the stronger the MAGA preference, the higher the morbidity and mortality.[10]

For the deluded president, when all else failed, press coverage was the villain, not the virus. He petulantly announced from the Oval Office, "I am sick and tired of how negative you all are. … I spend half of my day responding to what Tony Fauci has to say, and I'm the president of the United States!" He snapped at Dr. Debora Birx, "Every time you talk, I get depressed. You have to stop that." Instead of evidence-based policy from the top, we got policy-based evidence. And of course, it was all China's fault, blaming the National Institutes of Allergy and Infectious Diseases (NIAID) for partially funding, years before the outbreak, a research program designed to investigate just such outbreaks and, if possible, to head them off before they occurred.

It should not be forgotten, however, that China may well have been guilty of its own COVID-producing oops. When it comes to the initiation of the pandemic as a disease in humans, three possibilities exist. One is that it jumped from one of the notorious "wet markets" in which animals—many of them wild-caught and hence possible virus hosts—are kept in unsanitary conditions and then slaughtered on the spot, with body fluids splattering all over the place. A second is that it was an accidental release from a virus research lab, in which "gain of function" studies were underway. This research, conducted in the United States and Russia as well, seeks to add genetic traits to existing viruses; these traits could have included engineering viruses that could infect human beings. The third is that COVID emerged from a wholly natural situation, namely bat droppings. Of these, only this one would exonerate China from being complicit in the pandemic's origin.

- When a travel ban was finally imposed on Jan 31, 2020, it applied only to non-US citizens, and only to people coming from China, even though at that time, COVID was known to be proliferating in most of Europe. No screening for symptoms and no quarantines were established for Europeans; research later established that the great majority of COVID cases entering the United States came not from China but from Europe, presumably by way of China. By the time European travelers were restricted, it was too late: by then most new cases in the United States came from other states, having already entered the country. The barn door was closed too late, one of many tragic consequences of administration denial and outright lies.

- Trump tapped his son-in-law, Jared Kushner, to be the overall coordinator of the government's COVID response. Prior to 2017, the thirty-six-year-old Kushner had zero experience in government. His sole qualification? Being married to Trump's fashion-plate daughter, Ivanka, and having inherited a real estate fortune from his convicted felon, multi-millionaire father. But by COVID time, the cocky Kushner had already demonstrated his remarkable competence, giving nepotism a good name by his spectacular success in solving these problems to which he had been assigned: bringing permanent peace to the Middle East, modernizing the Department of Veteran's Affairs, solving the opioid crisis, and orchestrating Trump's "beautiful" infrastructure plans. (Remember "infrastructure week"?) He also served as primary liaison to Mexico, where he was tasked with blocking immigration and helping the Mexicans to ignore his father-in-law's disparagement of their country and its people. Oh yes, he also distinguished himself by smoothing relations with China, with North Korea, and with the Muslim community within the United States and worldwide.

So, it only made sense to add COVID to the first son-in-law's list of triumphs. He was immediately confronted with hospitals dealing with a lethal shortage of ventilators and desperately needing basic personal protective equipment (PPE). Emergency room personnel, for example, had been reduced to wearing garbage bags in lieu of sanitary gowns. At a meeting of private enterprise heavy-hitters, the head of General Motors offered to reconfigure assembly lines to produce ventilators and other hardware in short supply. Instead of organizing this and other essential transitions ASAP, Kushner stunned the participants by announcing that "the federal government is not going to lead this response. It's up to the states to figure out what they want to do." Moreover, "Free markets will solve this. It isn't the role of the federal government." Lacking direction and meaningful assistance from the federal government, states were accordingly left to compete with each other for critical supplies and devices.

One of the participants pointed out the desperate plight of New York State, which had initially been the hardest hit, at which Kushner expressed his dislike of the NY governor and shrugged that "his people are going to suffer and that's their problem."[11] Early on, COVID was ravaging mostly urban areas concentrated in blue states, because they received the greatest number of travelers, as well as having the largest and most dense populations. In addition to using COVID response (i.e., non-response) to punish blue states that hadn't voted for his father-in-law, Kushner's cynical approach had the additional narrow-minded benefit of giving Trump the opportunity to profit politically by laying blame on progressive governors nationwide. Deflecting the obvious political motivations, Kushner kept repeating that private enterprise alone would solve the problem. As a result, federal capacity to conduct vigorous contact tracing went largely unused and detailed plans for testing were vetoed and then delayed, a further triumph of political calculation over public health. With 4 percent of the world's population, the United States soon accounted for more than 20 percent of COVID deaths.

Although Kushner was a surrogate for Trump, his father-in-law wasn't shy about putting in his two cents' worth of ignorance, political vengeance, and a never-ending need to be admired. On March 26, he informed Sean Hannity that "a lot of equipment's being asked for that I don't think they'll need,"[12] in reference to the governors of New York, Michigan, and Washington (all blue states) who were requesting medical equipment for their people. The following day he used a task force briefing to complain that these state leaders "ought to be appreciative. . . . We've done a great job."[13]

- Notwithstanding the brutal political gamesmanship from the top, the federal government possessed an immense reservoir of career officials with perhaps the world's finest organizational and public health competence, but these experts were largely denigrated or bypassed as being part of the anti-Trump "deep state." Rather than unleashing the immense powers headquartered in Washington, DC and on the NIH campus, opportunities for a prompt, effective, and life-saving response were squandered while people sickened and died. The wasted resources included, paradoxically, the ballyhooed power of private enterprise, with major corporations eager to help (and, to be sure, also to help their bottom lines). But a major investment by private enterprise required federal funds to at least prime their waiting pumps. By contrast, although military procurement similarly relies on corporate contracts and subsequent production, the government orders and pays for what it needs. It never relies on the invisible hand of free markets to deal with immediate threats.

In fairness, the Trump Administration deserves a wee bit of credit for funding Operation Warp Speed, a public-private partnership intended as a crash program to develop an effective COVID vaccine. The good news is that such a vaccine (actually, vaccines) were developed and distributed. But as usual, Trump tried to take credit—lots of it—for these successes. Far more than he deserved. And not nearly enough to make up for his calamitous mishandling of the pandemic generally.

Moderna was already conducting its ultimately successful vaccine research program while Trump was still hitting the airwaves claiming that COVID wasn't spreading in the United States. And as for Pfizer, whose vaccine he claimed was "a result of Operation Warp Speed," it wasn't. Pfizer had explicitly opted to forgo US government funding and instead partnered with BioNTech, a German pharmaceutical firm, in March 2020. That collaboration began its first human study in April of that year. Operation Warp Speed, intended to fast track the research, wasn't even announced until May. A Pfizer spokesperson explained that "Pfizer's COVID-19 vaccine development and manufacturing costs have been entirely self-funded. We decided to self-fund our efforts so we could move as fast as possible."[14] Considerably faster, it turned out, than "warp speed."

Nonetheless, Trump continues to demand accolades for both the Pfizer and Moderna vaccines: "The vaccines were me!" So, the most anti-science president in modern times, dragging behind him a history of dysfunction, denial, and dissimulation—not to mention a devastating lack of leadership—suddenly began claiming that he was the conquering COVID hero after all. In fact, Moderna did take some government funding, and Pfizer, too, to help with distribution, but not development.

Forbes magazine—which typically supports a conservative approach to everything—published the following after the 2020 election, under the headline: "Trump Takes Credit For Vaccine Created By Others, Including Immigrants":

> Donald Trump did not invent or develop the vaccines to combat COVID-19, despite his claim he should receive the credit. Ironically, immigrants played the crucial role in developing the vaccines, a group Trump as president has vilified. It's fair to say if Trump administration immigration policies had been in place years earlier, including policies on international students, employment-based immigrants and H-1B and L-1 visa holders, the individuals instrumental in making the COVID-19 vaccines a reality would never have lived or worked in America.[15]

For example, Warp Speed's chief scientific adviser was Moncef Slaoui, a Moroccan-born immigrant; the Moderna chairman and cofounder was Noubar Afeyan. Dr. Ugur Sahin founded BioNTech with his wife, Dr. Özlem Türeci, both originally from Turkey, and both are (heaven forbid!) Muslims. As president, Trump had issued executive orders that banned approval of nearly all immigrants seeking employment-based admittance.

The *Forbes* article went on to conclude that: "There is nothing in the record that warrants him taking credit for the vaccines. A review of events shows immigrants and immigrant-led companies created them."[16] Moreover, the Trump White House pressured the FDA to approve Trump's discredited hobby-horse, hydroxychloroquine, as well as lobbying hard to bypass safety so as to be able to brag about a vaccine breakthrough in advance of the 2020 elections: yet another example of cynically putting politics ahead of public health.

- To mask or not to mask: that should never have been the question. And yet, to a degree never experienced before, manufactured ideology and political allegiance (to you know who) conflicted with scientific evidence and sound medical necessity. The result: an unknowable but tragically large amount of unnecessary morbidity and mortality, and not among those who followed sound medical advice as it evolved. Anthony Fauci, director of NIAID, initially recommended *against* masks, in part because aerosol transmission of the virus hadn't been clearly demonstrated at the time. It was believed that contaminated surfaces were the main culprits, Also, an early, desperate shortage of masks led to fear that mask hoarding by the public would leave front-line health care workers, who were especially exposed, without crucial protection. Then, when availability of good quality masks increased, as did understanding of how the virus was transmitted, the advice changed, as was good and proper.

But PR people within the administration—led by Trump—latched onto this as some sort of politically motivated flip-flopping rather than the way science works when confronted by novelty: adapt as information accumulates. Seizing an opportunity to change the narrative rather than adjusting policy accordingly, masks became politicized, notably when Trump objected to wearing them, initially because they offended his vanity and also because he feared that his cherished media exposure—which he couldn't imagine giving up—would italicize the pandemic's reality.

Trump continued to give unmasked media interviews and to hold large-scale rallies at which he conspicuously refused to wear a mask, as did most of the attendees. The result was a series of super-spreader events. Then, in a brazen act of dumb defiance, Trump's entire family removed their masks after being seated at the first presidential debate in 2020, violating rules established by the Cleveland Clinic and the Commission on Presidential Debates. These rules weren't legally enforceable, but they had been developed to provide maximum possible security for everyone in attendance.

By this time, refusal to take the pandemic seriously had become a badge of honor, *de rigueur* among Trump's followers. Red states were less likely to follow CDC guidelines and suffered higher per capita rates of the illness. They still do. Moreover, ignorance combined with growing belligerence toward mask-wearers became hallmarks of American conservatism. It still is.

In the spring of 2020 as COVID deaths surged, the Trump Administration could have invoked the Defense Production Act to turbocharge production of masks and other PPE, which would have helped clarify that masks were a national need and that the federal government recognized this and was acting accordingly. But it didn't happen. Trump verbally invoked the Act, but waited weeks before actually using it and then only haphazardly. In fact, he did almost nothing, other than blaming China and continuing to downplay the pandemic, falsely claiming that it was no worse than the common cold and that, in any event, it would peter out in the summer. He also cast blame on the media, medical experts, and especially the Democrats, who, he suggested, might have somehow caused the pandemic itself, just to make him look bad. He certainly ended up looking bad, for which he needed no outside help.

As described by Dr. David Holtgrave, dean of the University at Albany School of Public Health:

Even after states like New York showed that physical distancing (in many forms), mask use, avoidance of large gatherings, hand sanitization, staying home when ill, and other basic techniques served to bring down cases, hospitalizations and death rates, the administration encouraged states to abandon such effective strategies even in the face of widespread community transmission (such as in Florida) and if they did not, the President encouraged residents of jurisdictions such as Michigan to "liberate" their state.[17]

That word is revealing. Disdaining to wear a mask became, in addition to a mark of political allegiance, a statement of personal liberation, of resistance to the "nanny state." This lunatic combination of stubborn ignorance and occasional chest thumping is supposed to derive from a doctrine of individual rights, even though the right to keep your face exposed to a lethal pandemic does not appear to derive from the Bill of Rights and is thus inconsistent with the right-wing legal doctrine of constitutional originalism. Moreover, it flies in the face of the conservative mantra that, along with rights, comes responsibilities. Refusal to mask ignores the reality that in an airborne pandemic, masks not only offer protection to the wearer by filtering inhalations and thereby accepting responsibility to keep oneself safe, but, at least as important, they also reduce virus transmission during exhalations, which is to say, they reflect a responsibility: to help keep *others* safe. Those who demand freedom without responsibility are being, well, irresponsible.

- Dr. Scott Atlas, a Trump acolyte and MRI specialist with no background in virology, epidemiology, or public health, was tapped as special coronavirus adviser to the president. His superpower was saying whatever Trump wanted to hear. Also, he had an appointment at the right-wing Heritage Foundation think tank and, perhaps most important, Trump admired his appearance: for all his ignorance and ideological blindness, Atlas looked like a male model for the Navy Seals. It was thought that he would literally put a good face on the administration's efforts.

This particular Atlas did a terrible job holding up America's world. Notably, his influence greatly delayed the roll-out of testing and then discouraged true believers from being tested once the option was available. Without testing, it is almost impossible to control the pandemic, because in the absence of severe symptoms, there is no way to know who is contagious. Trump hated testing and complained, more than once, "Keep the testing down, please," because he didn't like the results, which made him look bad: "The more we test, the more cases we find." Funny thing about that.

Dr. Atlas advocated a controversial variant of the herd immunity hypothesis, which maintains that once a sufficient proportion of a population contracts the disease, the pathogen—whether virus or bacteria—cannot spread and eventually dies out. There are problems with that, however: notably, for herd immunity to take effect, even theoretically, many people—no one knows how many—must get sick, which means many additional deaths, especially among the elderly or otherwise medically compromised. In addition, with a disease such as COVID, which mutates often and produces novel variants, it isn't clear whether herd immunity can even work, given that the virus becomes a moving target. Dr. Atlas was not deterred, despite being almost alone in claiming that COVID could be knocked out if only a small percentage of the United States population contracts it. He said there was a "likelihood only 25 or 20 percent of people need the infection."[18] Trump, of course, applauded, although neither Atlas nor he revealed how they came upon this number.

Atlas and Trump also opposed testing asymptomatic people, an unknown number of whom harbor the disease and could pass it along to others, who may or may not experience symptoms. Epidemiologists were essentially unanimous that without this information, the pandemic could not be halted, never mind turned around. Nonetheless the Atlas/Trump plan prevailed, at least at the outset. Dr. Atlas and other administration officials playing influential roles in the government's virus response argued that more widespread testing would infringe on Americans' privacy and hurt the economy, by keeping potentially infected workers who show no symptoms from reporting to their jobs. To repeat, infected people who show no symptoms were nonetheless liable to infect others, and they still are.

- It is painfully clear that the administration disastrously fumbled the ball, putting public relations over public health, balking at a national strategy and instead practicing denial, diversion, and downright deception, and then, when reality could no longer be ignored, kept ignoring it anyhow. A week before the 2020 elections, the White House Office of Science and Technology Policy trumpeted the Trump Administration's achievements, a self-congratulatory series of claims that included "ending the COVID-19 pandemic." It is nothing short of amazing that such a loony-tunes assessment could have been made with a straight face at precisely the time that the pandemic was still bad and getting worse.

When Trump became deathly ill with the disease, even that didn't break through his shell of denial and braggadocio. No insight about how he might have acquired the disease (such as by refusing to mask and by attending crowded, mostly unmasked events), or any advice to Americans about how they might learn from his experience, and certainly not a hint of accepting responsibility for what had happened to him. Instead, he crowed about his personal recovery, claiming that similar heroic accomplishments are available to all Americans, oblivious to the fact that as president he had received the most up-to-date treatments and twenty-four/seven monitoring. Trump showed himself confident that everyone else had the same opportunity for high-end treatment and recovery, *fully paid in his case by the US government*. This all happened even as he had been trying to kill the Affordable Care Act, which provides at least minimally affordable care for millions of Americans who are in a less fortunate situation than the president of the United States. In a twenty-first-century version of "let them eat cake," Trump breezily told the country not to fear COVID or to let it dominate their lives.

Shortly after being released from the hospital and while still contagious, Trump theatrically removed his mask and later urged Americans to get back to work, pandemic or no. Naturally, he also took credit (for what? his own recovery?): "You're going to beat it [COVID]," he told the country, bragging that "We're going to be out front. As your leader, I had to do that."[19] What a guy!

- In addition to the administration's witches' brew of free market abracadabra, wishful thinking, and outright lies, there were Trump's own wacko fantasies. One involved hydroxychloroquine, a chemical legitimately used to treat malaria and certain autoimmune diseases such as lupus and rheumatoid arthritis. When Anthony Fauci was asked during a press briefing whether hydroxychloroquine was an effective antiviral treatment for COVID, he said "the answer is no." Trump was displeased and chimed in with "But I'm a big fan, and we'll see what happens." Then he added. "I feel good about it. That's all it is, just a feeling, you know."[20]

Hydroxychloroquine came to Trump's attention when a staff member heard about a small French study appearing in the out-of-the way *Journal of Antimicrobial Agents* that tentatively suggested some possible effectiveness. Two weeks after the article appeared, the French scientific society that published it disowned the research and apologized for giving it their *imprimatur*, pointing out that it "does not meet the Society's expected standard."[21] This didn't stop the guy in the White House from ardently pushing hydroxychloroquine as a miracle cure, tweeting to his then eighty-four million followers that in combination with azithromycin, an antibiotic, it promises to be "one of the biggest game changers in the history of medicine," so it should be "put in use immediately."[22] In the original, subsequently disavowed French study, only six people had been given the two-drug combo, and in Texas, a man died after ingesting a form of the drug used to clean fish tanks. The victim's wife reported that they had heard about it during one of Trump's press conferences at which he had said, "If it works, that would be great. But it doesn't kill people."[23]

Meanwhile, at a clinical trial in Brazil involving increased doses of hydroxychloroquine plus azithromycin, physicians noted irregular heartbeats three days after initiating treatment, and by day six, eleven people had died.

The president wasn't at all discouraged, announcing that "We don't have time to go and say, 'Gee, let's take a couple of years and test it out. And let's go and test with the test tubes and the laboratories.'"[24] His gleeful ignorance and derogation of medical science influenced more people than the Texas victim. It was a baleful contribution to millions of Americans who had originally admired Trump in part because of his open disdain for elitist intellectuals, including scientists of all stripes. They felt they were given permission, indeed encouragement, to try any number of looney tunes home remedies, consistently to their detriment.

Meanwhile, Trump's enthusiasm for hydroxychloroquine continued unabated. He pushed the FDA to put the drug on a fast track for approval, which diverted attention within the public health and research communities and delayed progress toward finding genuinely beneficial treatments and preventative agents. He also fired Dr. Rick Bright, head of the task force charged with developing a vaccine, when Bright complained that he was being pressured to push hydroxychloroquine. Bright reported that he had been axed "in response to my insistence that the government invest the billions of dollars allocated by Congress to address the COVID-19 pandemic into safe and scientifically vetted solutions, and not in drugs, vaccines and other technologies that lack scientific merit."[25]

After Trump announced that he had been taking hydroxychloroquine, Washington, DC and at least twenty-two states responded to a hurricane of constituent demand and obediently stockpiled in the neighborhood of thirty million doses of Trump's now-favorite drug. All the while, studies confirmed that hydroxychloroquine can cause cardiac arrest and, moreover, that its efficacy against COVID was…zero. The FDA, which had been pressured into establishing an Emergency Use Authorization, soon revoked it, which led Peter Navarro, Trump's trade representative—and whose knowledge of epidemiology, virology, and of medical science generally mirrored hydroxychloroquine's effectiveness in combating COVID—to complain to the *New York Times* that "This is a Deep State blindside by bureaucrats who hate the administration they work for more than they're concerned about saving American lives."[26]

At a press briefing shortly after the FDA had withdrawn its Emergency Use Authorization, and the National Institutes of Health (NIH) terminated its clinical trials of the drug, Trump doubled down on his enthusiasm for it, adding a dose of self-pitying paranoia. He complained at a press briefing that "Hydroxy has tremendous support, but politically it is toxic, because I supported it. If I would have said, 'Do not use hydroxychloroquine under any circumstances,' they would have come out and they would have said it's a great thing,"[27]

Amid this remarkable string of absurdities, let's not forget bleach-gate. On April 23, 2020, the president of the United States suggested that the country's premier health officials look into the prospect of injecting bleach into the human body. Here's how it happened. Shortly before a press meeting, Trump had been briefed about the possible role of sunlight in killing the virus on exposed surfaces. It was believed at the time that surface contamination was the main source of infection. As it turned out, Trump didn't get it. The official press meeting began with a report from an official at the Department of Homeland Security who described the effectiveness of household bleach *on exposed surfaces*. It was quickly evident that once again, Trump didn't get it, when he promptly wandered into no-man's-land with:

So, supposing we hit the body with a tremendous—whether it's ultraviolet or just very powerful light—and I think you said that

that hasn't been checked, but you're going to test it. And then I said, supposing you brought the light inside the body, which you can do either through the skin or in some other way, and I think you said you're going to test that, too. It sounds interesting. And then I see the disinfectant, where it knocks it out in a minute. One minute. And is there a way we can do something like that, by injection inside or almost a cleaning. Because you see it gets in the lungs, and it does a tremendous number on the lungs. So it would be interesting to check that.[28]

Even coming from someone so chronically off the rails, this was shocking in its lunacy. His opponents had a field day; make that many field days. His staff was painfully embarrassed, but kept dutifully quiet. Physicians around the country and across the globe warned anyone who could listen not to try this lethal "treatment." Trump was completely correct in one way: chlorine bleach in the lungs really would "do a tremendous number," one that victims would be fortunate to survive. The Clorox Company and Reckitt Benckiser, manufacturer of Lysol, immediately stated that their products must not be used in this way. Nonetheless people did begin consuming dangerous disinfectants, and within a few days, poison control centers reported increased numbers of emergency phone calls. No one seems to have taken Trump's other bizarre suggestion seriously: using light inside the body, perhaps by sticking a lightbulb up their butt. (Or if they did, they kept mum.) Even the president evidently recognized that he was on thin ice, and tried to walk it back, claiming that he was merely being sarcastic. But anyone who saw or heard this particular brainstorm could have no doubt that the COVID-Curer-in-Chief had been completely serious.[v] Observers were also left with no doubt that the president was in over his head, not for the first time.

He nonetheless felt that he had just identified a miracle cure that all those medical professionals with their research grants, technical

---

[v] You can watch it on YouTube; judge for yourself.

publications, fancy degrees, pointy heads, and high-tech laboratories had missed. After first announcing his path-breaking suggestion, Trump acknowledged that he wasn't a doctor, but then he pointed to his own head: "I'm like a person who has a good you-know-what."[29]

Focusing on such bizarre and off-the-wall events might seem to be making a PR mountain out of a molehill of a mental lapse—which sometimes happens even to people with a good you-know-what. After all, he was universally lambasted by the medical profession; shouldn't that have been the end of it? But even aside from the real danger that some deluded people might take Trump seriously and likely die as a result, the consequences were and are severe. For one thing, presidential credibility matters, not only within the country but as it impacts the standing of the United States worldwide. Notwithstanding almost four years of the Trump presidency at that time, the office of the president still received respect and even deference, but with his credibility unraveling, so did the country's reputation. Beyond this, comments of this sort cannot help but resonate with a large number of credulous people,[vi] with the effect—whether or not intended— being to undermine confidence in medical science, replacing it with an anything-goes ethos. Not a healthy development when the country is facing a dire once-in-a-lifetime pandemic, in which sober advice, soberly received, was crucial.

It isn't clear, and will never be known, how much additional suffering and how many unneeded deaths resulted from President Trump's dereliction of his duty to keep the country safe, or at least, to explore all avenues of improving public health. Serious estimates go into the hundreds of thousands. Our various highlighted mistake-makers—Adam and Eve, Pandora, those horse-humbled Trojans, even perhaps Napoleon—would likely acknowledge their errors if given the chance. But not Donald John Trump, who will doubtless go to his grave without ever saying oops. But we can and must say it for him.

[vi] At one point during Adlai Stevenson's unsuccessful presidential campaign against Dwight Eisenhower, a supporter assured him that he had the vote of all intelligent people," to which Stevenson replied, "That's not enough, madam. I need a majority."

4.8. A Mistaken Medical Mouthful That Made a Terrible Cancer-Causing Oops

The cause of Sudden Infant Death Syndrome (SIDS) is unknown, although the awful phenomenon has been known for more than a century: sometimes, seemingly healthy infants suddenly die. But because of a widespread taboo regarding death, few autopsies were performed on SIDS victims; this remains true today. In fact, it has long been difficult to get a handle on even normal adult human anatomy. This is because when a middle- or upper-class person dies, there's no autopsy, unless the circumstances of death are unusual or suspicious. Poor people are another story. Their bodies are frequently unclaimed or "buried" in the shallow graves of Potter's Fields. And so, medical knowledge of human anatomy has long been based on the bodies of the poor. (Please be patient: we'll get to SIDS and cancer soon.)

The story goes that when F. Scott Fitzgerald said to Ernest Hemingway, "The rich are different from the rest of us," Ernie replied "Yes, they have more money." They also tend to have different bodies, for a number of reasons including poor nutrition and healthcare, along with various sources of chronic stress. But this wasn't known in the late nineteenth and early twentieth centuries, when it was found that the bodies they dissected had small thymus glands. (Please be yet more patient; this medical misadventure demands that we connect the dots, of which there are many.) The thymus, not to be confused with the nearby thyroid gland, is part of the lymphatic system and is complexly involved with immune function, including the body's response to stress. Poverty, often also associated with being an ethnic or racial minority, leads to chronic stress, which impacts the thymus. It responds by shrinking. And so, it became received medical wisdom that normal thymus glands are rather small, whereas in reality they are fairly large in people who live healthy, happy lives, and are abnormally shrunken in poor people who became the poster-children for "normal."

When a poor baby died of SIDS, medical authorities paid little attention and only rarely bothered to ascertain the cause of death. But when the victims were from well-to-do families, pressure developed to figure out what was going on. Upon autopsy, these thymuses from otherwise well-func-tioning babies were found to be large . . . quite different from the diminished thymuses found in autopsies of the disregarded poor. But since those stressed, shrunken thymus glands were thought to be normal, a connection was soon made: SIDS must be caused by a pathologically enlarged thymus that presses against a baby's trachea and causes death by suffocation. Twentieth-century physicians were so confident of their analysis that they even devised a term for the non-existent condition: *status thymicolymphaticus*. Furthermore, early in the 1900s, some hardworking professionals conducted retrospective psychological profiles of children who died of *status thymicolymphaticus*, and sure enough they were described as having stoic personalities when it came to dealing with their imaginary disease.[30]

Because it was already known that radiation shrinks certain body tissues, the obvious way to guard against SIDS was to irradiate the thymuses of otherwise normal, healthy infants. And so, it became commonplace during the 1920s and 1930s to irradiate the throats of perfectly healthy infants, to protect them from SIDS. It took years for physicians to realize that this procedure was worse than useless. Recall that the thyroid gland neighbors the thymus. It is also liable to develop cancer as a result of excessive radia-tion.[vii] That's exactly what happened. Before these radiation "treatments" were discontinued, more than ten thousand babies had died of medically induced thyroid cancer. Even though pediatric textbooks in the late 1930s had already reported the dangers of irradiating the necks of infants, the procedure continued to be used in parts of the Deep South into the 1950s.

4.9. *The Tuskegee Tissue of Lies*

The official US government title of the despicable pseudo-research tells the terrible story: "The Tuskegee Study of Untreated Syphilis in the Negro Male."

[vii] This is why potassium iodide is prescribed to protect the thyroid after radiation exposure. The thyroid accumulates iodine and uses it in its normal function. By saturating the gland with potassium iodide, it is made less liable to gather up cancer-causing radioactive iodine.

It occurred from 1932 to 1972 under the benighted auspices of the CDC, the US Public Health Service, and Tuskegee Institute, now Tuskegee University, a historically Black university in Alabama. Six hundred impoverished Black sharecroppers were enrolled, of whom 399 had been diagnosed with latent syphilis, while the remaining 201 were not infected. All were induced to enroll by the promise of free medical care, which was a blatant, bold-faced lie. The subjects (i.e., victims) were given placebos—treatments known to be ineffective—and told that they suffered from "bad blood," but not syphilis. They were told, however, that the research would last for six months; instead, it continued for forty years, during which time the men were never treated, despite the fact that by 1947, penicillin was known to provide an effective cure. One hundred of the men died from complications resulting from syphilis, which include mental illness, bone deterioration, and collapse of the central nervous system, along with deafness and blindness. Twenty-eight of those enrolled died directly from the disease, and forty wives of the enrollees were infected, resulting in nineteen children born with congenital syphilis.

Doctor drawing blood from a "patient" (actually, a victim) as part of the Tuskegee Syphilis Study (anonymous photographer, 1932).

This abomination was only terminated after a leak to the media. The racist monstrosity had violated all known ethical standards and would have been right at home in the phony research conducted by the infamous Nazi doctors such as Josef Mengele, a.k.a. the "angel of death." It was justified at the time by the claim that no direct harm was inflicted on the "patients" and was ostensibly motivated not by racism per se but to assess the then-prevalent belief that syphilis impacted Blacks differently than whites. Yet after penicillin was available as an effective treatment for the disease, it was intentionally withheld. In addition, victims were also induced to undergo a spinal tap—painful and potentially dangerous in itself—by the further lie that it was their "last chance for special free treatment." When, during World War II, more than two hundred of the infected men registered for the military draft, they were promptly diagnosed with syphilis and told to get treatment. The Public Health Service intervened and prevented this, claiming that it would invalidate their ongoing research.

The underlying nature of the Tuskegee experiment was italicized by Taliaferro Clark, then-head of the US Public Health Service, who explained that: "The rather low intelligence of the Negro population, depressed economic conditions, and the common promiscuous sex relations not only contribute to the spread of syphilis but the prevailing indifference with regards to treatment."[31] Unlike the other medical blunders chronicled in this chapter, which at least occurred because of ignorance untainted by malice, there is nothing that can justify "The Tuskegee Study of Untreated Syphilis in the Negro Male." Much more than an oops, it is a permanent blot on the history of the United States.

In 1996, President Bill Clinton issued what appears to have been a heartfelt apology, which was probably better than nothing, but not by much.

Chapter

5

Science

This chapter won't deal with things thought to be true but subsequently corrected, such as earlier belief in a geocentric universe, or Aristotle's explanation of why objects accelerate as they get closer to the ground: because they become ever more "jubilant" as they approach their home substance. Such mistakes are inevitable in an undertaking that is constantly self-correcting and never congratulates itself for having achieved ultimate, static perfection. Accordingly, errors of this sort are more like healthy growing pains, a sign that development is going nicely. It is legitimate to criticize mistakes based on carelessness, insufficient attention, or stubborn refusal to accept reality, including evidence that contradicts a previously held opinion. But mistakes themselves aren't bad; as Samuel Beckett advised, "fail, fail better." Better to fail than to flail, or not to try at all.

In this chapter, we examine occasions in which scientists *did* something—as distinct from *thinking* something—doing things that in many cases they (and their victims) had reason to regret.

5.1. Radium's Regrettable Rays

Once upon a time there was a magical element. It had recently been discovered by the greatest husband-and-wife science team, then or now. But this substance was still largely a mystery. It was like a UFO that had landed, with a space alien inside. It was known, however, to glow in the dark and to send out special, mysterious rays—appropriate for its name—that produced beautiful effects. Moreover, it was (1) entirely harmless and (2) even good for you. These were lies.

RADIUM
EMANATION WATER
Drives Out Uric Acid

Suffering from too much uric acid and diseases caused by faulty elimination—**Rheumatism, Gout, Periodical Headaches, Neuralgia, Constipation, Neurasthenia, Auto-Intoxication and Lack of Bodily Vigor**—quickly relieved in a natural way without drugs or chemicals by our new discovery

THE WAY TO MAKE RADIUM WATER IN YOUR OWN HOME

with our Rayode. A little device containing Radium enough to supply 2,700 Mache Units of Radio-activity, in two quarts of water every twenty-four hours, for less than 10c a day. The Rayode will last a lifetime.

SEND FOR FREE LITERATURE

Tells how you can buy or rent a Rayode to make Radium Water in your own home, with your own ordinary drinking water. Address:

THE COLORADO RADIUM PRODUCTS COMPANY
635 First National Bank Building   Denver, Colo

Advertisement for Radium Emanation Water (produced by The Colorado Radium Products Company, 1918).

But the stuff was useful, especially for manufacturers of watches and clocks, who recognized that money could be made catering to customers who wanted to know what time it was in the dark. Sometimes it was a matter of life and death for soldiers during World War I, who needed to coordinate actions while in a blacked-out trench. When radium atoms are struck by photons, some of their electrons are kicked into a higher energy orbit. Then, in the dark, they fall back into their usual, low-energy state, giving off photons, which produce the glow. But there's also a downside: as the radium nuclei resume their unexcited state, they throw off subatomic alpha particles, which are relatively heavy as subatomic things go, so they move somewhat slowly. When outside the human body, alpha particles can barely penetrate our skin, so people wearing a radium dial watch were not at significant risk, but inside, and even outside in sufficient quantities over sufficient time, alpha particles wreak havoc.

Radium provided good wages for the women who worked in bustling factories in Illinois and especially New Jersey, painting dials for the US military as well as for night owl civilians. Hickory Dickory Dock, the radium went on the clock . . . and into the bodies of the employees (nearly all young women), who would eventually become known as Radium Girls, not as a moniker of admiration but a patronizing reminder of the horrors of science gone wrong when combined with corporate greed.

The male employees—mostly chemists and technicians—wore heavy gloves and lead aprons and used tongs. The women, no protective gear. Initially known as dial painters, they were advised to "point" the tips of their camel hair brush in their mouths to sharpen the lines they drew on clock and watch faces. The mantra was "Lip, Dip, Paint." The first time each day, when the brushes were dry, this would have been innocuous; from then on, using the same already-dipped brush hundreds of times, was catastrophic. The women were paid by piece work, 1.5 pennies per dial. They were repeatedly told that the mixture they applied was harmless: just water, gum Arabic, and powdered radium. Having been assured (i.e., lied to) that the brew was harmless, the dial painters often adorned their fingernails, faces, and even sometimes their teeth with the glowing wonder-stuff, to "give their kiss a pop." The lovely, other-worldly aura thereby conveyed led to the additional moniker Ghost Girls, meant as a compliment. As years went by, it became all too accurate. But initially, many of the Ghost Girls took to wearing their finest gowns to work on Fridays, so as to be belles of the dancing balls over the weekend. These dancing queens glowed and shimmered like Cinderella, flashing smiles that could only be described as radiant.

From its opening in 1917, a large factory in Orange, New Jersey, operated by the Radium Dial Company, employed something like three hundred painters. Eventually there were three humming factories, two in New Jersey and one in Illinois. The first large-scale purification of radium from raw ore was by the Radium Luminous Material Corporation, later renamed the US Radium Corporation (USRC). It marketed, as you might expect, luminous paints, sold as "Undark." Appropriately, for a much-lauded modern miracle that turned out to be a disaster, the raw ore from which the radium was extracted came from Paradox Valley in Colorado.

Dentists were among the first to notice that something was terribly wrong among the Radium Girls. A young woman named Mollie Maggia had a toothache and went to a dentist in January 1922. The tooth had to be pulled, but the wound never healed. Then Ms. Maggia returned with another toothache and the molars next to the first one couldn't be saved either. Soon, the dentist concluded that his patient must have a large abscess but upon probing the area and the bone underneath, he was horrified to find that there was no bone there. Instead of bone, the patient's entire lower jaw was like a mass of sawdust; it crumbled into a limp pile and Ms. Maggia's entire jaw literally fell apart and was no more. By September of that year, eight months after her initial toothache, Mollie Maggia died. She was the first of many.

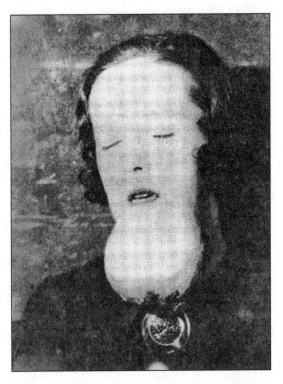

Mollie Maggia, shortly before she died (anonymous photographer).

In rapid succession the Radium Girls experienced loss of teeth, severe oral abscesses, failure of tooth extractions to heal, and necrosis of the jaw. Even with women dying in large numbers, the US Radium Corporation continued to lie about the effects of radium, claiming that Mollie Maggia and then others had died of syphilis. It seemed that USRC's employees, certainly not the company, were of low moral character. As the deformities and deaths piled up, physicians and dentists were either pressured or paid off to keep their findings secret. The other manufacturer, the Radium Dial Company, sponsored research to assess their product's toxicity, but kept the results secret from the public and especially from the workers. It's a tactic that major corporations of today, such as Big Tobacco and Big Oil, have "pointed" to their own benefit.

Eventually, workers at one of the New Jersey factories sued the owner, although it took years for them to find an attorney sufficiently brave, public spirited, and willing enough to work for a reduced fee. The trial was dramatic. The five women bringing suit were all so ill that not one could raise her hand to take the oath. Radium Dial kept appealing and delaying, during which courts found against them eight different times, until the company finally settled out of court and agreed to pay some compensation plus medical and legal costs, as well as funeral expenses. Years later, when one of the victims was exhumed, her corpse glowed faintly—a Ghost Girl indeed.

In 1924, with dozens of young women sick or dead, an independent research study established that radium is indeed hazardous when consumed. USRC was infuriated and sponsored its own study, which unsurprisingly found no negative effects of radioactive paint and concluded that it should qualify as a health food. The ruse didn't work, especially after 1925 when Dr. Harrison Martland, medical officer of Essex County, New Jersey, conducted his own independent investigation and found clear evidence that radium exposure was extremely hurtful and dangerous. (Martland would later coin the term "punch drunk," to describe the concussive damage boxers' brains suffered in fights.)

The lawsuits were among the first cases in which a corporation was held legally liable for providing an unsafe workplace. A significant result was tightening of worker's compensation laws, initially in New Jersey and Illinois. So-called occupational disease labor law was soon established on a national level as well, along with the Occupational Safety and Health Administration. Nonetheless, radium paint was still being used to paint glow-in-the-dark dials into the 1970s, albeit with no more "dip, lick, paint."

In 1895, the German chemist/physicist William Röntgen had discovered something that he called "X-rays," which had the astounding property of passing through barriers that blocked visible light. It caused a sensation, among his colleagues and the general public, leading Röntgen, looking back, to write "... und nun ging der Teufel los" (*and now the Devil was let loose*), an observation that was true in more ways than one. It also set the stage for Marie Curie and her husband Pierre to discover the important element that produced these mysterious and exciting rays. The Curies identified what was subsequently labeled radium in 1898, but it wasn't until 1910 that Marie Curie isolated enough to work with. Radium was quickly ballyhooed as a wonder drug, with, inexplicably, a potential for curing cancer. In the first two decades of the twentieth century, hundreds of thousands of people eagerly drank radium-infused tonic water. It was soon incorporated into cosmetics, toothpaste, and even anal suppositories (the glowing consequence of which boggles the mind). The rest is history, along with much pain and suffering, and, of course, those marvelous, shining dials.

5.2. How a Midwife Toad Birthed a Suicide and How a World-Class Mountebank Duped Some World-Class Blackguards

Scientific fakery is blessedly rare, and, when revealed, it's a career-ending oops. In this case, it was life-ending as well. Our tragic anti-hero is an Austrian biologist, Paul Kammerer (1880–1926), who was a passionate proponent of Lamarckism, the theory that when organisms obtain a trait during their lifetimes, they somehow pass it along to their offspring. And that, my dear

Dr. Watson, is how evolution was supposed to work. We all learn about Lamarckism in biology class, a.k.a. "the inheritance of acquired characteristics."

It had a kind of common-sense logic, and still does, today. Tall people grow tall and tend to have tall children. Smart people study a lot, learn a lot, and tend to have smart kids. The iconic biology-class example is the giraffe, who— according to Jean-Baptiste Pierre Antoine de Monet, chevalier de Lamarck— stretch their necks to reach leaves high up in trees, and as a result, their offspring became increasingly long-necked until *Voila!*, the animals we know today. Alas for Lamarck's devotees, there were some serious problems with this scientific scenario, starting with the reality that biological information flows from DNA to RNA to proteins and thence to each organism's body, not vice versa as would be required for the body's experience to influence its genes and thereby its descendants. If a body-builder builds a majorly muscled body, their children will not find themselves similarly endowed—unless they similarly build their own bodies. Hundreds of generations of male circumcision among Jews and Muslims has not diminished the length of a newborn's foreskin.

Nonetheless, faith in Lamarckism persisted, in part because genetics was poorly understood in the early twentieth century, so scientists hadn't yet grasped the "fundamental dogma of biology" (genes to proteins to body structure, rather than vice versa). Paul Kammerer had been highly regarded for his research on amphibians, having manipulated the reproductive behavior of certain egg-producers to bear live young and vice versa. He then worked to get midwife toads, which normally breed on land, to reproduce in water by the simple expedient of raising the temperature of their tanks so that the females spent most of their time in the water, in order to cool off. But it takes two toads to tango, then and now, and the males were adapted to mating on dry land and had not evolved to do so in water, where they had great difficulty toadally performing their husbandly duties. They kept slipping off the females' wet backs. Kammerer reported, however, that after just two generations, some males developed distinct black "nuptial pads" on their forearms that enabled them to gain purchase on top of female toads while mating, a new trait that was inherited by their offspring. Lamarck would have been delighted and Kammerer's colleagues were transfixed with excitement.

Midwife toads mating, on land (photo by Pierre-Yves Vaucher, date unknown).

But then, Dr. G. Kingsley Noble, curator of fish and amphibians at the American Museum of Natural History and a renowned amphibian maven, carefully examined Kammerer's specimens and announced—in the journal *Nature*, the world's most prestigious and widely read science journal worldwide—that Kammerer's stunning discovery was a fraud. Rather than exemplifying Lamarckian inheritance, the black pads were due to subcutaneous injections of India ink and their enlargement most likely because of irritation caused by the ink rather than to a hitherto undocumented case of Lamarckian inheritance of acquired sex toys, er, mating aids. To his credit, Kammerer looked again (or maybe for the first time) at his specimens and acknowledged that indeed *someone* had injected India ink into the male toads' thumb pads, but certainly not himself, and he had no idea who might have been the culprit. Probably one of those pesky, irresponsible (and never identified) lab assistants.

Making matters worse, subsequent attempts to replicate Kammerer's finding ranged from inconclusive to complete failure. Lamarckism—already shaky among biologists as natural selection was increasingly understood and repeatedly verified—was in tatters, along with, even more, Paul Kammerer's credibility, never to recover in his lifetime. That turned out to be short, as he committed suicide at age forty-six.

In recent years, Lamarckism has revived somewhat, at least under highly restrictive circumstances and rather differently from how the early nineteenth-century chevalier and the hapless early twentieth century biologist had envisioned. Commencing especially in the 1990s, a new subdiscipline known as epigenetics has revealed a mechanism whereby experience can indeed influence genes, notably the experience of pregnant mammals (but alas, not toads). Epigenetic changes during early embryonic development are now known to occur especially when a pregnant mother is exposed to stress of various sorts. These changes are most often associated with a chemical process known as methylation in which a methyl group—the same molecular substance responsible for methyl alcohol—attaches to various parts of a developing organism's DNA. The effect is to alter gene expression, but without changing the underlying nucleotide sequence. This is quite different from Lamarck's original conception and also from Kammerer's, in which the environment was said to directly change an adult's body, with these changes then passed along to offspring.

Kammerer's posthumous reputation has not improved, because even if there might be a smidgeon of modified validity to Lamarckism, no quarter is given to fakery. Having acquired the characteristic of fudging one's data, or at least a reputation for doing so, it is nearly impossible to get back on the right side of one's colleagues. Once burned, twice shy, and the great majority of today's biologists who still recall Paul Kammerer's oops regard him as beyond the pale, and probably always will.

Yet the polymath Arthur Koestler had long been sympathetic to Lamarckism and he attempted to rehabilitate Kammerer's reputation in a 1972 book titled *The Case of the Midwife Toad*. In it, Koestler argued that one of Kammerer's lab assistants may well have sabotaged the research so as to undermine the lab's director. After all, this was a time when fascism was on the rise in central Europe, including in Austria, and, Koestler maintained, because Kammerer was known to have leftist sympathies (as did Koestler), such behavior would have been consistent with an unknown fascist's effort to sabotage his reputation. Although *The Case of the Midwife Toad* was persuasive among the lay public, it didn't change the minds of many biologists; perhaps not any.

Kammerer's oops had a serious consequence, but its impact did not go beyond the unfortunate perpetrator. And it is at least possible that he got a raw deal from his professional colleagues. This was definitely not true of another devotee of Lamarckism, a truly nefarious character named Trofim D. Lysenko. This charlatan and lickspittle to Josef Stalin had genuine blood on his hands, compared with Kammerer's India ink. The history of science reveals few genuine bad guys, but Lysenko is an exception.

T. D. Lysenko (anonymous photographer, date unknown).

Despite the pall cast by Kammerer's midwife toad debacle, Lamarckism had remained popular in the Soviet Union because it appeared to offer the prospect that a generation or two of socialist governance could engender a "new Soviet citizen," devoid of the competitive inclinations implied by Darwinian evolution. This provided an opening for Lysenko, a biological mountebank who claimed that his techniques would revolutionize Soviet agriculture. He gained Stalin's confidence (no easy feat), and indeed changed Soviet agriculture . . . dramatically for the worse.

During the 1930s and after, the Soviet Union was ripe ground for Lysenko's blend of fake science and real politics. Soviet agriculture was in disarray following the mass collectivization of peasant farms. There was simply not enough food. Enter T. D. Lysenko, who claimed that he had a technique for increasing crop yields; not only that, but his brilliant discoveries were shining examples of "Marxist-Leninist science" (an oxymoron if ever there was one). A fervent believer in Lamarckism, Lysenko trumpeted that by exposing wheat seeds to moisture and cold, he achieved "vernalization," producing adult plants that behaved as though it was spring, a useful transformation given that the climate in Soviet Russia was anything but. This abracadabra was yet another fanciful example of Lamarckism in action. In addition, Lysenko claimed that he had pulled another rabbit out of his hat: transforming one species of wheat into another, notwithstanding that the two species had different chromosome numbers, and legitimate plant geneticists knew that such a claim was bullshit.

But Lysenko's genius wasn't science but politics. His "Marxist-Leninist science" was nonsense, but "Lysenkoism" blended perfectly with Marxist-Leninist *politics*. Genuine genetics was a capitalist, bourgeois plot, whereas Lysenkoism (Lamarckism plus communist ideology) got rid of the awkward capitalist/bourgeois implications of Darwinism, namely that individuals really are genetically different, and that natural selection favors some variants over others. In Lysenko's telling, heritable changes could be made not by favoring certain genes, but by subjecting everyone to appropriate experiences. In that way, not only could plants be "bred" to flourish in any climate, but by extension, the ideal Soviet citizen could be similarly produced in just a generation or two. Stalin loved it—results be damned—and Lysenko loved Stalin's love.

Lysenko's crackpot notions became official Soviet dogma, and Trofim the Terrible became czar of Soviet agriculture. Under his sway, valid genetics became anathema and more than three thousand competent Soviet biologists were either exiled, imprisoned, or killed, including most notoriously the head of the Soviet Agriculture Academy, Nikolai Vavilov, a geneticist of international repute, who died in a Siberian prison. Lysenko became head of the Lenin All-Union Academy of Agricultural Sciences, while real agricultural sciences in the USSR withered and died, not to be resuscitated until the 1960s. Even then, the malign ghost of Lysenko continued to strangle progress. It is likely that Lysenko's death grip on the throat on Soviet biology was to some extent responsible for Nikita Khrushchev's downfall in 1964, by which time agricultural production in the USSR had fallen so disastrously that the country was importing grain from the decadent West, whose "fascist Mendelian genetics" generated bumper crop yields.

Lysenko's stench penetrated Mao's China as well, especially from 1949 until the late 1950s. That country's Great Leap Forward (1958–1962)

SCIENCE

resulted in the starvation of incalculable numbers of people, variously esti-
mated at between ten and forty-seven million during the Great Chinese
Famine. This Great Leap Backward was brought about by adverse weather,
socio-economic mismanagement, and, not least, Lysenko's stubborn lunacy.
It's a heavy burden for one biologist, however incompetent, to bear, but
Trofim Lysenko remained steadfast to the end, never acknowledging his
massive, murderous oops. He never got around to killing himself, à la Paul
Kammerer, whose blunder was far less consequential.

*[Before we proceed to an entertaining account of one case of purported
scientific fraud in the United States, I must note that although I recall these
events from the late 1960s, in researching the present book, I haven't been able to
confirm them. If anyone can do so, or provide contrary evidence, I'll be grateful.]*

Research conducted at Duke University's one-of-a-kind Parapsychology
Lab, first established in 1935, was attempting to evaluate the possibility of
psychokinesis, the phenomenon whereby some living things are alleged to move
objects by their mental powers alone. The experimental design involved rats. No
surprise here: anyone who has had to deal with rats is likely to suspect that they
possess powerful and mysterious powers, such as the ability to appear and disappear instantly, to find food wherever it might be, and, always, to breed without
our permission. The experimental design at Duke involved an early-generation
computer that had been programmed to come up with something close to
random numbers.[i] When it came up even, the rats got a food reward; when odd,
they got nothing. After a large number of runs, the read-out became skewed
toward even numbers, far more than would be expected based on chance alone.
The stunning conclusion was that the rats were telekinetically manipulating the
computer! Much excitement, enthusiasm, and skepticism ensued.

But then it was realized that a laboratory assistant had been spending an
inordinate amount of time apparently fiddling with the computer, after which
he confessed that indeed, he had reprogrammed it to bias the output in favor
of even numbers, just what the experimenters had been looking for. Oh rats!

---

[i] Generating truly random numbers turns out to be extremely difficult, even with
today's super-computers.

129

My take on this seeming case of pseudoscience fakery was somewhat different, however. Just as Kammerer had pinned the blame on one of his anonymous lab assistants, perhaps the academic world was too quick to blame the Parapsychology Lab's assistant, even as that assistant had been too quick to plead guilty for faking the results. Let's imagine that those hungry and parapsychologically endowed rats had in fact contrived to get more food for themselves by biasing the arithmetic in their favor. What better way to "kinetically" achieve this than by manipulating the hapless lab assistant to do the work for them? And so, instead of a scientific fraud a la Kammerer, the Duke University rats might have been flexing their telekinetic superpowers after all.

For our final case of scientific fakery, we turn to recent times, and the almost biblical fall from grace of Hwang Woo-suk, a South Korean veterinarian and biologist whose research had made him something of a national hero, especially when, in 2006, he cloned human embryonic stem cells. Rather, he claimed to have done so. Things began to unravel when he was accused of having used eggs from his graduate students, an ethical violation, as well as from the black market: a legal gray zone at best. After initially denying the charges, he soon copped to them. Shortly afterward, the roof caved in. His human cloning "results" were exposed as thoroughly fraudulent, and Dr. Hwang was also charged with embezzlement (misuse of research funds). He received a suspended sentence from the criminal charges but was fired from his professorship at the prestigious Seoul National University after an investigative panel concluded that his fabrications were "a grave act damaging the foundation of science."1 But Mr. Hwang was unquestionably a gifted researcher, having been the first to clone a dog. Really. After keeping a low profile, he returned to various laboratory projects involving cloning of other animals. But no more monkeying around with *Homo sapiens* for him.

Okay, enough fake science. Time now for something all too real.

5.3. When Physicists Sinned, and We're All Screwed

The Manhattan Project was initiated and then carried out for many reasons: concern that Nazi Germany might develop atomic weapons before the

Allies, the scientific appeal of working on problems that are "technically sweet," simple pride, ambition, patriotism, and income. The inventors of nuclear weapons must have foreseen the real-world consequences of their work, although it appears that the more thoughtful ones were genuinely shocked and even apologetic about what they had done. "Despite the vision and farseeing wisdom of our wartime heads of state," wrote J. Robert Oppenheimer, scientific director of the Manhattan Project, "physicists have felt the peculiarly intimate responsibility for suggesting, for supporting, and in the end, in large measure, for achieving the realization of atomic weapons. . . . In some sort of crude sense which no vulgarity, no humor, no overstatement can quite extinguish, physicists have known sin; and this is a knowledge which they cannot lose."[2]

In short, the invention of nuclear weapons was a real-life case of uncorking a dangerous genie. During a BBC interview some years after witnessing the first atomic bomb test, at Alamogordo, New Mexico, Oppenheimer reflected that, "We knew the world would not be the same. A few people laughed, a few people cried. Most people were silent. I remembered the line from the Hindu scripture, the *Bhagavad Gita* . . . 'Now I am become Death, the destroyer of worlds.'"[3]

Some maintain, of course, that whatever the dangers, we should be grateful for nuclear weapons; rather than an oops, nuclear weapons are a godsend, albeit not from a Hindu god of destruction. They have kept us safe and have ushered in peace. And so, nuclear enthusiasts maintain that nuclear weapons are a modern miracle, one that eluded Christ: ushering in peace on earth *without* goodwill toward men.

Let's see.

A frequent claim by those who refuse to see nuclear weapons as a huge, dangerous mistake is that they prevented war between the United States and the former Soviet Union. But there are many credible reasons why the United States and the USSR avoided destroying each other, most notably because neither side wanted to go to war in the first place. True, the two didn't go to war after nuclear weapons arrived on the international scene; but then, they didn't go to war *before* that either.

Singling nukes out as the reason the Cold War never became hot is like saying a junkyard car, without an engine or wheels, never sped off the lot because no one turned the key. There are lots of other reasons. There is no way, moreover, to demonstrate logically that nuclear weapons kept the peace during the Cold War, or that they do so now. By contrast, there is plenty of historical evidence of narrowly avoided disaster by mistake, malfunction, or miscalculation. And there have been—and still are—many conventional wars as well.

In ancient China, it was widely believed that solar eclipses were caused by a dragon swallowing the sun, so people responded to sudden darkening by making as much noise as possible—banging pots and gongs, yelling loudly—in order to scare away the dragon. And guess what? It worked! Every time. If, for some reason, people had refrained from all that noise-making and the eclipse resolved anyhow, the worst outcome would have been a loss of respect for the appetite of dragons. But if nuclear deterrence fails, its advocates will not be around to acknowledge that they were wrong.

In some cases, it only takes one failure for an entire scaffolding, previously thought safe, to come crashing down. The Concorde supersonic transport entered service in 1976 and flew flawlessly throughout the late 1970s and 1980s. In fact, it was lauded as not only the fastest, but also the *safest* passenger plane of all, having a zero accident and fatality rate. Then, in 1990, one of them crashed on a runway in Paris, killing all 109 people on board and ultimately grounding the entire fleet, which was subsequently abandoned. The Concorde's safety record instantly jumped from the best to the worst (because only a handful of the planes were ever built and flown). The disaster occurred after a tire blew out, which initiated a chain of multisystem failures whereby the fuel tanks ruptured, from which there was no return.[4]

The crash of the Concorde was certainly an oops. The idea that nuclear weapons are a boon, not an oops, relies on their supposed role in preventing World War III, and the related claim that nukes have helped keep the peace more generally. Both versions of happy talk are, at best, premature. The so-called "nuclear peace" has been fairly brief so far; the interval between World War II and the end of the Cold War covers about five decades. More than twenty years separated World Wars I and II; before that, there had been more than forty years of relative peace between the end of the Franco-Prussian War (1871) and World War I (1914). Fifty-six years elapsed between Napoleon's defeat at Waterloo (1815) and Bismarck's war with France. Or, taking a broader look at the historical record when it comes to big, pan-European wars, there had been a gap of nearly one hundred years from the end of the Napoleonic Wars to the beginning of World War I. Even in war-prone Europe, decades of peace have not been so rare—yet they always concluded with war, during which the combatants used the weapons available.

Even when possessed by just one side, nuclear threats have not kept the non-nuclear side from fighting, and often winning. The Chinese, Cuban, Iranian, and Nicaraguan revolutions all took place even though a nuclear-armed United States backed the governments that were eventually overthrown. Similarly, the United States lost the Vietnam War, just as the Soviet Union and then the United States lost in Afghanistan, despite the fact that both superpowers not only possessed nuclear weapons, but also more and better conventional arms than their adversaries. Nor did the implicit threat posed by its nuclear weapons aid Russia in its initially unsuccessful war against Chechen rebels, from 1994–1996, or later from 1999 to 2000, when Russia's conventional forces devastated the Chechen Republic. It was a nuclear-armed United States that "lost" China in 1949 and a nuclear-armed Soviet Union that lost China again during the late 1950s and early 1960s. (Isn't it odd that such a huge nation can have been so frequently misplaced?)

Nuclear weapons did not enable the United States to achieve its goals in Iraq or Afghanistan, which have become costly failures for the country with the world's most advanced strategic forces. During the Cold War, each side engaged in conventional warfare: the Soviets, for example, in Hungary (1956), Czechoslovakia (1968), and Afghanistan (1979–1988); the Russians in Chechnya (1996–2009), Georgia (2008), Ukraine (2014–present), as well as in Syria (2015–present); and the United States in Korea (1950–1953), Vietnam (1962–1974), Beirut (1982), Grenada (1983), Panama (1989), the Persian Gulf (1990–1991), the former Yugoslavia (1999), Afghanistan (2001–present), and Iraq (2003–2016), to mention just some of the more prominent cases.

OOPS!

In 1948, the USSR restricted access to West Berlin, which was jointly administered by the United Kingdom, France, and the United States. At that time, the United States had a nuclear monopoly, but this didn't inhibit Stalin from initiating the Berlin Blockade, one of the most provocative and aggressive actions of the Cold War. In fact, the USSR was most aggressive vis-à-vis the United States between 1945 and 1949, when only the United States had nuclear weapons. It was then that Stalin consolidated Soviet control over its Eastern European satellites, violating the promises he had made to Roosevelt and Churchill during their Yalta summit. All this while the United States "enjoyed" a worldwide nuclear monopoly.

Nor has the threat of another side's atomic and then hydrogen arsenals deterred actual attacks by nonnuclear opponents upon nuclear armed states or their avowed strategic interests. In 1950, China was fourteen years from developing its own nuclear weapons, whereas the United States had dozens, perhaps hundreds, of atomic bombs. US military and civilian officials also judged that China's military was exhausted by decades of civil war and would not dare intervene against the world's sole nuclear superpower. They were spectacularly wrong. As the Korean War's tide shifted against the North, Mao's China felt threatened that General MacArthur's forces wouldn't stop at the Yalu River and would invade China in an attempt to overthrow its communist government. To the surprise and consternation of the US leadership, the American nuclear arsenal did not deter China from sending more than three hundred thousand "volunteers" southward.

When it comes to countries without nuclear weapons making war against nuclear-armed states, the saga continues—which hardly breeds confidence in the deterrent value of nukes. In 1956, nuclear-armed Great Britain warned nonnuclear Egypt to refrain from nationalizing the Suez Canal. It happened anyhow and the United Kingdom, France, and Israel ended up invading the Sinai in an unsuccessful effort to reverse it. Argentina attacked the British-held Falkland Islands in 1982, even though the United Kingdom had nuclear weapons and Argentina did not. Following the US-led invasion in 1991, conventionally armed Iraq was not deterred from lobbing thirty-nine Scud missiles at nuclear-armed Israel, which did not retaliate, although it could have vaporized Baghdad. It is hard to imagine how doing so would have benefited anyone. The fact that Israel had this capacity did not stay Saddam Hussein's hand, perhaps because he realized that Israel would have had more to lose than to gain by "making good" on its unstated but universally understood nuclear threat. Moreover, nuclear weapons obviously did not deter the terrorist attacks of September 11 on New York and Washington, DC, just as the nuclear arsenals of the United Kingdom and France have not prevented repeated terrorist attacks on those countries.

The failures continued. Nuclear-armed France couldn't prevail over the nonnuclear Algerian National Liberation Front. The US nuclear arsenal didn't inhibit North Korea from seizing an American intelligence-gathering vessel, the USS Pueblo, in 1968. Even today, this ship remains in North Korean hands. Its nuclear arsenal didn't enable China to get Vietnam to end its invasion of Cambodia in 1979; a conventional invasion did. Nor did US nuclear weapons stop Iranian revolutionary guards from capturing US diplomats and holding them as hostages from 1979 until 1981, just as fear of American nuclear weapons didn't prevent Iraq from invading Kuwait in 1990.

Thus far, the historical record is also clear that even when a nuclear state is losing in an armed struggle against a nonnuclear one, nukes don't help. The United States unequivocally lost in Vietnam, but accepted this defeat rather than flailing about with its atomic and hydrogen bombs. Ditto for the USSR in Afghanistan. It remains to be seen whether, if Putin's invasion of Ukraine continues to go badly, he will resort to battlefield nuclear weapons, and if he does, whether it will do him any good. When the United States "lost" Afghanistan, no one expected this outcome to be reversed by incinerating Kabul.

By the end of the twentieth century, both India and Pakistan had nuclear weapons, which might have inhibited each side—thus far—from using them. But it certainly didn't make their confrontations less dangerous, nor, it seems likely, any less frequent. In 1999, Pakistan snuck military units—disguised as Kashmiri militants—into an area known as Kargil, a high-altitude region on the Indian side of the Line of Control that separates India and Pakistan in the disputed regions of Jammu and Kashmir. The Pakistanis apparently thought that their nuclear arsenal would force India to accept the move as a *fait accompli.* Pakistan had tested its first nuclear weapons the previous year, and it seems likely that its military was emboldened by this addition to its arsenal, expecting that the threat of going nuclear would inhibit an Indian response. If so, it didn't work. India responded by mobilizing two hundred thousand troops, initiating an air campaign (not answered by Pakistan), and preparing a naval blockade of Karachi.

Pakistan's next step was to begin issuing nuclear threats. Prime Minister Nawaz Sharif announced, "If there is a war, or if the present confrontation continues on the borders, it will bring so much devastation, the damage of which will never be repaired."[5] This did no good at all and, by mid-June, Indian forces had retaken all of the key positions in Kargil. India's nuclear arsenal had not deterred the Pakistanis from their military adventuring, just as Pakistan's didn't prevent India from retaking its lost territory.

It should be clear that nuclear weapons haven't helped those possessing them to get their way in the world. But the real reason that nuclear weapons are an enormous oops isn't simply because they haven't been useful to their possessors, but from the danger that they pose. We have come close to disaster many times, far more often and much closer than most people realize. There have been computer errors, radar images of migrating geese mistaken for a floc of incoming missiles, an explosion on a natural gas pipeline interpreted as the exhaust signature of a missile launch, a war games tape perceived as the real thing, and many more. Let's review the three most harrowing nuclear near-oops so far.

The Cuban Missile Crisis of 1962—when, by most accounts, we were closest to nuclear Armageddon—is often cited as evidence for the peace-keeping role of nuclear weapons. But that crisis wasn't so much ended by nuclear weapons and the threat of Mutually Assured Destruction as it was *caused* by them, specifically the Soviet attempt to base nuclear-armed missiles in Cuba, close to the United States. This, in turn, occurred because the United States had placed nuclear-armed medium-range Jupiter missiles in Turkey, close to the USSR. It may seem a truism that absent nuclear weapons there wouldn't have been any crisis, but that's precisely the point.

Here's how it played out. JFK demanded that the initial Soviet deployment be removed and ordered a naval "quarantine" of Cuba. The world held its breath as Soviet naval vessels approached those of the United States and exhaled with collective relief when the USSR turned around and both sides agreed to some future restraints and a "hotline" was established to minimize miscommunication between the two countries. Also, the United States withdrew those Turkish missiles, which were obsolete and that JFK had decided to remove long before the crisis unfolded.

Prior to this resolution, things had been touch-and-go. The readiness level of US strategic forces was raised to DEFCON 2, one notch short of war at the time, and the only time this was done during the Cold War. For the only time before or since, one eighth of the B-52 bomber fleet was placed on continuous airborne alert while B-47 bombers, also fully loaded with nuclear bombs, were dispatched to various military and civilian airfields. High-level negotiations between the two countries proved to be immensely stressful and confusing, and although the American public widely believes the Soviets simply backed down, the truth was much more complicated, with several events bringing the two countries even closer to nuclear war than was reported at the time. Here is a brief summary.

Let's start with a crucial oops, one that is little known even today, except among historians recently granted access to what had been secret Soviet archives. It was a blunder that set the stage for the whole desperately dangerous business. Before Khrushchev green-lighted his decision to station ballistic missiles in Cuba, he sent the commander of the Soviet Strategic Missile Forces—one Sergei Biryuzov—to meet with Fidel Castro. Biryuzov returned with Castro's enthusiastic agreement, but also with a proposed solution to what had been acknowledged to be a potentially serious problem: for the scheme to work, it would be necessary to implant those missiles without the Americans knowing what was going on, so as to present the United States with a *fait accompli,* something unveiled as complete before those affected could do anything about it. Biryuzov reported that the missiles could be hidden from U-2 spy planes by putting them under Cuba's abundant palm trees. He forgot to mention that in the proposed location, these trees were spaced forty to fifty feet apart, and, moreover, their foliage provided very little camouflage. As a result, the missiles stuck out like large, pointy, sore thumbs. When detected by US overflights, and their presence reported to JFK, the crisis erupted—long before the Kremlin had planned, and thereby aborting Khrushchev's hope to present Washington with a situation for which they had no recourse.

As the crisis intensified, a different American U-2 spy plane was shot down by a Soviet-made anti-aircraft missile fired from Cuba. US officials believed this had been ordered by the Kremlin, leading some to conclude that war was imminent. It was subsequently revealed that the order had been given by Cuban officers at the scene, without knowledge or approval by the Soviets. As things heated up, important members of JFK's military and civilian structure—notably Air Force Chief of Staff General Curtis LeMay—began urging an immediate preemptive strike against the Soviet missile sites in Cuba.

Unknown to US authorities, the Soviets had already put at least twenty nuclear-tipped missiles in Cuba, capable of reaching as far as Washington, DC, and each carrying a one-megaton nuclear warhead—equivalent to roughly seventy Hiroshima-size bombs. Had the president followed the advice of his military leaders, a nuclear war would almost certainly have resulted. JFK's resistance to the war-mongering advice of his own military appears to have been due, in part, to the searing experience of the Bay of Pigs disaster, which played out a year earlier. At that time, Kennedy had green-lighted a hare-brained scheme, inherited from the Eisenhower Administration, that called for an invasion of Cuba by 1,500 Cuban exiles, but without effective air or naval support, and grossly under-estimating Cuban support for Castro's government. It failed miserably, but paradoxically, that blunder had at least one positive outcome: it immunized Kennedy against relying on trigger-happy and over-confident military recommendations. So, he didn't follow his most hawkish advisers—a paradoxical benefit of a prior oops.

About the same time that the U-2 was shot down, a Soviet submarine that had been submerged off the Cuban coast was being harassed by a US Navy surface flotilla, which was firing small depth charges of the sort used in training exercises—trying not to destroy the sub, but rather to announce that it had been located and get it to surface. The submarine's officers, however, believed they were under full attack; the US military was unaware that it was equipped with at least one nuclear-tipped torpedo. Unable to communicate with its military leadership in the Kremlin, the officers in the Soviet submarine had previously been given permission to use its nuclear weapon in "dire circumstances."

Accordingly, the captain, Vassili Savitsky, wanted to put the ship's fifteen-kiloton nuclear torpedo in operational condition. He told his crew, "We're going to blast them now! We will die, but we will sink them all. We will not disgrace our Navy."[6] Two out of the three officers with launch responsibility voted to fire their nuclear torpedo at the US fleet, believing a war had already started, and even though it hadn't, nuking the US Caribbean fleet would have done it. But the third officer, one Vasily Arkhipov, voted no, and so the Soviet submarine didn't devastate a chunk of the US Navy, the United States did not retaliate, and the world remained intact. A multi-megaton oops avoided. Barely.

Forbearance by the Soviet undersea threat was, coincidentally, followed by a US challenge to the Soviet "Air Defense Forces." That same day, a different U-2 spy plane accidentally went off course and overflew Soviet Siberia. As a result, MIG fighter jets were scrambled, leading the United States, in turn, to launch F-102 interceptors armed with nuclear air-to-air missiles. By good fortune, the U-2 got out of Soviet airspace before this incident escalated. When told of the events, JFK grumbled, "There's always some sonofabitch that doesn't get the word."

Another particularly harrowing episode occurred twenty-one years later, during the Reagan Administration and that of Yuri Andropov in the USSR. The details have been kept under wraps for decades, and even now much is classified, with the Russians being particularly close-mouthed about their side of the story. Here is a short version: in 1983, the Soviets mistook a NATO war-gaming exercise as a prelude to the real thing and came dangerously close to preempting the expected nuclear attack with one of their own.

US–Soviet tensions had nearly maxed out in 1983. Ronald Reagan took office as a strenuous anticommunist whose rhetoric was often downright bellicose. Early during the Reagan years, many in the Soviet hierarchy were convinced the United States was preparing for a first strike. Once in office, Reagan had authorized development and production of the Trident II submarine-based missile, B-1 and B-2 bombers, neutron bombs; doubling of the US military budget; increased funding for blast and fall-out shelters; and so forth. Moreover, the United States had been initiating a series of probes to test Soviet response times and capacities, with naval vessels attempting to get as close as possible to Soviet nuclear facilities and aircraft, and periodically approaching Soviet airspace at high speeds, only to veer off at the last minute. The result was an increasingly paranoid atmosphere in the Kremlin.

During the late 1970s, the USSR had begun deploying intermediate-range SS-20 missiles that could reach Allied forces in Western Europe. In response, NATO elected to field its own Europe-based ground-launched cruise missiles, along with Pershing II ballistic missiles. The United States avowedly intended these actions to induce the Soviets to withdraw their SS-20s, but, from the Kremlin's perspective, they constituted a serious threat as part of a possible decapitating first strike. After all, the Pershing IIs could reach Moscow in less than ten minutes. Commenting on the advanced age of the Kremlin hierarchy, the vice chairman of the US National Intelligence Council observed at the time that these missiles could strike in "roughly how long it takes some of the Kremlin's leaders to get out of their chairs, let alone to their shelters."[7]

In 1981, the Soviets had initiated Operation RYaN (Russian acronym for "Nuclear Missile Attack"), the most extensive and far-reaching espionage undertaking in their history. Its motto, according to KGB General Oleg Kalugin, was "do not miss the moment when the West is about to launch war."[8] Soviet foreign agents accordingly began monitoring anything considered relevant to a surprise attack, which comprised 292 identified indicators, ranging from late-night pizza deliveries at the Pentagon (seriously!) to the movements of key military and political figures, as well as recording traffic in and out of nuclear facilities themselves. Misunderstandings were rife, such as the time Pentagon lights were on all night, which suggested to the Soviet spooks an episode of feverish war planning, but was actually routine janitorial work. Soviet intelligence also reported, incorrectly, that US bases had suddenly been placed on high alert; coincidentally, this was within the precise window Soviet planners had estimated would elapse between a decision to launch an attack and when it would be carried out.

Making matters worse, a few months previously, in May 1982, someone at the Department of Defense had leaked a document to the *New York Times* that contained plans for conducting a six-month-long nuclear war, with orchestrated sequences of reloading missile silos that even included retaining enough warheads to continue fighting yet another war, or possibly to deter future attacks. In any event, whatever their intention, these announcements ratchetted up the tension in the Kremlin. So, the stage was set for some near-miss misunderstandings.

It got worse.

An enormous naval exercise was conducted during April and May 1983, which turned out to be a particularly fraught year, with three Pacific-based carrier battle groups simulating total war against the USSR. By design, US forces began probing the sensitivity (and restraint) of Soviet air defenses. Especially provocative was a mock bombing exercise in which US Navy aircraft flew over a Soviet military base on Zeleny Island, which led Premier Andropov to order that any subsequent overflight of Soviet territory be shot down. In addition, the Soviets countered by flying over the Aleutians. At the time, the United States was about to deploy its Pershing II missiles in Europe. And then, sure enough, in September of that same fateful year, Soviet radar reported what they believed was a US spy plane in Soviet airspace over Siberia.

A Su-15 interceptor was ordered to shoot it down. The intruder was no spy plane, but Korean Airlines (KAL) flight 007, a commercial airliner bound for Seoul that had gone off course and whose communications with the scrambled Soviet jet were garbled. There were 269 civilian passengers, all of whom perished, including sixty-two Americans (one being a sitting congressman who was chairman of the bellicosely anticommunist John Birch Society) and twenty-two children younger than the age of twelve.

The West was outraged. President Reagan denounced Soviet "barbarity," and then things got even more dangerous. On September 26, three weeks after shooting down KAL 007, a newly installed Soviet early-warning satellite system sent an alert that a US intercontinental ballistic missile (ICBM) had been launched and was heading toward the USSR, followed by a possible four more. The mid-ranking duty officer, Lieutenant Colonel Stanislav Petrov, decided—on his own and counter to protocol—not to report this incident, which he judged to be a false alarm. And so it was. (Part of his reasoning was that a real first strike would have involved hundreds of missiles, not just a handful.)

Had Lieutenant Colonel Petrov informed his superior officers, General Secretary Andropov et al. would have had just minutes to decide whether to "retaliate" and, given the tense state of US–Soviet relations at that time, the outcome could easily have been disastrous. Petrov was nonetheless officially reprimanded. Shortly thereafter, he left the Soviet military and, in May 2017, died in relative poverty. Interviewed for the film *The Man Who Saved the World*, Petrov said this about his role in the incident, "I was simply doing my job . . . that's all. My late wife for ten years knew nothing about it. 'So, what did you do?' she asked me. 'Nothing. I did nothing.'" Petrov's "nothing" likely saved the world from one hell of an oops.

One might think that after this harrowing event things couldn't have gotten worse, but they did. As incredibly bad luck would have it, just six weeks after the Petrov close call, and at precisely the time that the USSR's intelligence services were desperately looking for early indicators that the West might be about to initiate a nuclear attack, NATO began to simulate just such an attack. An extensive war game, called Able Archer 83, began on November 7, 1983, mimicking a full-fledged nuclear assault on the USSR. It was nothing less than a dress rehearsal of how a first-strike nuclear war would be conducted. The formal exercise ended four days later; but, during that interval, life on Earth was in the balance. Able Archer 83 involved not only a formal handoff from conventional to nuclear authority, but it also simulated loading nuclear warheads aboard strategic bombers, along with heightened alert status on the part of missile silo crews and forward-deployed medium-range missiles.

Able Archer had also been preceded by a sudden increase in coded communications between Washington and London, which was exactly what the KGB anticipated would occur before a coordinated US–UK nuclear attack. In fact, the flurry of diplomatic to-and-fro had concerned the US invasion of Grenada at the time, a Caribbean Island that was officially under the sovereignty of the United Kingdom's Queen Elizabeth.

In 1990, the US President's Foreign Intelligence Advisory Board conducted its own investigation of the Soviet response to these events, the results of which were only made publicly available in 2015, after a more than decade-long battle with the National Security Archive. The review revealed that the USSR had conducted thirty-six intelligence flights, "probably to determine whether US naval forces were deploying forward in support of Able Archer 83,"[9] while all civilian air flights in Eastern Europe had been canceled, probably to facilitate use of emergency aircraft as needed. Soviet military activities at the time suddenly escalated to an "unparalleled scale" that included Soviet fighters in Poland and East Germany placed on high-alert status for the only time during the Cold War and Soviet helicopters transporting nuclear weapons from their storage sites to missile launch pads. At the same time, Soviet spy satellites were reporting that NATO bombers, conspicuously armed with nuclear weapons, had been leaving their hangars; it was subsequently revealed that these were dummies, intended to add realism to the ongoing Able Archer exercise. Verging on too much realism.

This set the stage for the West's own unsung hero who may also have saved the world. Leonard Peroots was assistant chief of staff for US Air Force Intelligence in Europe during Able Archer 83. He noted how, in response to NATO's war game exercise, Soviet military forces—most assuredly not playing games—had increased their alert. Peroots reasoned that if he ordered a correspondingly heightened real-world strategic response by NATO, this would have risked confirming the Soviets' worst fears, leading to tit-for-tat escalations that might have become unstoppable. And so, like Petrov, he did nothing, and, by the skin of our nuclear teeth, the greatest of all possible oops didn't happen.

The point of the preceding is that the invention of nuclear weapons was an oops in itself because it hasn't done anyone any good while using up precious resources of all kinds and, most crucially, threatening to bring about precisely the outcome they allegedly prevent. Unlike the other oops explored in this book, the nuclear oops is a double-header: first, just making the weapons turns out to have been a blunder in itself, albeit maybe an understandable one given fears at the time that Hitler's scientists might produce nuclear weapons first. (As it happens, they weren't even close.) Second, the nuclear enterprise threatens to cause the infinitely greater oops of nuclear war, something that hasn't happened yet, but if it ever did, would be the most calamitous oops in history. It might even end history.

Here is one last, especially well-documented case, for anyone who still doubts the potential for that humongous, ginormous oops-of-all-oops. It occurred four years after the end of the Cold War, on January 25, 1995, when fear of nuclear war may have been, ironically, at an all-time low. It's known as the Norwegian Rocket Incident, or the Black Brant Scare. US and Norwegian atmospheric scientists had launched a four-stage rocket designed to study the aurora borealis. Its northbound trajectory carried the rocket briefly along the route outlined for Minuteman III ICBM launches if they were to target Moscow. It also attained an altitude of more than nine hundred miles, which suggested it could constitute the kind of high-altitude nuclear attack designed to incapacitate Russian early-warning radar. Russian nuclear crews went to high alert and the famously alcoholic President Boris Yeltsin was handed the Kremlin's equivalent of the US presidential "football," which contains nuclear launch codes.

Maybe he was just sober enough, or a nonbelligerent drunk. In any event, Yeltsin decided not to respond. It turned out that Russian authorities had been notified ahead of time about this launch, but the information had not been conveyed up the command chain. ("There's always some sonofabitch that doesn't get the word." Or who doesn't send it.) Russian observers eventually ascertained that the rocket wasn't entering their airspace and was not a threat. Twenty-four tense minutes after it had been launched, it fell to earth, as planned, near Spitsbergen.

Thus far, and contrary to Robert Oppenheimer's dark vision, nuclear weapons have not destroyed the world. But given how many times we have come terribly close—even without destroying the world—and how little, if any, positive payoff they have provided, it is hard not to see them as an enormous mistake. Anyone who chooses to see nuclear weapons as anything other than a looming cataclysmic blunder might consider the optimist who jumps off the top of the Empire State Building and who, passing the thirty-seventh floor, shouts "So far, so good."

5.4.Bees in Their Bonnets, Exotics in Our Environment

Honeybees originated in temperate Europe. In the 1950s, a group of Brazilian geneticists sought to develop a strain that would be adapted to tropical South America. So, they hybridized relatively easy-going European honeybees with their African relatives, which thrive in a warm climate. They succeeded. However, the African species is also highly aggressive, and so, the next stage of the research had been to reduce this unwanted trait by selective breeding. But some of the newly-created Africanized honeybees had other plans: they escaped first. These "killer bees" have now been reported in Arizona, California, Nevada, New Mexico, and Texas. They are continuing to move north, thanks to global warming. If the hybridization wasn't an oops—and in retrospect it might have been—letting them escape certainly was.

Africanized "killer" bees (photograph by Lorraine Beaman, USDA ARS Honey Bee Breeding Lab, 2007).

OOPS!

As environmental problems go, invasive non-native species are promi-nent, although they often don't get the critical attention they deserve. There's nothing especially bad or even unusual about species expanding their range; it happens all the time. And of course, mistakes happen, such as accidentally letting animals or plants escape into environments where they cause trouble. The blunders are especially blameworthy, however, when they derive from carelessness, or intentional acts that turn out badly. Often non-native species have been introduced for seemingly valid reasons—generally pest control—only to have the liberated species go rogue and, rather than controlling their targets, proliferating and becoming serious pests them-selves, frequently worse than the "problem species" they were expected to control. Among the many examples are cane toads introduced into Australia and parts of the United States in the hope of controlling sugar cane beetles. The beetles didn't much care, but the toads, having toxins in their skin, have killed many native species as well as domestic dogs that commit their own oops and eat them.

There are also myriad examples of pets that escaped or were released when they grew too large or unmanageable; e.g., Burmese pythons, which have become severe pests in southern Florida, threatening much of the Everglades' unique wildlife. Others have been introduced for inane reasons (e.g., starlings originally released in Central Park as part of a project to seed the United States with all birds mentioned in Shakespeare's plays). Many unwanted non-natives have arrived as accidental hitch-hikers (zebra mussels, brown tree snakes, Japanese "murder hornets"). There are also plants brought in for ornamental purposes which became destructive invasives (e.g., kudzu, honeysuckle, English ivy, purple loosestrife) many of which have initiated ecological catastrophes. And this is just a brief list of troublesome species introduced into North America where they didn't evolve and where local ecosystems are not adapted to incorporate them. It's a problem worldwide, induced by careless and heedless human beings and powered by the fact that, frequently, species that are part of a local, smooth-functioning ecosystem proliferate out-of-control when introduced into environments where they have no natural predators or other natural restraints. The next step, surprisingly often, is to compound the blunder by introducing yet another organism in an effort to control the would-be controllers.

5.5. Haber: Hero and Horrible

There was once a syndicated cartoon character called Hagar the Horrible. He was comical and fictional. Fritz Haber was altogether real, both a global hero in the struggle to provide food for hungry people, and Horrible, an unintentional facilitator of the Holocaust. Few scientists have such a contradictory legacy. A brilliant and pioneering German chemist, Haber the Halfgood/Halfbad figured out how to synthesize ammonia from hydrogen and atmospheric nitrogen. The process yielded inexpensive fertilizer that was widely

Fritz Haber (anonymous photographer, 1906).

lauded as making "bread from air." Most of the fertilizer used worldwide is still based on his discovery, which earned Haber the Nobel Prize in Chemistry in 1918 and revolutionized global agriculture. Some estimates hold that more than one-third of the human population is alive today because of the tremendously increased crop yield due to the chemical process that bears Haber's name. Vaclov Smil, a historian of global agriculture at the University of Manitoba, makes a credible argument that Haber's discovery was nothing less than the most important technological advance of the twentieth century. His place in the pantheon of great scientists who have benefitted humanity would have been secure if he had stopped there. Alas, it was not to be. Haber was like those Manhattan Project physicists who were entranced by solving problems that were technically sweet, and that also promised to be in some way useful and even laudable. But that also had a downside.

Haber was also endowed with what his godson, the renowned historian Fritz Stern, called an "excess of patriotism,"[10] and accordingly, he used his chemist's genius to research the weaponization of chlorine gas. After studying various methods, Haber settled on the simplest; namely, waiting until the Goldilocks winds were blowing: strong enough to carry the gas away from the German lines but not so strong as to dissipate its effectiveness. Haber personally oversaw its first use during the Second Battle of Ypres at which an estimated five thousand Allied troops, caught completely by surprise, are estimated to have choked to death within minutes. A Canadian soldier, who survived being gassed at Ypres, described the horror as "an equivalent death to drowning only on dry land. The effects are there—a splitting headache and terrific thirst (to drink water is instant death), a knife edge of pain in the lungs and the coughing up of a greenish froth off the stomach and the lungs, ending finally in insensibility and death. It is a fiendish death to die."[11]

And so, Fritz Haber is currently known as not only one of the great benefactors of humanity but also as one of the most reviled: the father of chemical warfare.

Haber's wife, the former Clara Immerwahr and another brilliant chemist (the first woman to receive a doctorate in chemistry from the University of Breslau), became increasingly despondent over what she saw as her husband's misuse of science. She publicly condemned his work on chemical weapons as a "perversion of the ideals of science" and "a sign of barbarity, corrupting the very discipline which ought to bring new insights into life."[12] She begged him to turn his genius to other pursuits, but he refused. After the Battle of Ypres, Haber returned to Berlin in time to be feted for his contribution to the German war effort, just before he was to leave for the Eastern front to oversee the use of poison gas against the Russians. During the party, his wife took Haber's service revolver into a garden and shot herself. Haber nonetheless went on to the Eastern front as planned. German patriotism *uber alles*.

In the 1920s, he and his colleagues continued to research gases, this time for use as pesticides. Killing insect pests was less ethically fraught than killing human beings. But this change of focus gave rise to a kind of grisly poetic justice when the work of Fritz Haber, a German Jew, was ultimately extended (by others) to develop the "Zyklon process," leading to the infamous gas used to murder millions in German concentration camps. That's correct: a German Jew was ultimately behind the invention of the gas used to kill millions of German Jews. And included among the victims were members of Haber's own extended family. Fritz Haber was certainly a patriotic German, but because of his Jewish heritage (although he had converted to Christianity), he felt obliged to resign his directorship of the prestigious Kaiser Wilhelm Institute for Physical Chemistry over his refusal to fire his Jewish colleagues. He became a refugee, washing up in England where he indeed found himself washed up: shunned by fellow scientists, his Nobel luster and humanitarian accomplishments insufficient to overcome his ignominy. Albert Einstein observed that, "Haber's life was the tragedy of the German Jew, the tragedy of unrequited love."[13]

5.6. Fire and Ice

The *Hindenburg* was a German rigid airship or dirigible (zeppelin in German), the largest ever built and the pride of Nazi Germany. It has been said, however, that "Pride goeth before a fall." After crossing the Atlantic and docking in Lakehurst, New Jersey in 1937, the *Hindenburg* suddenly burst into flames, one of the most dramatic and widely reported civilian disasters of the twentieth century. "Oh, the humanity!" an anguished reporter exclaimed on live radio, in perhaps the most famous extemporaneous broadcast of all time. There are many hypotheses as to what initiated the explosive fire, but one thing is clear: the *Hindenburg* had been filled with highly flammable hydrogen gas, which, in retrospect, was—at minimum—unwise.

The *Hindenburg* burning (from the San Diego Air and Space Museum Archive).

That pride going before a fall thing just might have some validity. Early in the morning of April 15, 1912, the *RMS Titanic* sank in the north Atlantic, just four days into its maiden voyage. Like the *Hindenburg*, the *Titanic* was the largest of its kind and it, too, carried a nation's pride: in this case, the United Kingdom. It was 882 feet, nine inches long, and had approximately 2,200 people on board, of whom an estimated 1,500 died. Comparable to the *Hindenburg*, which couldn't possibly crash and burn (make that, burn and collapse), the *RMS Titanic* had loudly been declared unsinkable. As a result, it carried barely enough lifeboats to enable transferring its occupants to another ship in the inconceivable event of a serious problem, but because no one seriously considered that an outright sinking could happen, especially in peacetime, there weren't nearly enough to evacuate everyone at once. The day before the sinking, the ship had received six—count 'em, six—warnings of serious sea ice, but didn't change course and didn't even slow down.

Because of some confusion before the *Titanic* departed the United Kingdom, its lookouts hadn't been outfitted with binoculars. By the time the first iceberg was spotted, it was too close, the *Titanic* was too big and was going too fast to avoid a catastrophic collision. There is no evidence, by the way, that anyone spent any time rearranging the deck chairs on that ill-fated ship.

The *Titanic* and *Hindenburg* had some similarities. The *Hindenburg* was only slightly shorter (804 feet vs. the *Titanic*'s 882 feet). Both carried mail; the *Titanic*'s prefix RMS stood for Royal Mail Ship. Both were considered indestructible, but destructible they both were, in part because of some lethal blunders. They were both destroyed very quickly, the *Hindenburg* in thirty-four seconds and the *Titanic* in less than three hours. Both vessels offered fancy accommodations, especially the *Titanic*: e.g., a heated swimming pool and eleven-course meals. The *Hindenburg* was also no slouch; included among its amenities was a pressurized smoking room and a dedicated writing room. Whereas the *Titanic* was designed for super-luxury, not speed (maxing out at about twenty-four knots), the *Hindenburg*—although super-luxurious compared to current airplanes—had a top speed of about 82 mph, extraordinarily fast compared to any other commercial trans-oceanic options at the time.

The *Titanic* sinking (painting by Willy Stöwer, 1912).

Both had design deficiencies, albeit recognized only by twenty/twenty hindsight. The *Titanic*'s rudder was too small, its overall structure too big, and its crew overconfident. The *Hindenburg* was designed to be helium-filled, but was using highly flammable hydrogen instead. It attempted to dock between two electrical storms. Both vessels represented big-time technological hubris. The *Titanic* was essentially a conservative creation, based on pre-existing tried-and-supposedly-true engineering features (just scaled up). It has since been dwarfed by generations of genuinely titanic vessels and doesn't even make the list of the sixty-four largest modern cruise ships by gross tonnage. The *Hindenburg* was a marvel of technological innovation, but unlike the *Titanic*, which has spawned many much larger offspring, the Hindenburg's fiery demise marked the end of dirigible passenger travel.

The demise of the *Hindenburg* and the *Titanic* will forever resonate, in turn, with Robert Frost's poem, "Fire and Ice." Add oops.

5.7. NASA's Miserable Metric Martian Mishap

In 1999, after a seemingly flawless journey that took ten months, the Mars Climate Orbiter broke into pieces just short of its goal. The spacecraft had been designed and built by Lockheed Martin (LM), its mission to send data back regarding, as you might surmise, the Mars climate. Lockheed Martin's engineers used standard English measurements such as inches, feet, and pounds. The navigation team at California's Jet Propulsion Laboratory (JPL), which was responsible for controlling the orbiter's movements, used the metric system of millimeters, meters, and grams. And therein resided the making of an oops. The JPL team mistook the English-based numbers provided by Lockheed Martin as referring to the metric system; e.g., if LM had said that acceleration should occur over a distance of one hundred, they would have meant one hundred feet, while JPL would have perceived these instructions to mean one hundred meters. As a result, reality was lost in non-translation: navigational instructions sent from Earth to the orbiter used the metric system when they should have involved the same numbers, but referring to English units. Also lost was NASA's $327.6 million investment (roughly $500 million in 2022 money) when the orbiter, robotically following the incorrect instructions, missed its intended orbit and either disintegrated when it hit the Martian atmosphere or ended up orbiting the sun, to be eventually swallowed up, leaving a universe of red faces among senior NASA officials. *Wired* magazine ran this headline: "Metric Math Mistake Muffed Mars Meteorology Mission."[14]

Ironically, the initial mission of the ill-fated Mars Climate Orbiter was to serve as a communication link between the Mars Polar Lander and Deep Space probes, via JPL on Earth. As the brutal chain-gang boss snarkily observed in the movie *Cool Hand Luke,* "what we've got here is failure to communicate." Edward Weller, NASA associate administrator for Space Science at the time, explained the blunder, sorta (or maybe he tried to explain it away): "The problem here was not the error; it was the failure of NASA's systems engineering, and the checks and balances in our processes, to detect the error. That's why we lost the spacecraft."[15] So, if you add two numbers and get a wrong answer, the problem "isn't the error," it's your failure to detect the error. Nice to know.

The Mars climate orbiter (artist's rendering by NASA/JPL/Corby Waste, date unknown).

Here's a similar, earlier case: an Air Canada flight ran into trouble in 1987 when the plane's ground crew, instead of calculating how many liters were needed to fulfill its necessary fuel allotment of 22,300 kilograms, instead ended up loading its tanks with the number of liters needed to total 22,300 pounds. Since it takes 2.2 pounds to make a kilogram, the plane had less than one-half the fuel it needed, a discovery made only when it was flying at 12,500 meters (metric) = 41,000 feet (English). Fortunately, the captain was also an experienced glider pilot who was able to land the plane safely.

It's always good to be on the same page. But it's essential to be on the same measuring scale.

5.8. A Bunch of Errors by Some Great Scientists

The introduction to this chapter claimed that it would look only at scientific blunders that caused bad *actions*. Surprise! This final section violates that promise. We'll consider a few *conceptual* errors made by some great scientists.

As a twenty-four-year-old math genius, Galileo was approached by the Florentine Academy to calculate the precise dimensions of hell, using Dante's *Inferno* as underlying data. Although known to be poetic fiction, *The Divine Comedy* was so revered that in Italy it was widely considered to have been divinely inspired and so, many sophisticated scholars took it as literal truth. In 1588, Galileo presented his results in two lectures to his Florentine sponsors. Using proportional scaling from Dante's poem, Galileo calculated that Satan was 1,180 meters (3,870 ft) tall, and, taking Dante's claim that Satan's naval was at the center of the Earth, he determined the exact depth of hell and the thickness of its dome.

Did the brilliant Galileo Galilei, widely revered today as perhaps the preeminent founder of modern Western science, believe all this? We'll never know, but it may be significant that what remains of him now is a bony finger—the middle one—from his right hand, on public display in Florence's science museum, where it points upward to the universe or perhaps issues a defiant obscene gesture toward the Church that subsequently persecuted him for demonstrating that the Earth moved and not the sun.

Then there was Isaac Newton, Galileo's most eminent scientific descendant. The poet Alexander Pope wrote the following "Epigram on Sir Isaac Newton": "Nature, and Nature's laws lay hid in night./God said, Let Newton be! and all was light." To this a more scientifically inclined twentieth-century writer, one J. C. Squire, responded, "It did not last: the Devil, howling 'Ho!/ Let Einstein be!, restored the status quo."[16] (This refers to Einstein's theory of relativity, which overthrew Newton's laws of motion and of universal gravitation . . . at least for very small things traveling very fast.) Like Galileo, Newton had an interesting relationship with religion. Newton was a devout Christian but an extremely unorthodox one, who believed that his unusual theology was, if anything, more important than his contributions to mathematics and physics. He wrote more on the biblical prophecies of Daniel and of John than in his immensely influential *Principia Mathematica*—at least more words, whether or not more accurately. Newton did not see his biblical investigations as taking a back seat to his pioneering work on gravity, motion, color, or the invention of calculus, and there is no reason to think that he thought that his theological exegeses were in any way a mistake. Others may think differently.

Charles Darwin was the most important biologist, ever. To him (and to a lesser extent, Alfred Wallace) we owe what philosopher Daniel Dennett called "the best idea anyone ever had"[17]: evolution by natural selection. But even Darwin wasn't infallible. Today, every reputable biologist knows that natural selection is the mechanism behind evolution, but in Darwin's day, the mechanism behind natural selection itself wasn't understood. The biggest conceptual problem arose because scientists at the time didn't know how heredity operates. Darwin's explanation of natural selection was persuasive. But because there was no science of genetics, there was no understanding of precisely how adaptive traits—those favored by natural selection—could be inherited. And this led to a logical inconsistency, one that greatly troubled Darwin.

The prevailing view was "blending inheritance," that in each new generation, the essential characteristics of mother and father were blended together to form their children. The offspring of a tall father and a short mother would typically be medium height. The result of crossing a red flower with a white one would often be pink. Inheritance was thought to be a matter of combining the characteristics of one parent with those of another, with the offspring a mix of the two, like mixing two different buckets of paint. The problem was that under blending inheritance, natural selection couldn't produce an evolutionary change because a new trait, no matter how useful, would be swamped by the less favored characteristics already present in the larger population. Worse than being lost in a crowd, a new, adaptive trait would be chewed up, swallowed, and then pooped out as part of an undifferentiated next generation. Imagine that you have many buckets of paint, but all of them are yellow, and you want to paint a wall blue. Then, just by chance (let's call it a mutation), a bucket of blue paint shows up. If you mix the nicely adapted contents of that blue bucket—one parent—with that of another parent, the yellow bucket, the blue is swamped by the yellow and can't be found in the resulting green offspring.

If you dump the blue paint into a huge vat of yellow, the result may show a teeny, tiny tinge of green, but certainly no blue. In this way, blending inheritance would make adaptation by natural selection nearly impossible: you'd need a helluva lot of sudden blue paint to get the desired result, and new, potentially adaptive mutations—in Darwin's day called "sports"—arise rarely and not by the bucket-full. Houston, we have a problem.

With the discovery of Gregor Mendel's work, around the end of the nineteenth century, it became clear that heredity worked quite differently, and that it was completely consistent with natural selection as Darwin originally envisioned it. Charlie D never learned about the particulate nature of genes. It would have made his day, because it answered the most cogent biological critique of evolution by natural selection by showing that inheritance doesn't blend. Ironically, he had a book that described Mendel's scientific findings in his study, but he hadn't cut the pages, and so, it escaped his notice.[ii] Yet, he had already intuited that blending inheritance couldn't be all that it was cracked up to be. In a letter to Alfred Wallace, he observed that

---

[ii] In those days, books were published as folded pages, to be cut open by the reader.

among all sexually reproducing species, the offspring are either sons or daughters and not hermaphrodites. But he had no idea how inheritance actually worked. As a result, he argued (briefly, to his credit) for a confused notion called "pangenesis," by which each body part somehow sent some sort of messages to the reproductive organs, which then somehow influenced the next generation. It was a shot in the dark, and it missed.

Mendel's studies gave the first clear evidence that there were distinct particles of inheritance, a phenomenon that is digital rather than analog. Instead of being thrown into a reproductive blender, with everything smooshed together, those entities that we now call genes remain independent rather than being blended into indistinguishable reproductive mush with each passing generation. To be sure, genes sometimes change (i.e., mutations happen), but mostly they are like playing cards that are dealt out, with each offspring given a different hand each generation. So, Darwin made a big mistake, one that has since been corrected and the right answer smoothly incorporated into biology's key concept. But no one blames him for not knowing what was, in his day, not known.

Darwin got off lightly. There are other cases, however, in which the errors of great scientists have somewhat diminished their luster, although plenty of shine remains.

Take William Thomson, First Baron Kelvin (1824–1907), widely known as Lord Kelvin, and mostly today as just Kelvin. As a scientist, he really was lordly, a brilliant British mathematician and physicist, one of the United Kingdom's most eminent scientists, then and now. Kelvin flourished just before the Golden Age of physics in the early twentieth century; his work was foundational in several ways. Kelvin is one of the founders of the field of thermodynamics and is widely known today for the scale of absolute temperatures,

Lord Kelvin (photographed by Messrs. Dickinson, London, New Bond Street, UK, date unknown).

called in his honor, "degrees Kelvin." Temperature is defined by the movement of particles and absolute zero is the temperature at which atoms and molecules stop moving. Kelvin was the first to calculate its objective value: −273.15 degrees Celsius or −459.67 degrees Fahrenheit. Kelvin was the first British scientist to join the House of Lords based on their accomplishments rather than their ancestry.

In a few respects, however, he goofed.

Kelvin was publicly skeptical of Röntgen's discovery of x-rays, but quickly acknowledged his error. In a newspaper interview printed in 1902, he predicted that "no balloon and no aeroplane will ever be practically successful."[18] He also threw a temporary monkey-wrench into the scientific acceptance of evolution. In Kelvin's day, there was great debate about the age of the Earth, with some geologists maintaining that our planet had been around forever. Literally. Kelvin disagreed and was correct: the Earth had only existed for a finite time. But he was wrong about how long that had been. Calculating based on the heat transfer from the sun to the Earth, Kelvin came up with between twenty million and a hundred million years old. As with Darwin, whose error derived from what was not known at the time, Kelvin's error also came from what wasn't known: the reality of plate tectonics, the role of nuclear fusion, and the heat-generating effect of radioactivity within the Earth. With these considerations factored in, it turns out that the Earth has a significant and previously unknown source of heat, so its age can't be calculated merely by looking just at static heat transfer. Considering the additional heat sources, unknown to Kelvin, it turns out that the Earth's heat loss has been much slower than even the great physicist had realized. And so, we now know that its correct age is a bit more than 4.5 billion years.

The connection to Darwin was not only coincidental, but consequential. One of the roadblocks to the scientific acceptance of evolution had been that the Earth was thought too young to have allowed evolution's necessarily slow pace. Before Kelvin's calculations, there had also been an abundance of biblical bullshit, notably the determination by Archbishop Ussher in 1650 that the Earth was created on October 23, 4004 BC. Using rather different methodology than counting biblical "begats" and employing other extracted Old Testament "data," Kelvin's calculations were considerably more reliable and up-to-date, but they nonetheless seemed to confirm the existence of a problem, one serious enough to cast doubt on Darwin's theory. Once corrected, however, there was plenty of time for natural selection to work. Regrettably, Darwin didn't live long enough to witness this additional confirmation of his insight, or at least, the removal of one of the few remaining substantive objections.

Richard Goldschmidt (1878–1958) was an accomplished geneticist and developmental biologist who proposed an idea intended not as a substantive objection to evolution, but rather, a variation on its major theme. He maintained that evolution occurred not only within species via small steps ("micromutations," consistent with accepted evolutionary theory) but also via large leaps ("macromutations"), the latter being necessary to explain the gaps between different species and between larger taxonomic units. For example, how dogs became different not only from wolves, but from cats. In 1940, Goldschmidt wrote that "the change from species to species is not a change involving more and more additional atomistic changes, but a complete change of the primary pattern or reaction system into a new one, which afterwards may again produce intraspecific variation by micromutation."[19] He also suggested a colorful phrase for those creatures that he believed appeared rarely, but were substantially different from their ancestors: "hopeful monsters." Suffice it to say that even though a few possible major genetic leaps have been suggested, among modern evolutionary biologists Goldschmidt's idea is a hopeless monster.

Lord Kelvin wasn't the only renowned physicist who made a boo-boo. Another was Fred Hoyle (1915–2001), an English astronomer who was a genuine polymath, having written plays, short stories, an autobiography, and more than twenty science fiction novels, including his first, the now-classic masterpiece, *The Black Cloud*. He became Astronomer Royal and did pioneering work on "stellar nucleosynthesis," proving that nearly all of the known elements were created inside stars and were then distributed throughout the universe as a result of supernovae (intra-stellar explosions). Hoyle vigorously opposed the emerging theory that the universe developed from a single spectacular expansion event, presenting theory and data supporting the alternative steady-state model. He even coined the term "Big Bang" to disparage the concept of an expansionary universe; ironically, his verbal invention has subsequently been adopted as the mainstream phrase describing precisely what he had opposed. And what is now recognized pretty much, to coin a phrase, universally among cosmologists.

Hoyle gloried in taking positions that were, to put it mildly, out of the mainstream and which seemed kooky then and even more now. For example, he suggested that influenza epidemics occurred when the Earth passed through an interstellar cloud of viruses left behind by the tail of a comet. He claimed that the precise conditions needed for the production of carbon could not be achieved by natural forces and that "the laws of nuclear physics have been deliberately designed with regard to the consequences they produce inside stars."[20] Not that he believed that God was responsible; rather, that the universe's physical laws were generated by an earlier, extremely advanced interplanetary civilization. Hoyle also argued that evolution by natural selection was all wrong and that new organisms were produced when viruses from outer space collided with existing life forms on Earth. (He evidently had something about viruses.) Despite these wacky ideas, Hoyle's serious science was so impressive that many observers, including fellow astronomers and physicists, are convinced that his work on stellar nucleosynthesis alone deserved a Nobel Prize, which was denied him because his personality was so obstreperous.

Some scientists are so brilliant that even their mistakes ultimately turn out to be correct. And so, we come to a mathematical physicist who certainly deserved his Nobel and whose contributions were such that his name has become synonymous with scientific genius: Albert Einstein. As developed in his theory of general relativity, gravity isn't some mysterious force acting through space, but rather, the mass of any object warps the curvature of space, causing movement of anything that possesses mass. Furthermore, the geometry of space-time is determined by the amount of mass and energy nearby. Gravity changes space in its vicinity and objects move by the shortest path in that curved space. As physicist John Archibald Wheeler puts it, mass tells space how to curve, and those curves tell matter how to move. Initially, Einstein was working pre-Big Bang under the widespread assumption that the universe was static, something like the steady state that Fred Hoyle was later to espouse so vigorously. But if gravity causes everything to attract everything else, how can it be that the universe doesn't collapse onto itself, making a Big Crunch or what we would now call a universal black hole?

So, Einstein added another term to his general relativity equation, the so-called cosmological constant, which represented a repulsive force. This repulsive force had to exactly equal the attractive force of gravity, keeping things—i.e., the cosmos—constant. But there was also a problem with this proposed repulsive force: gravity decreases inversely with the square of the distance (it gets much weaker as the objects are farther away from each other), and yet Einstein's repulsive force is linear with distance. As a result, the universal attraction due to gravity should poop out rapidly as distance increases whereas the repulsive force, although also weakening, should do so less rapidly than the decline in gravity's impact. As a result, repulsion should exceed attraction among objects already distant from each other and this disparity should become greater the more spread out things are. So, the universe should expand.

Yet according to scientific understanding and data in the early twentieth century, it was static. When, in the late 1920s, Edwin Hubble and the Belgian priest and astronomer Georges Lemaître showed that the universe is, in fact, expanding, Einstein concluded he didn't need his repulsive force because gravity would merely slow this expansion, just as if you throw a rock into the air, gravity will slow its ascent. Einstein reasoned that all the forces didn't need to be balanced and so he removed the term for repulsion that he had added earlier—his "cosmological constant"—from the equation for general relativity. Not surprisingly, he regretted having introduced this term in the first place, supposedly calling it his "biggest blunder." It has been suggested, incidentally, that he didn't use that phrase; rather, astronomer George Gamow did. No matter. There's no doubt that Albert E regretted having introduced an arbitrary fudge factor—that cosmological constant calling for a repulsive force—into his relativity equation.

This regret arose in part because he believed that scientific truths expressed in equations must be elegant, and yet, in this regard, he may well have been wrong. Modern physicists and philosophers of science now seem to agree that elegance should reside in the theory, not necessarily in the equations expressing that theory. Moreover, in 1998, it was found that the universe was not only expanding (as Hubble and Lemaître had shown) but the *rate* of this expansion is increasing; that is, it is accelerating. This, in turn, has become a major conceptual pillar for the existence of dark energy, which provides the "vacuum energy" of outer space. What of the mathematical factor that accounts for this vacuum energy and that is driving the universe's acceleration? It turns out to match remarkably well the term that Einstein had originally introduced as his cosmological constant. His blunder, insofar as there was one, wasn't putting it in but taking it out. So, it looks like Einstein's greatest mistake was thinking it had been his greatest mistake.

Chapter

6

Athletics

There has been a ton of athletic oops, most of them comical when viewed retrospectively and particularly when divorced from the emotional connection with which so many sports fans are blessed. (Or afflicted.) Here are a few.

6.1. Tossing Out the Babe for Some Bathwater

In January 1920, the Boston Red Sox announced that they had sold Babe Ruth to the New York Yankees for $100,000. Although this seemed like a huge amount of money at the time, so that many people thought the Yankees had been fleeced, the fleecing was the other way around. An economist calculated that during the fifteen years that Ruth wore Yankee pinstripes, the team made $3.4 million in profits, of which roughly 40 percent was attributable to this one man. (We should all be fleeced like that!)

When Red Sox president H. Harrison Frazee informed Red Sox manager Ed Barrow of the sale, Barrow replied: "I thought as much. I felt it in my bones. But you ought to know you're making a mistake."[1] Indeed. Yup. You betcha. Right on. True dat. The Red Sox had won the Major League Baseball Championship in 1918, with Ruth on their roster, but after trading him, the Sox went eighty-four years without a comparable success, reaching the Series just four times: in 1946, 1967, 1975, and 1986, but losing each time in the final seventh game. Pouring salt on Boston's wounds, during that time the Yankees won thirty-nine American League pennants and notched twenty-six World Series wins. Even today, the Red Sox front office continues to be Ruthlessly derided for having Rendered their team Ruth-less, with fans Ruing the day they gave up Ruth.

While the Red Sox suffered the "Curse of the Bambino," Babe Ruth became the most famous ballplayer of all time and the money he made for the Yankee organization enabled them to build their own ballpark. (Previously they had shared the Polo Grounds with the more renowned and better financed New York Giants.) That new ballpark was Yankee Stadium, which opened in 1923, offering Mr. Ruth (a left-handed batter) a tantalizingly accessible right-field fence. It didn't take him long to access it, and the new stadium shortly became known as The House That Ruth Built, which also italicized what we might call The Blunder that Bedraggled Boston. Here's a bit more on all that.

George Herman ("Babe") Ruth was kind of a baby himself, all of twenty-four years old, when the Red Sox sold him. He didn't have much of a belly at the time, but he did have a reputation as a home-run hitter, having just the year before (1919) transitioned from star pitcher to star slugger as an outfielder. Looking at his pitching statistics, it's surprising that he ever tried the outfield. His career pitching stats are extraordinary: Earned Run Average of just 2.28, ninety-four wins verses forty-six losses. He pitched just three times for the Yankees (won three games, lost none), but he batted a whole lot more and even more successfully. He retired in 1935, as the most revered home-run hitter in history, with a lifetime total of 714. The next closest was 378 (Lou Gehrig). He was almost literally in a different league. In his first year with the Yankees, he hit fifty-four homers, more than any other American League *team* that season. Little known fact: he was also the Yankees' best bunter. Babe Ruth bunting sounds like an oxymoron.

Babe Ruth as a pitcher for the Boston Red Sox (photograph by Frances P. Burke, prior to 1919).

He played left field, batted left-handed, and, in 1919, his first year as an outfielder for the Red Sox, the "Sultan of Swat" (that moniker hadn't yet been coined) hit twenty-nine home runs, at the time a new major league baseball season record. That "record" wouldn't turn many heads today, and it didn't last long then, either. Almost single-handedly he changed the focus of baseball, which previously had been a game of tactics and strategy: get a runner on base, have him advance by a sacrifice bunt, or maybe stealing a base, or hit-and-run, and end up with final scores that looked more like soccer games than today's baseball. Once Ruth opened the floodgates, it turned out that fans loved home runs more than what had been called "inside baseball," a change in the sport that persists today.

Everything about the Babe was outsized: his home-run hitting, his waist-line, his personality, his fondness for strong beer and eager women. When the Yankee co-owner once asked him to tone down his lifestyle, Ruth said, "I'll promise to go easier on drinking and to get to bed earlier, but not for you, or for fifty thousand dollars, or two-hundred and fifty thousand dollars will I give up women. They're too much fun."[2] The Yankees proceeded to hire a private detective to follow him one night in Chicago; he reported that Ruth had been with six women. He played the next day; no indication whether he had any (more traditional) home runs.

Also larger than life was the money coughed up by the Yankees to obtain him; $100,000 was a sizeable fortune in 1920, and the Red Sox owner justi-fied the sale by pointing out that when so much money was dangled before him, he couldn't say "No." In retrospect, of course, he coulda, shoulda, woulda had he only known what we do today. The bargain that the Yankees got came close to matching the Louisiana Purchase engineered by President Thomas Jefferson in 1803: $15 million for 828,000 square miles, or roughly eighteen dollars per square mile, a shopping spree that doubled the size of the then-United States. Or perhaps "Seward's Folly," arranged by Secretary of State William Seward in 1867, whereby the United States purchased what is now the state of Alaska from Russia for $7.2 million.

As his popularity soared along with his home-run totals, the Bambino's enormous appeal was enhanced by his personal story. At the age of seven,

Ruth had been sent to St. Mary's Industrial School for Boys, a reformatory and orphanage. Previously, he had rarely attended school, and, even as a pre-teen, Ruth drank beer and roamed the streets. At St. Mary's he started playing baseball, staying there until age nineteen, while being recorded as "incorrigible." His rags-to-riches, in-America-anyone-can-succeed story added to his luster as one who succeeded mightily. One sportswriter dubbed him "the patron saint of possibility." Although he was clearly a one-of-a-kind athlete, even his body was just strange-looking enough to suggest that the average Joe could aspire to greatness. Another reporter once described him as a refrigerator with four toothpicks stuck into it, testimony to his oddly thin lower legs and wrists.

When he was sold to the Yankees, Ruth had just signed a three-year contract with Boston for $10,000 per year, and he shocked the country (and doubtless the Red Sox management in particular) when he announced that he thought he was worth double that. The Babe's salary demands may well have been part of why Red Sox owner Harry Frazee elected to sell him. Hoping to assuage the anticipated anger of Sox fans, Frazee announced that:

> No other club could afford to give the amount the Yankees have paid for him, and I do not mind saying I think they are taking a gamble. With the money, the Boston club can now go into the market and buy other players and have a stronger and better team in all respects than we would have had if Ruth had remained with us. I do not wish to detract one iota from Ruth's ability as a ballplayer nor from his value as an attraction, but there is no getting away from the fact that despite his twenty-nine home runs, the Red Sox finished sixth in the race last season.[3]

In the ensuing years, they didn't do better without the Colossus of Clout, and, in addition . . . they no longer had Ruth and his growing star appeal. Nor did they have to meet his salary demands. To keep their new star happy, the Yankees agreed to the princely sum of $20,000 per year. (It was later revealed that as part of the deal, Yankee co-owner Jacob Ruppert loaned the Red Sox owner $300,000, who put up Boston's Fenway Park as collateral.)

There's no indication that existing Yankee team members resented the Babe's humungous salary, although such restraint is hard to imagine. Pitcher Bob Shawkey, who had faced Ruth as a Red Sox, was ecstatic to be on the same team at last. "Gee, I'm glad that guy's not going to hit against me anymore," he rhapsodized. "You take your life in your hands every time you step up against him, You just throw up anything that happens to come up into your head, with a prayer, and then duck for your life with the pitch."[4]

6.2. Why Did the Corrigan Cross the Ocean? (Hint: He was going the "Wrong Way," but at least he got to the other side.)

On July 17, 1938, thirty-one-year-old Douglas Grace Corrigan took off from Brooklyn's Floyd Bennet Field in a single-engine Curtiss Robin airplane, with two boxes of fig bars, a quart of water, two chocolate bars, and a map on which he had marked up the route from New York to California. His first choice had been to fly across the Atlantic, but permission was denied. He was told, however, that he could attempt to fly nonstop to California, which itself would be quite an accomplishment. After taking off from Floyd Bennett Field in Brooklyn, Corrigan flew straight into a fog bank, and then, twenty-eight hours later, he landed. In Dublin. Corrigan was promptly met by an Irish army officer. "I left New York yesterday morning headed for California," he explained. "I got mixed up in the clouds, and must have flown the wrong way."[5] Hence, his moniker, Wrong Way Corrigan, and the rest, as they say, is history.

Wrong Way Corrigan (photograph by Harris & Ewing, 1938).

For the next fifty-seven years, until his death at age eighty-eight, Corrigan insisted that his wrong-way flight was unintentional: heavy clouds made it impossible for him to know that he was over ocean rather than land, and low visibility kept him from correctly reading his compass. Yeah, sure. His "navigational error" was almost immediately suspect. He was a skilled and experienced aviator, having barnstormed all over the country, and was also a highly regarded aircraft mechanic who had built a substantial part of Charles Lindbergh's trans-Atlantic *Spirit of Saint Louis*. Corrigan was of Irish descent, and, inspired by Lindbergh's feat, he dreamed of being the first to fly solo and nonstop from the United States to Dublin. Moreover, Corrigan had spent the previous three years attempting to get permission from the Federal Bureau of Air Commerce, predecessor to the Federal Aviation Administration, to make the flight of his dreams.

Each time, he was turned down. But he nonetheless made numerous modifications to his plane—a Curtiss Robin purchased for $325—that would only be needed for a nonstop, transoceanic flight. Wrong-Way had made the plane his own do-it-yourself project, modifying it by, for example, adding extra fuel tanks in front of the cockpit that also made it impossible for him to see directly below. Only out of either side. Afterward, Corrigan recounted that on his epic journey, after flying for about ten hours, his feet had felt suddenly cold and he found that the floor of the cockpit had filled with an inch of gasoline, coming from a leak in one of the fuel tanks. Losing fuel was bad enough, although not as dire as the prospect of a mid-air explosion. The only tool he had with him was a screwdriver. He used it to punch a hole in the cockpit floor so the gasoline would drain out as it collected, being careful to do so on the side opposite the super-hot exhaust pipe.

He didn't have a radio and his compass, if he ever bothered to consult it, was two decades old. One journalist who met Corrigan when he landed called the plane a "jalopy" and marveled that "anyone should have been rash enough even to go in the air with it, much less try to fly the Atlantic. He built it, or rebuilt it, practically as a boy would build a scooter out of a soapbox and a pair of old roller skates. It looked it. The nose of the engine hood was a mass of patches soldered by Corrigan himself into a crazy-quilt design. The door behind which Corrigan crouched for twenty-eight hours was fastened together with a piece of baling wire."[6]

He became a celebrity, getting a ticker-tape parade (with a larger audience than Lindbergh had generated.) He also played himself in a movie based on his exploit, and, in his later years, endorsed a range of "wrong way" products, including a wristwatch that ran counter-clockwise. He even appeared on the TV show *To Tell the Truth*.

Front page of *The New York Post*, 1938, with headline suitably printed the wrong way.

Intentional or not, Corrigan's adventure ended up doing him a lot of good, despite the near-certainty that he lied about his actual intent. Others were not so fortunate, having made their genuine oops before a large and stupefied crowd. Moreover, to some extent they became objects of ridicule rather than bemused admiration. Mr. Corrigan wasn't the first wrong-wayfarer. Before him, there was Wrong-Way Roy Riegels.

6.3. How Many Wrong-Way Rascals Make a Right?

It was the second quarter of the 1929 Rose Bowl, and all-American Roy Riegels was playing for the University of California Golden Bears ("Cal") against the Georgia Tech Yellowjackets. Riegels adroitly recovered a Georgia Tech fumble around the Tech thirty yard line and then even more adroitly raced—you guessed it—the wrong way, sixty-five yards, toward the Cal end zone. It was a magnificent effort, chased all the way by one of his teammates, screaming at him to turn around. All the while, Georgia Tech head coach Bill Alexander burbled delightedly: "He's running the wrong way. Let's see how far he can go." (Reminiscent of Napoleon's quip "Never interrupt your opponent when he's making a mistake.")

But it's a good idea to interrupt *your own side* when they're making a mistake. Riegels's teammate pursuer finally collared him at the Cal ten-yard line, but Riegels could taste an impending triumph and broke free, shouting "Get away from me. This is my touchdown." Grabbed again at the three, Roy Riegels finally realized his blunder and tried to turn and run the other way, but too late. He was tackled by the Yellowjackets on Cal's one-yard line. His team soon had to punt, but it was blocked and resulted in a safety (two points for Georgia Tech).

Roy Riegels was so distraught over his oops that he almost couldn't bring himself to emerge from the locker room for the second half. But he was a stand-up guy, to be elected team captain the next year. So, he showed up, played a strong second half and even managed to block a punt. But that earlier safety, courtesy of Roy R., made the difference in the final score: Georgia Tech 8, Cal 7. A Rose Bowl with thorns for Mr. Riegels, who was quickly dubbed Wrong-Way Riegels, a decade before the country celebrated Mr. Corrigan. Like Corrigan, Riegels also benefitted from his oops (although not as much). He went on to coach high school and college football, was inducted into the Rose Bowl Hall of Fame, and in 2003, CBS Sports designated Roy Riegel's wrong way Rose Bowl run in the Rose Bowl one of a half-dozen "Most Memorable Moments of the Century."

He also went from team goat to compassionate father figure. In 1957, a high school student intercepted a pass and then accidentally ran fifty-five yards into his team's end zone, scoring a safety for the other side and resulting—as did Riegels's mistake—in the other team winning, in this case, 9 to 7. Riegels wrote to the abashed oopser: "For many years I've had to go along and laugh whenever my wrong-way run was brought up, even though I've grown tired listening and reading about it. But it certainly wasn't the most serious thing in the world. I regretted doing it, even as you do, but you'll get over it."[7]

When, during a 1964 NFL game between the San Francisco 49ers and the Minnesota Vikings, another superb athlete, Vikings defensive end, Jim Marshall, recovered a fumble and ran it into his own end zone—again, scoring a safety for the other team—Riegels wrote sympathetically to him: "Welcome to the club." Unlike Roy Riegels, Jim Marshall didn't realize his mistake until he had actually scored for the opposing side. He even triumphantly threw the ball into the stands. The first player to reach him in the end zone was a San Francisco player, who gave him an ironically congratulatory pat on the back. Marshall later lamented that, "I had made the biggest mistake you can probably make," although his team eventually won the game, thanks in part to Marshall later forcing a fumble and recovering it . . . after which he didn't try to run, in either direction.

Jim Marshall, at right, having realized that he ran the wrong way (anonymous photographer, 1964).

The annals of Wrong-Way-ness are surprisingly crowded. Early in the third quarter of a basketball game between the NBA's Washington Wizards and the Orlando Magic, on Dec. 23, 2020, Washington center Thomas Bryant slam-dunked into his own team's basket, scoring two points for Orlando. In a National Hockey League 1986 playoff game, defenseman Steve Smith of the Edmonton Oilers accidentally scored an "own goal" against the Calgary Flames, leading to a Flames' victory and eliminating the Oilers from the playoffs. In addition, it happened on the twenty-three-year-old Smith's birthday; a present from him to the opposing team. "Own goals" are especially common in soccer, when, in the heat of the action, defending players, working just in front of their own goal and seeking to keep the other side from scoring, accidentally kick the ball into their own net. These next two wrong-way athletic feats are, however, considerably more unusual.

During the Commonwealth Games in July 2022, Ugandan marathoner Victor Kiplangat was just a mile from the finish line when he accidentally veered off course and found himself running away from it. Fortunately for him, he had built up such a commanding lead that after realizing his mistake,

Kiplangat was able to double back and still win the gold medal, finishing in an extraordinary time of 2:10:55, a full one minute and thirty-four seconds ahead of the second-place finisher. One never knows what will happen in an athletic contest; that's what makes horse races.

And speaking of horse races, this final wrong-way oops is the most dangerous one ever, although disaster was narrowly averted. It was the ninth race at Louisiana Downs on September 4, 2011, when a horse named Secretfly tossed his rider right at the starting gate, and began galloping, riderless, in the opposite direction around the 1 1/16-mile racetrack. He was going along the rail, heading right for the on-rushing mounted stampede when the oncoming rider, also on the rail, narrowly avoided a head-on collision by moving, at the last second, to the outside. The race was promptly annulled, but not the crowd's hyperventilation, and especially not among the jockeys who experienced the near miss.

6.4. When Willie Should Have Stuck to Shoemaking

Just as Jim Marshall is renowned as one of the finest defensive ends in football history (ultimately elected to that sport's Hall of Fame), Willie Shoemaker is widely recognized as the greatest jockey in the history of horse racing. But unquestioned greatness doesn't necessarily insulate someone from an occasionally embarrassing and costly error. It was the 1957 Kentucky Derby. The favorite was Bold Ruler, ridden by another horse race legend, Eddie Arcaro. But coming down the final stretch, it was Shoemaker—riding Gallant Man—versus Iron Liege, ridden by another justly renowned jockey, Bill Hartack. Shoemaker finally took the lead, and then suddenly, inexplicably, he stood up in anticipated triumph at the sixteenth pole. Willie had misjudged the finish line and engaged in premature ejockey-elation. Quickly realizing his oops, he resumed all-out pursuit, but Hartack and Iron Liege won by a nose. In his autobiography, aptly titled *Shoemaker*, the great jockey wrote that "I knew I had made a big boo-boo."[8]

Willie Shoemaker, at right, with Jayne Mansfield, center, and jockeys Johnny Longden and Eddie Arcaro (photo from *The Los Angeles Times*, 1957).

6.5. Billy Buckner's Blunder and Other Baseball Boo-Boos

This book has already given the notorious trade of Babe Ruth to the Yankees at least some of the attention it deserves. It was a management mistake that still echoes a century later. But baseball players make plenty of errors, too. In fact, more than any other sport, baseball reports regularly on players' oops: not only how many runs, and hits, but also how many errors every time a half-inning is over. There have been so many errors that it is challenging to choose just a few. Our first wasn't technically an error but it sure was a mistake.

Rick Stuart, son of former major league ballplayer Dick Stuart, was playing for the minor league Johnson City Cardinals. By 1981, he had never hit a home run in his professional career, but one day he knocked one over the left field fence. His teammates thronged around to congratulate him but during the celebration, he neglected to touch home plate, and was eventually called out. He never hit another homer.

Next, the most infamous officially designated error of modern times, at least among fans of the Boston Red Sox. The Sox were underdogs against the Mets, and yet were leading in Series games, three to two. One more win and they'd finally defy the "Curse of the Bambino." It was the sixth game of the 1986 World Series. The game had been tied and was into extra innings. A Boston miracle seemed in the offing, as the Sox scored two runs in the top of the tenth, but then the Mets tied it with two runs of their own in the bottom of the inning, and they had a runner on second. With two out, the Mets' Mookie Wilson hit a slow ground ball toward first base. Wilson was known for his speed, which may have induced first baseman Bill Buckner to rush the ball. It rolled between his legs, allowing the runner on second base to score and the Mets to win the game, evening the series at three and three. They then proceed to win game seven and Buckner becomes an outcast, perhaps baseball's most infamous "goat."

Bill Buckner famously flubbing a ground ball (anonymous photographer, 1986).

The television play-by-play was by the usually restrained Vin Scully, but in this case he got louder and more agitated as the play developed: "So, the winning run is at second base, with two outs, three and two to Mookie Wilson. [A] little roller up along first . . . behind the bag! It gets through Buckner! Here comes Knight and the Mets win it!" A veteran sportscaster, Scully also knew when to keep quiet, which he did for nearly three minutes, deferring to the wild cheering of the deliriously happy New York crowd. "If one picture is worth a thousand words," he finally said, "you have seen about a million words, but more than that, you have seen an absolutely bizarre finish to Game Six of the 1986 World Series. The Mets are not only alive, they are well; and they will play the Red Sox in Game Seven tomorrow!"[9]

Chapter

7

Business

Business people are reputed to be especially hard-headed. So, they shouldn't figure prominently when it comes to notable blunders. But of course they do, as demonstrated, for example, by the Great Recession of 2008,[i] and also by the following fascinating flubs.

---

[i] Although many big businesses, notably some banks, emerged from that debacle quite well.

7.1. Stepping on Beatles

Back in the day (in this case, 1962), when musicians were signed by "record labels," Decca was searching to sign the next successful band. Maybe even a blockbuster. The Deccan wizards invited two groups of young singer-songwriters to audition in their London recording studio. They signed Brian Poole and The Tremeloes. Who did they reject? A not very promising bunch from Liverpool called The Beatles.

The Tremeloes, not quite as successful as The Beatles (trade ad by Epic Records, 1968).

7.2. They Should Have Googled It!

Two brash Silicon Valley types had recently designed an Internet search engine they called BackRub, hoping it would compete with (or at least maybe carve out a tiny fraction of) the market share enjoyed by behemoths Altavista, Netscape, and Yahoo. But by 1999, the two men, graduate students at Stanford University, figured that their internet project was taking too much time from their studies, so they approached George Bell, CEO of Excite, offering to sell their baby for one million dollars. Mr. Bell balked. One of Excite's venture capitalists negotiated the two eager sellers down to $750,000; still no sale. The disappointed duo, Larry Page and Sergey Brin, eventually renamed the creation they were stuck with, calling it Google. As of early 2020, its parent company, Alphabet, was worth more than $1 trillion. So, had Excite taken up Messrs. Page and Brin, it would have made a profit of $999,999,250,000.

7.3. The Red Queen in Real Life

At one point in Lewis Carroll's *Through the Looking Glass*, the Red Queen tells Alice "My dear, here we must run as fast as we can, just to stay in place. And if you wish to go anywhere you must run twice as fast as that." The world changes and we have to change, too, or be left behind.

Eastman Kodak was for decades the Big Gorilla when it came to photos. It brought out the first mass-market cameras and Polaroid, the first quick-developing photo system—all using traditional film. For all its innovations, the company never caught up with the digital revolution in photography, despite the irony that the first digital camera was invented by a Kodak engineer. When the inventor brought his idea to upper management in 1975, the bosses knew better and told him it would never fly. He should deep-six it, which he did. Years later, when digital photography became the rage, Kodak couldn't catch up, and, as it appears, never even tried. It filed for Chapter 11 bankruptcy protection in 2012. The company still exists, but only as a dim negative image of its former robust self.

Back in the day, movie rentals were mostly handled by Blockbuster brick-and-mortar stores (you had to go in, choose your movie, bring it home, watch it, and then return it to the store). Then came Netflix with its own DVD-by-mail service. In the early 2000s, when Netflix was new and still relatively small, it approached John Antioco, Blockbuster's CEO, proposing that Blockbuster buy Netflix for $50 million. This would establish a synergy that covered the only two routes for watch-at-home movies: get them in-store, or by mail. They were net-flicked away. Former Netflix CFO Barry McCarthy recalled that, "They [Blockbuster] just laughed us out of their office."[1] Blockbuster soon went belly up and Netflix is a movie-making and subscription-selling industry leader with a market cap of more than $25 billion. Maybe they should consider a streaming series titled "Who's Laughing Now?"

Finally, here's a big one that should have gotten away. In the late 1990s, Chrysler was struggling to establish an international market. Daimler-Benz (Mercedes) rubbed its corporate hands, anticipating that like the proposed Blockbuster/Netflix merger that should have happened but didn't, merging with Chrysler would produce a powerful hybrid with automotive roots in both national and international markets. They orchestrated a fifty/fifty merger with Chrysler in 1998, for mere chicken-feed: $30.7 billion. By 2006, however, sales of Chrysler vehicles accounted for roughly 30 percent of the combined company, so after much *sturm und drang*, Daimler decided to sell 80 percent of its Chrysler holdings for $7.4 billion. Its turn into this particular merging lane cost Daimler something on the order of $20 billion.

7.4. Fat Finger Financial Flubs

The financial industry lives in fear of so-called "fat finger trades," in which an errant keystroke—whether precipitated by carelessness or a finger allegedly too wide for its keyboard—makes an errant trade. The mother of all fat finger trades—so far— was committed by a Japanese trader employed by Misuho Securities when, in 2005, he sold 610,000 shares in a job-recruiting firm that was just going public. The problem was that he sold them for one yen each (a bit less than a penny), when he intended to sell one share at 610,000 yen. The trade cost the company $342 million, because of quick-witted customers with a yen to buy these shares as soon as the offer appeared.

Misuho Securities appealed to have the deal canceled but officials at the Tokyo Stock Exchange ruled that the sale was, albeit a tad unusual and something of a good deal for the buyers, entirely legal and enforceable. The employment status of the fat-fingered fellow remains obscure, but the head of the Tokyo exchange resigned a few weeks later, acknowledging his failure to have appropriate oversight mechanisms in place. (The fact that this person resigned, even though he wasn't directly responsible for the oops, says a lot about the Japanese cultural tradition of higher-ups accepting blame—and about the contrasting Western tradition of ducking it.)

A worker at Samsung Securities, one of the biggest brokerages in South Korea, had been instructed to pay Samsung's employees a bonus of 1,000 won (just under one US dollar) per share. Instead, he gave each employee 1,000 shares in the company. The paper value of the entire windfall was 112.6 trillion won (US $100 billion), which exceeded the company's total market value more than thirty-fold. Before Samsung detected the oops and stopped honoring attempted sales by the surprised recipients, sixteen had already sold their windfalls, getting about US $9 million apiece. So far as can be determined, the original fat-fingered flubber was not among those who rushed to benefit by his own oops.

Yet another renowned fat-fingered foul-up victimized Citibank in 2020. The intent was to transfer an interest payment of $8 million to Revlon Lenders. Instead, they bestowed a whopping $900 million. As of 2022, the bank has recovered less than half and has attempted to define itself as being a lender to Revlon, rather than paying money owed. In the meanwhile, Revlon filed for Chapter 11 bankruptcy in June of 2022 and fully intends to keep the remaining money. One more: in 2006, an employee of the Italian-based airline, Alitalia, absent-mindedly left out two zeros when setting the price for flights from Toronto to Cyprus. Friendly skies indeed.

7.5. Products That Didn't Produce

There's much to be said for innovation. But sometimes, "if it ain't broke, don't fix it." The Coca-Cola Company had been worried, as ever, about Pepsi. Their flagship product wasn't broke, but the higher-ups in Atlanta decided to fix it anyhow. So, in 1985, the company announced that it was going to change the secret formula of America's best-selling soft drink. The public was unimpressed, and that's an understatement. Columnists and comedians mocked it; more than four hundred thousand outraged soda pop slurpers deluged company headquarters with letters and phone calls. After a few months of customer abuse (and plummeting sales), Coke rethought its brainstorm and, with its corporate tail between its legs, unveiled Coke Classic, which was what it had been before this embarrassing, costly, and now-classic screw-up.

Toys "R" Us used to be the country's premier toy retailer; it went bankrupt, having closed all of its seven hundred-plus stores by 2021. The following year it was purchased by WHP Global and has gradually been making a comeback, notably in Macy's stores. But in 2014 it was still going strong, when it pulled a bonehead move, which didn't cause its later troubles, but certainly didn't help. It introduced four collectible dolls based on that heart-warming children's classic that ranks with *Charlotte's Web* and *Alice in Wonderland*: *Breaking Bad*. For anyone who's been hibernating through the twenty-first century, *Breaking Bad* was the story of a high school chemistry teacher who, well, broke bad and became a crystal meth cooker and ultimately a big-time drug dealer and murderer. The dolls in question came with their own adorable bag of crystal meth and a detachable sack of cash. A Florida mom was, for some reason, a bit perturbed and initiated a petition on change.org demanding that the sweet little figurines be withdrawn, claiming that: "A show celebrating the drug trade ...[is] unsuitable to be sold alongside Barbie dolls and Disney characters."[2] Bryan Cranston, who played the main character in the long-running show, tweeted in response: "I'm so mad, I'm burning my Florida mom action figure in protest."[3]

Finally, the Disaster in Dearborn. Ford's biggest flop. A car catastrophe. Wait for it: Ta Da!—The Edsel. Even the name sounds weird. When it was name-tested even before the car proved its mettle, "Edsel" often evoked "weasel" and "pretzel," which should have alerted someone. Actually, this terrible moniker was chosen after months of intense searching, during which the company even consulted Pulitzer Prize–winning poet Marianne Moore, tasking her to suggest something that conveyed "some visceral feeling of elegance, fleetness, advanced features and design."[4] Ms. Moore obliged with such sure-fire winners as the Utopian Turtletop, the Intelligent Whale, Pastelogram, Mongoose Civique, and Andante con Moro, whereupon the Ford functionaries flaunted their wisdom by rejecting all of these and coming up with Edsel. (Which, purely by coincidence, happened to be the first name of one of Henry Ford's sons.)

On Sept. 5, 1957, the breathlessly waiting world was introduced to the 1958 Edsel, as part of an unprecedently large ad campaign. There were two rollouts, one for men and one for women (this was, after all, the 1950s). The men's involved all sorts of he-man accelerations and rapid-turn automotive contortions, during which the showcased vehicle once almost flipped over. The women's was presented as a fashion show. The Edsel was envisioned as the perfect medium-priced car for middle class families, with such innovative features as push-button transmission and a super-safe rear seat designed for children, whose rear doors could only be opened from the outside, with a key. According to one account, they were also "delivered with oil leaks, sticking hoods, trunks that wouldn't open, and push buttons that . . . couldn't be budged with a hammer."[5] These features didn't exactly take the country by storm. In fact, the Edsel flopped so spectacularly that the name has become synonymous with a failed product, proving that sometimes even ostensibly intelligent people are not very smart. Even by 1950s standards, it had been perceived as an uneconomic gas guzzler, ill-designed, wrong for the market, and with virtually no redeeming features. Nonetheless, marketing manager J. C. Doyle had no hesitation blaming the American public for the debacle. "What they'd been buying for several years encouraged the industry to build exactly this kind of car," he complained. "We gave it to them, and they wouldn't take it. Well, they shouldn't have acted like that . . . And now the public wants these little beetles. I don't get it!"[6]

By the time Robert MacNamara—soon to become JFK's secretary of Defense—finally pulled the plug in 1960, the Edsel had cost the Ford Motor Company about $350 million, and had truly run out of gas.

1958 Edsel Citation (photograph by Greg Gjerdingen).

7.6. Best Sellers, Worse Decisions

Once there was a single mother, unemployed and, according to her own account, delivered in a 2008 commencement speech at Harvard, "as poor as it is possible to be in modern Britain without being homeless."[7] She wrote a book that was rejected by twelve publishing houses before being picked up by Bloomsbury with an advance of £1,500 (about $2,250 at the time). Her books have now sold more than 500 million copies, grossing $7.7 billion and the author—who you've doubtless guessed is J. K. Rowling—is a billionaire and one of the wealthiest people in modern Britain. This true story, starring Harry Potter and colleagues, may be unique in the degree of oops committed by eleven different publishers (herein unnamed), but the basic pattern has happened often: books, both of great literary merit and/or providing great financial return once published, have been turned down by presumably savvy editors and their publishing houses.

Here is a severely abbreviated list of some of these authors and their first books:

- Stephen King, *Carrie*, rejected thirty times
- Dr. Seuss (Theodore Geisel), *And To Think That I Saw It On Mulberry Street*, rejected twenty-seven times

- John Le Carré, *The Spy Who Came in from the Cold*, initially rejected by an editor who wrote to the would-be author's agent: "You are welcome to Le Carré. He hasn't got any future."
- Louisa May Alcott, *Little Women,* initially rejected with the note "Stick to your teaching, Miss Alcott. You can't write."

Little Women, cover from first edition (1868).

- Margaret Mitchell, *Gone With The Wind*, thirty-eight rejections
- Richard Bach, *Jonathan Livingston Seagull*, initially rejected and told, "Nobody will want to read a book about a seagull."
- Beatrix Potter, *The Tale of Peter Rabbit*, rejected so many times she self-published 250 copies

Peter Rabbit, cover from first edition (1902).

- *The Diary of Anne Frank*, sixteen rejections, the first stating, "The girl doesn't, it seems to me, have a special perception or feeling which would lift that book above the curiosity level."[8]
- Madeleine L'Engle, *A Wrinkle in Time*, twenty-six rejections
- L. Frank Baum, *The Wizard of Oz*, rejected with the note, "Too radical of a departure from traditional juvenile literature."[9]

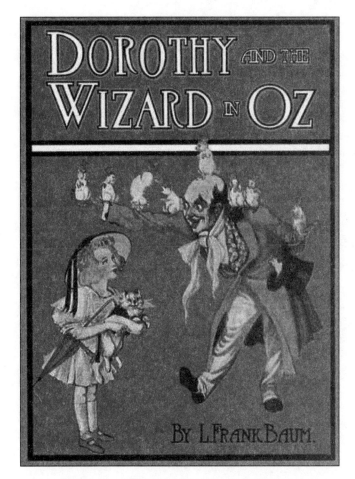

The Wizard of Oz, cover from first edition (1908).

- Kenneth Grahame, *The Wind in the Willows*, rejected as "an irresponsible holiday story that will never sell."[10]
- George Orwell, *Animal Farm*, turned down by Faber & Faber because its head, T. S. Eliot, objected to its "Trotskyite politics"
- Joseph Heller, *Catch-22*, so named because Simon & Schuster agreed to publish it after twenty-one others had turned it down
- Frank Herbert, *Dune*, twenty-three rejections
- John Grisham, *A Time to Kill*, rejected by sixteen literary agencies and twelve publishers

Chapter

8

Politics

When it comes to blunders, politics stands
out as an especially rich source of disasters.
It offers such an embarrassment of riches that
the problem isn't identifying what to include,
but rather, which of the stunning blunderers
and their impolitic errors can reasonably be
left out. Apologies, therefore, to those who
didn't make the cut, or whose notable oops
aren't about to receive the attention they
deserve.

8.1. The Travesty of Trump

Donald John Trump is, as he always insists, a special case. On the one hand, his life has been built of blunders. But on the other, he has in many ways been wildly successful (lots of money, president of the United States) even as he has left a path of destruction in his wake. So far, he has been able to avoid being held accountable for his many oops. *So far*. Sort of. Until now. As of this writing, he has been indicted in New York City on multiple counts for a scheme involving hush-money payments, violating campaign finance laws, and falsifying business records in the service of tax fraud. Other shoes are poised to drop.

Trump's many misbehaviors have been documented so many times, in so many books, articles, podcasts, congressional hearings, and the like that it would be redundant to pursue them here. Each time he steps— make that leaps, or stumbles—over the line, pundits proclaim that "this time, he's gone too far." But each time, following his latest gaffe, revelation, absurd and indefensible lie, along with the next inevitable avalanche of immoral, unethical, or downright illegal acts, he has managed, again *so far*, to be politically and legally untouchable, a zombie who, after being repeatedly shot by his own misdeeds and allegedly buried, keeps staggering on, covered with flies and stinking to high heaven yet also adored by millions. 'Nuff said.

Well, not quite. Among Trump's most serious transgressions have been politicizing the Department of Justice and trying to strong-arm Ukrainian president Volodymyr Zelenskyy by threatening to illegally withhold designated military aid unless he dug up dirt on Joe Biden. Looking just at his most egregious actions as of 2023, we find stealing highly classified documents belonging to the American people and lying (as usual) about what he had done, as well as trying to overturn Biden's clear victory in the 2020 election by engaging in a series of bizarre and likely illegal political coups and election law violations, notably but not limited to the state of Georgia, and, when they all failed, instigating the violent January 6 insurrection in an effort to prevent Biden's election from being certified.

Never before has a sitting president or ex-president constituted such a threat to US democracy. Maybe, just maybe, his heinous acts will finally come back to bite him.

Life is too short, however, to go down the rabbit hole of this man's innumerable fuck-ups. (And besides, depictions of his transgression already fill many a bookshelf.) Someday, perhaps even his deluded cultists will see him for the sociopath and dangerous malignant narcissist that he is. Maybe some fine day he'll get his comeuppance at last for a lifetime of oops, the consequences of which have thus far descended on many others, but, as of this writing, not yet on the actual perp. For all his malfeasances, he has not yet been convicted or served jail time. Indicted, yes, but not yet convicted. Maybe his spineless enablers in the Republican Party will also be held to account for having abandoned democracy, civil decency, and what presumably once passed for their conscience. In her opening statement as part of the The United States House Select Committee to Investigate the January 6th Attack on the United States Capitol, Liz Cheney captured their situation: "I say this to my Republican colleagues who are defending the indefensible: There will come a day when Donald Trump is gone, but your dishonor will remain."[1]

8.2. Derailed Campaigns (Even Before Being Nominated)

In 1859, a successful politician named William H. Seward was the odds-on favorite to be the presidential nominee of the Republican Party, even though his prickly, take-no-prisoners verbal style alienated some politicos. Seward was, nonetheless, so confident that he had the nomination sewed up that he took off for Europe and Asia and had a long and lovely trip, including a stop in Beirut where he added some prized Arabian horses to his stable. But he was in for a surprise when he got back to the United States: a gaunt, lanky, bearded, relative political newcomer and former congressman from Illinois with a quick wit and a surprisingly high-pitched voice had captured the imagination of the new political party.

Seward, having been out of the country too long, found himself out of the presidential nomination as well.

But all was not lost for the former New York governor. Lincoln selected him as secretary of state as part of what historian Doris Kearns Goodwin has called his "team of rivals." During the Civil War, Seward capably managed international affairs for the beleaguered republic, successfully keeping the United Kingdom and France from recognizing the Confederacy. Later, he was the driving force behind the purchase of Alaska from Russia, which was known at the time as Seward's Folly. This bit of retail shopping, however, turned out to be anything but a folly, ending up such a success that it has pretty much erased his genuine political folly—that earlier round-the-world jaunt—from the public mind.

Roughly a century after William Seward's presidential-hope-defeating international trip, another governor, George W. Romney, also made a trip, which also ended up dashing his presidential aspirations. (This Romney should not be confused with his son, Mitt, also a former governor and failed presidential wannabe.) George Romney, like Seward, had admirable civil rights credentials as a supporter of equal voting rights and integration, and an opponent of Jim Crow. Seward's trip occurred shortly before the United States found itself embroiled in the Civil War; George Romney's took place while the United States was fully engaged in the Vietnam War. Like Seward before him, Mitt's father had been a leading contender for the Republican Party's presidential nomination.

But then came "the Gaffe." In late summer 1967, Romney told a Detroit talk show host that while he toured southeast Asia in 1965, "I had the greatest brainwashing that anybody can get," orchestrated by US generals and aimed at getting him to support the US war effort in Vietnam. For a time it worked, but Romney explained that later, "since returning from Vietnam, I've gone into the history of Vietnam, all the way back into World War II and before. And as a result, I have changed my mind. I no longer believe that it was necessary for us to get involved in South Vietnam to stop communist aggression."[2] He ended up a dove, opposed to the Vietnam War, but by that time both supporters and opponents of the war came to distrust the three-term governor. After all, who would want a president who gets brainwashed, even when those doing the laundry are from your own country?

The damage had been done. Richard Nixon became the 1968 Republican presidential nominee who then, by narrowly defeating the Democrats' Hubert Humphrey, became president. After Nixon resigned during the Watergate scandal, Gerald Ford became president, and the oops continued when his re-election campaign came around. In 1976, Ford was debating the Democratic challenger, Jimmy Carter, when he blundered into a Romney-worthy gaffe by committing an unforced verbal error by claiming: "There is no Soviet domination of Eastern Europe."[3] The perplexed moderator gave President Ford—a former stand-out football player at the University of Michigan—an opportunity to pick up his fumble. But Mr. Ford unaccountably remained firm, and Jimmy Carter won the election.

Joe Biden has been especially gaffe-prone, although his verbal infelicities haven't kept him from becoming president and for the most part they have come less from stupidity or ignorance than from the bane of many politicos: speaking one's mind. Sometimes, however, those minds are simply addled, although addle-patedness has not been inconsistent with high political office. Witness former Nevada senator Chris Hecht, a reliable gaffe-machine who once opposed plans to locate nuclear waste repositories in his state, calling them "nuclear suppositories," something likely to be rejected by even the most fervent atomic advocates.

Gaffes aside, infants in their infancy aren't as persistent as adults in their adultery. So, let's get to that.

After two terms of Reagan, the Democrats were looking for a presidential candidate, and Colorado Senator Gary Hart was the clear frontrunner. He was a smart, experienced, and attractive politician who had successfully managed George McGovern's presidential nomination campaign and also his failed presidential effort. (But hey, nobody's perfect.) Hart had long been dogged by persistent rumors of "womanizing." But in 1987, the *Miami Herald* reported that the rumors were true, and that the married Hart was having an affair with Donna Rice, a twenty-nine-year-old model. The newspaper had staked out Hart's Washington, DC townhouse and recorded him coming and going with Ms. Rice. The gamey senator gamely denied a sexual liaison, and even famously told a journalist, "Follow me around. I don't care. I'm serious. If anybody wants to put a tail on me, go ahead. They'll be very bored."[4] It appears that Sen. Hart wasn't literally—and foolishly—challenging the media, as many people thought, but rather, expressing the hope that if he broke off the relationship (and any others), that he could still salvage his potential candidacy. But it was too late. Almost immediately, the next shoe dropped: a photo showing him on a chartered yacht aptly christened "Monkey Business," on a voyage to Bimini with the lovely Ms. Rice perched seductively on his lap. His campaign collapsed immediately, with the senator finally acknowledging: "I've made some mistakes. Maybe big mistakes, but not bad mistakes."[5] When trying to secure a presidential nomination, that seems to be a distinction without a difference.

Michael Dukakis (remember him?) became the Democratic nominee, running against George H. W. Bush in 1988. In that campaign, he committed a notable gaffe, but it was more like speaking honestly, which, in politics, can be a huge blunder. During a presidential debate, CNN moderator Bernard Shaw asked Dukakis, "Governor, if Kitty Dukakis were raped and murdered, would you favor an irrevocable death penalty for the killer?"[6] The Massachusetts governor had been a life-long opponent of capital punishment, knowing that it did not deter violent crime. Massachusetts had abolished the death penalty and had one of the lowest violent crime rates in the country, much lower than George Bush's Texas, which had long embraced killing killers.

But Dukakis didn't point that out. Rather, he responded coolly to Shaw that he would not change his view on the death penalty, "And I think you know, Bernard, that I've opposed the death penalty during all of my life."[7] This was true, and was in fact sound policy even if not, at the time, good politics. But the oops was immediately evident to nearly all observers: his answer was altogether lacking in warmth (make that, heat) and emotion.

Better to have said something like, "If someone raped and murdered my wife, I'd want to rip off his balls and then tear out his heart." It's one thing to support a national policy to be administered by the federal government, quite another to show the country that you're capable of personal emotion and even anger. The Bush campaign knew immediately that it had won, even without its own despicable, race-baiting television ad that linked Dukakis to a black former prison inmate who had committed murder while on parole. And even without the greatest photo-op oops in American history, the hapless Dukasis's Great Tank Trip.

Michael Dukakis had been accused of being not only soft on crime (he wasn't) or lacking in relatable emotion (well, maybe he was), but also soft on national defense (which he wasn't). So, his genius campaign managers thought it would be just the ticket if he were filmed riding in an M-1 Abrams Main Battle Tank. What could go wrong? The problem was that during his phony joy-ride Dukakis not only wore a goofy smile but an absurdly large tanker's helmet that made him look like a parody of a children's action figure. It tanked his campaign.

Dukakis recounted that for years after that debacle, when he would arrive at a speaking venue he'd often get the snide question whether he had come in a tank. He'd reply, "No, but I've also never thrown up all over the Japanese Prime Minister."[8] (Bush had. But the voters evidently preferred barfing over blandness.)

When Gary Hart's philandering was revealed, thereby opening the nomination for Michael Dukakis, it was the most notable adultery-infused campaign meltdown in recent times. There have been innumerable others, especially "down-ballot." For example, Cal Cunningham was a promising Democratic senate candidate in North Carolina, whose opponent, Thom Tillis, appeared vulnerable. Cunningham was leading in the polls when, just a month before the 2020 election, sexually suggestive emails emerged between the married Cunningham and a woman, also married. Soon, Cunningham and his lover acknowledged that they had had "a physical relationship," and Tillis won. The ever-present adultery oops has a long history of bringing down politicians of both parties. Mark Sanford, Republican governor of South Carolina, inexplicably disappeared from June 18 to June 24, 2009. It evoked nationwide news coverage, which isn't exactly what a married man (politician or not) generally wants when he is spending time with his mistress. Sanford's spokesman said that he was hiking the Appalachian Trail, but after Sanford resurfaced, he eventually admitted that he had been in Argentina with his extramarital lover, and not for the first time. "Hiking the Appalachian Trail" became a substitute phrase for you-know-what.

Newt Gingrich had been a major force in Republican politics and was for a time speaker of the House. He also led the charge against then-president Bill Clinton's adulterous relationship with White House intern Monica Lewinsky during which time—you guessed it—he was himself cheating on his second wife, as he had on his first. Gingrich ended up resigning his speakership in 1999 but it wasn't until 2007, as he was beginning a brief, failed campaign for the presidency, that the Republican congressman admitted his own adultery, but not his hypocrisy. Bill Clinton's adulterous liaison while president was certainly an oops, as were his associated lies. The scandal became national and international news, eventually leading to his impeachment, the first since Andrew Johnson more than a century earlier. (It was also, for better or worse, the first time that fellatio went from being of largely private interest to public recognition.) All things considered, and blow-jobs aside, coverage of Clinton's transgressions was so extensive it became a widespread obsession, internationally as well as nationally. And so, to spare the readers of this book what Yogi Berra once called "déjà vu all over again," we'll stop here.

8.3. Corruption? Will Wonders Never Cease?

It is said that money is the lifeblood of politics. If so, corruption is the heart that pumps that blood. It's possible that corruption isn't any greater in politics than in other areas such as business or athletics, that it simply garners more attention when a spotlight is shined upon it. A cynical electorate nonetheless pretty much expects the worst from most politicians and only claims to be "shocked, shocked" when it is revealed. Although political corruption often involves dipping hands in that lifeblood, it's not limited to money. Nepotism, lust for power and influence—and, of course, sex—have significant roles. And insofar as corruption is an oops for those involved, it's only when the perpetrators get caught. Let's start with the most infamous case of corruption in America.

Warren G. Harding was elected president in 1920 under the slogan "Return to normalcy." (World War I had ended barely two years earlier.) Harding's election included an interesting sidebar. In addition to his Democratic opponent, there was a third party candidate, the socialist Eugene V. Debs, who got 3 percent of the national vote. Moreover, Debs campaigned from prison, having been convicted of what was then a federal crime: opposing the war. Then, as now, there was no law against running for president while incarcerated, something that might conceivably happen again in 2024.

Harding's normalcy turned out to include a full menu of corruption, although bribery, nepotism, and self-dealing had been rampant during the war as well. One needn't be a cynic to acknowledge that this happens whenever large amounts of money are involved, with wars offering especially fertile soil. Cutting to the chase, Harding's secretary of the interior, Albert Fall, accepted $400,000 in Liberty Bonds under the table from oil magnate Henry Sinclair. In return, Sinclair's Mammoth Oil Company received drilling rights to a reserve in Wyoming called Teapot Dome, the oil wherein had been designated as a strategic reserve for the US Navy. There had not been any competitive bidding, allegedly because military preparedness had been involved, but in fact, the only real preparedness had been Secretary Fall's preparedness to fill his wallet.

As a congressional investigation proceeded, it was revealed that Fall had spent lots of money on his fancy ranch in New Mexico, about the time that he had engineered the lease of Teapot Dome. Pure coincidence, of course.

Fall eventually fell, convicted of bribery. In 1931, he became the first member of a presidential cabinet to be imprisoned for crimes committed while in office . . . but not the last. (See Watergate.) It appears that President Harding was not directly involved in the scandal, which wasn't revealed until after his death. But he had plenty of his own, such that his name became, for a time, synonymous with financial corruption and cronyism. During his tenure, the Harding Administration was shot through with both, the most notable being the Veteran's Administration scandal, in which Charles Forbes, director of the Veteran's Bureau, defrauded the government too many times to be recounted here. Among these was a deal whereby Forbes and two construction company owners split the proceeds from federal construction of veteran's hospitals, and others in which the prices for government hospital contracts were inflated and the "overhead" pocketed. In these scandals, once again Harding did not profit personally nor did he orchestrate the multiple frauds, but as the details came out, he worked hard (and unsuccessfully) to protect the perpetrators, especially Forbes, who was a personal friend.

Harding was, however, directly involved in one personal scandal—that old bugbear, adultery. Scrutiny of his personal life uncovered Harding's relationship with a mistress, the stress of which likely contributed to his death in office from a cardiac arrest.

The Watergate scandal may now be water under the bridge of DC scandals, but it persists as a major blemish to President Richard Nixon's already tarnished record. Its resonance is such that it has given rise to the suffix "gate," affixed to every newly revealed wrongdoing. In brief, prior to the 1972 election, at which the incumbent Nixon trounced the Democratic challenger, George McGovern, the White House may or may not have orchestrated a break-in at the Democratic National Committee in the Watergate Hotel. The attempted burglary occurred at the immediate behest of the Committee to Re-elect the President (which bore the apt acronym, CREEP).

But Nixon and crew were definitely involved in an elaborate, illegal cover-up. This was stunningly revealed when it was found that Nixon had secretly recorded conversations with his fellow conspirators in the Oval Office. The whole scheme eventually unraveled, shortly after Nixon famously announced, "I am not a crook." But he was, and he resigned his office—the only president ever to do so—before he could be impeached. The evidence against him had become incontrovertible and his support, even among fellow Republicans, had evaporated. The now ex-president was promptly pardoned by the newly inaugurated Gerald Ford, who proclaimed that "our long national nightmare is over." Many of Nixon's top figures, including the White House counsel, chief of staff, and attorney general did well-deserved prison time.

Not least was "Iran-Contra," so named because it involved (surprise!) Iran and the contras, the latter being right-wing revolutionaries attempting to overthrow the left-wing Sandinista government of Nicaragua. Many, although certainly not all, who had seen Ronald Reagan as a cheery and squeaky-clean political messiah ("Morning in America" and all that) were disabused of that perception when the Iran-Contra Affair came to light. Congress had set strict limits on funding the contras. In addition, the government had been prohibited from selling weapons to Iran and had a public policy of not paying ransom for hostages. All these were violated by

Aerial view of the Watergate Hotel, storied location of a major Nixon Administration oops (photograph by Carol M. Highsmith, sometime between 1980 and 2006).

an underhanded maneuver that included a secret deal to sell arms to Iran, via a connection through Israel, and to use the Iranian money to support the contras. Also included was that Iran would release American hostages, not those captured by the newly established Iranian government in 1979, but others who had been kidnapped by Hezbollah operatives in Lebanon, early in the Reagan years.

When the scandal became known, there was an immense hubbub, as part of which Oliver North, a staff member of the National Security Council, was indicted for multiple crimes: notably fraud and obstruction of justice. He was also convicted of illegally accepting a gift, lying to Congress about the timeline of events, and shredding government documents as part of an attempted cover-up. The charges were subsequently dropped, part of a scandal-based-on-the-scandal whereby essentially no one was held accountable for this pattern of misdeeds. North subsequently became a darling of right-wing talk radio. Dick Cheney, at the time a member of Congress, defended the whole debacle by arguing that the perpetrators had no alternative because Congress had expressed its will otherwise!

8.4. Unintended Consequences

Remember the Alamo? Lots of us do, with a "memory" that is simply wrong. It comes from a successful PR campaign that painted Santa Anna as the bad guy and Davy Crockett, et al, the good guys. Turns out these "good guys" were indeed fighting for a free and independent Texas, but not because of a sudden burst of local patriotism and laudable love of liberty; rather, they were mostly fighting *for slavery*. And Santa Anna? He was leading his army against establishing Texas as a sovereign slaver state and for his own country's territorial integrity. Years before, there had been a major oops, this one committed by the Mexican authorities.

Romanticized view of the fall of the Alamo (painting by Robert Jenkins Onderdonk, around 1903).

Like so many blunders, it seemed like a good idea at the time. After Mexico won its independence from Spain in 1821, the northern and western parts of the then-huge country weren't effectively controlled by the Mexican government, whose resources were stretched thin. Native Americans—Apache, Navajo, and especially Comanche—made devastating raids deep into the heart of Mexico, killing Mexicans, stealing cattle which they typically sold to US markets, and devastating what remained of the northern Mexican economy. The region was dry (still is) and sparsely settled (ditto), and what became effectively a state-within-a-state blocked trade and even communication with the then-Mexican regions now known as New Mexico and California.

And so, the beleaguered government in Mexico City encouraged US citizens to settle in their province of Tejas, granting instant citizenship to immigrants in the hope that they would provide a buffer between those obstreperous Native American lands, the "Commancheria," and the Mexican heartland. It worked. Too well. So many English-speakers migrated from the United States that soon gringos outnumbered Spanish-speaking Tejanos by roughly six to one. Worse yet, the new arrivals mostly chose not to settle in the northern and western regions (too few cowboys and too many Indians), but rather in east Tejas, where the farmland was better suited to agriculture and whose proximity to the slave state of Louisiana made trade with the rest of the United States relatively easy, converging conveniently with the settlers' own slave-holding.

In an effort to staunch the excessive influx of US settlers, who weren't protecting central Mexico, were simply hogging Mexican land, and not even trading with the country to the south, the central government abolished slavery in 1829. They also reinstituted a property tax that had earlier been removed to sweeten immigration from the United States, and they also raised tariffs on goods shipped from the United States to Mexican Tejas. The slave-holding settlers weren't happy (nor were the American exporters). The Mexican government tried to stop additional immigration, making the gringo "Tejanos" even unhappier. The result, ultimately, was the Texas Revolution and Mexico's loss of much of its territory, even before the Mexican American War, which lopped off even more.

We'll never know what would have happened if the Mexican government hadn't committed their early oops of welcoming US settlers onto their land.

We do know, however, what happened a few decades later, in 1864, after President Abraham Lincoln made what turned out to be a decision with bad unintended consequences. (Not when he went to Ford's Theatre, which was an oops of a different sort.) Like the Mexican government several decades before, Lincoln had what looked like a good geo-political strategy. By 1864, it was clear that the Union was going to win the Civil War, and Lincoln was eager for reconciliation with the losers. A former senator and governor named Andrew Johnson seemed the right person for the job of vice-president. He was a Democrat from Tennessee and the only major southern politician who stuck with the Union. But after Lincoln was assassinated, Johnson turned out to be a lousy, no-good, horrible, terrible, very bad choice. As president, he showed himself to be pretty much in line with his pro-slavery fellow southerners. He vetoed legislation designed to protect these newly freed Black citizens. He opposed the Fourteenth Amendment, which granted citizenship to formerly enslaved persons. He promptly granted amnesty to the Confederate states, and did whatever he could to keep Whites on top and Blacks below. Congressional Republicans tried to work with him—more like trying to get him to work with them—but became increasingly frustrated as he persistently vetoed their progressive legislation.

Johnson was eventually impeached by the House of Representatives and barely avoided being thrown out of office when the Senate failed to achieve the necessary super-majority by one vote. (It appears that the deciding vote was cast by a senator who received more than a few special favors in return. Corruption, anyone?) Lincoln was among the best US presidents. Andrew Johnson was, if not the worst, very close. Lincoln didn't make many blunders, but selecting Johnson—seemingly a good idea at the time—was probably his greatest oops.

Jumping ahead 120 years, we come to Mikhail Gorbachev, whose seemingly good idea had unintended, unforeseen, and—at least initially—undesired consequences as well. Gorbachev began his career as a devoted Marxist-Leninist and Soviet nationalist, rising to become general secretary of the Communist Part of the Soviet Union in 1985, to which was soon added head of state, chairman of the USSR's Presidium and of the Supreme Soviet, along with being the Soviet Union's first general president. All of these positions disappeared as the Soviet Union disintegrated, something that Gorbachev set in motion.

As general secretary and undisputed leader of the USSR, Gorby came to feel that his sprawling, increasingly dysfunctional country needed significant reforms, something that was anathema to the sluggish, top-heavy Soviet bureaucracy. Gorbachev announced two particular programs, embodied in the words *glasnost* (openness) and *perestroika* (restructuring). *Glasnost* involved undoing most of the existing restrictions on speech and publication, while *perestroika* called for loosening the state's highly centralized and inefficient decision-making apparatus. The Chernobyl nuclear disaster in 1986 (which occurred in then-Soviet Ukraine) was a particular spur to his thinking, italicizing the need for reform on many levels. Not all of his reforms were well-received. It appears that whereas the entrenched *apparatchiks* were appalled, the Soviet public was on board, at least initially . . . until Gorby touched the third rail of Soviet society: he sought to restrict the availability of vodka. Outrage was immediate, deep, and widespread. (Imagine if a US president came after Americans' cars, or, even more catastrophic, their guns.) In addition to the public opposition, Gorbachev's anti-alcohol crusade seriously diminished one of the Kremlin's main revenue sources.

Gorbachev also was, or became, convinced of the folly of nuclear weapons and of the need to diminish the prospect of nuclear war between the two world superpowers. Toward that end, he met several times with President Reagan, notching some success, notably agreement on the Intermediate-Range Nuclear Forces Treaty. At about the same time, the ethos of *glasnost* and *perestroika* spread rapidly through the Soviet Union, as previously banned books were published, previously prohibited movies were screened, and previously suppressed political views were permitted.

Gorbachev made it increasingly clear that he favored democratization of Soviet politics and liberalization of its economy, although he stopped short of endorsing capitalism. In foreign policy, he allowed reform-minded anticommunist nationalists to overthrow Soviet-backed governments throughout what had been the Warsaw Pact, without using Soviet armor to crush these movements, as had occurred years earlier in East Germany, Hungary, and Czechoslovakia. He refused to intervene militarily as the USSR's various Eastern European satellite states began discarding communism and Soviet domination, and he even green-lighted the unification of what had been East and West Germany, and didn't have a fit when the reconstituted Germany joined NATO. Within the USSR, the "nationalism question" had been fueled by Gorby's reforms, and as a result, former Soviet republics such as Estonia, Latvia, Lithuania, Georgia, Moldova, Ukraine, and the Asiatic "stans" (Uzbekistan, Kazakhstan, etc.) moved toward separation and full independence, along with the Russian Republic itself. Although

POLITICS

Gorbachev strongly opposed secession, the USSR was becoming the UFFR: The Union of Fewer and Fewer Republics. He didn't like it, but couldn't stop it. These and other events occurred with head-snapping rapidity, while Soviet communist hardliners—more and more pissed off—couldn't take it anymore and eventually plotted a coup, a *putsch*, an internal overthrow of the Gorbachev government.

In August 1991, while Mikhail and his wife were vacationing in the Crimea, the plotters cut communications with his dacha, and placed him and his family under house arrest. Fearing for his safety, Gorby ordered his still-loyal guards to barricade the dacha. Meanwhile, the coup was courageously opposed by one Boris Yeltsin, who favored taking Gorbachev's liberalizations further yet, and had become president of the Russian Republic (which, at the time, was part of the still-intact USSR). It soon became apparent to the *putschists* that they had insufficient support, so they capitulated. Mickey returned to Moscow, where he promised to reform—not dissolve—the Communist Party. But it was far too late. He quickly resigned as general secretary of the now-crumbling state party, while Yeltsin discontinued all formal Russian Communist Party activities. By the end of August 1991, communist rule in the Soviet Union (which still nominally existed, just as Gorbachev was still nominally its head) was over. An increasingly assertive Boris Yeltsin took over the Kremlin and clear-cut leadership of the increasingly assertive and independent-minded Russian Republic. Gorbachev, now named president of the more and more moribund Soviet Union, tried to retain a semblance of its previous existence as a technically unified state, this time with a loose federal structure. But the individual republics wanted out.

Gorby kept trying to preserve the "Union" in the face of overwhelming nationalist sentiment. But each republic had gotten the alluring scent of national autonomy. When Ukraine voted on a referendum—stay or secede—in late 1991, Gorbachev expected a "stay" vote. But 90 percent opted for secession and a legally independent state. (Looking at you, Putin!) Then, Boris Yeltsin met with the leaders of Ukraine and Belarus behind Gorby's back. They signed a treaty whereby as far as they were concerned, the Soviet Union was defunct, replaced by a Commonwealth of Independent States.

Gorby fervently but unsuccessfully tried to rally support for retaining the USSR, but no dice. Leaders representing eleven of the twelve remaining republics met in late December 1991, and formally agreed on the dissolution of the USSR and to accept Gorbachev's resignation as head of that no-longer-existing state-cum-empire. Russia became the de facto successor to what had been the Soviet Union, and Gorbachev's time in office was over.

We'll never know for sure whether if he had it to do over, Gorby would have led his country down the road of *perestroika* and *glasnost* (as well as tea-totaling), and ultimately to its dismemberment and his own fall from power. We do know that, at the time, he found himself holding a tiger by the tail, having unleashed forces that he hadn't anticipated and could not control. At the time he must have considered it an immense mistake. On the other hand, he did well in his premature retirement. He established the Gorbachev Foundation, for which he raised money by appearing in commercials for distinctly non-communist Pizza Hut, Louis Vuitton, and Apple, among others. He also ran in the 1996 election for the presidency of Russia, receiving a whopping 0.5 percent of the vote. He died in August 2022, having received plaudits for ending the Cold War, and, in his time at least, for ending the nuclear arms race, as well as for his eventual commitment to human rights, democratic socialism, and even a "green future." For this and more, he was mourned around in the world. But in Russia not so much, where he had long been thought responsible for the fall of the Soviet Union, for its people's loss of international prestige, and for the severe economic pains experienced by most Russians during the era of vampiric privatization during the 1990s. He didn't get a state funeral.

Vladimir Putin was not a fan. In 2005, he proclaimed that "The collapse of the Soviet Union was the biggest geopolitical catastrophe of the century. For the Russian people, it became a real drama. Tens of millions of our citizens and countrymen found themselves outside Russian territory. The epidemic of disintegration also spread to Russia itself."[9] Putin didn't attend Gorbachev's low-key funeral and hated, hated, and then hated some more not only what had happened to the former USSR, but the man he largely blamed for its demise. It is said that you can learn much about someone by their enemies, in which case we can safely conclude that Mikhail Sergey-evich Gorbachev, oops and all, was a pretty good guy.

Under him, the USSR broke apart. Thirty years later, under British Prime Minister David Cameron, the European Union didn't break apart, but the Brits broke out of it: Brexit. As of 2022, Brexit was the second most dramatic event in Europe following the collapse of the Soviet Union (Putin's Ukraine War being number one). The European Union was somewhat weakened by Brexit, which has hurt Britain even more, with that hurt becoming more painful as its economic and social costs consolidate. Just as Mikhail Gorbachev's oops led to the USSR's demise, one man—then Prime Minister David Cameron—was almost singlehandedly responsible. Without his oops, Brexit almost certainly wouldn't have happened.

There had long been some hyper-nationalists and angry right-wing populists in the United Kingdom who resented the European Union and wanted their country to get out. (Reminiscent of the road signs, still visible in parts of the United States in 2022, saying "Get the UN out of the US and the US out of the UN.") In 2016, Cameron recklessly called for a referendum on whether the United Kingdom should leave the European Union, fully expecting that the "leavers" would lose. But they won, by only about 2 percent of the vote, but still, in a democracy, a win is a win. Cameron had anticipated that the vote would put Brexit to rest, and also that by calling for the referendum he would secure greater support for himself and his political future among the right-wingers of his conservative (Tory) party. Although himself a Tory, Cameron was somewhat progressive when it came to some social policies and was therefore distrusted by those to his right. Immediately after the Brexit vote, Cameron took responsibility and resigned. His critics said that he resembled a character in an action movie that plants and sets off a bomb and then calmly walks away from the explosion.

The truth is that David Cameron wasn't at all calm about the Brexit explosion that he had unwittingly initiated, an unforced error that—whatever its effect on the United Kingdom's future—devastated his own. It was the first time, ever, that a national referendum had gone against the preferred outcome of a sitting UK government. Cameron had been the youngest UK prime minister in more than two hundred years and used to have a bright political future. Used to. Michael Portillo, a former Tory cabinet minister, opined that Cameron's decision to call that referendum "will be remembered as the greatest blunder ever made by a British prime minister."[10]

From his self-generated political exile, Cameron claimed that he didn't think that calling the referendum was itself a mistake, but that he blundered in not campaigning more effectively against its passage. "The greatest regret," he told National Public Radio, "is that we lost the referendum, that I didn't prevail, that we could've fought perhaps a better campaign, we could have conducted perhaps a better negotiation—perhaps the timing wasn't right—and that I didn't take the country with me on what I thought was a really important issue."[11] Part of the "remainers'" inadequate campaign was their failure to refute the many lies that were promulgated by the "leavers." Of these, the most notorious was that the United Kingdom sends 350 million pounds ($473 million at the time) per week to the European Union and that following Brexit the money would go back to the National Health Service. During the campaign, the UK Statistics Authority wrote to Vote Leave, the primary promotor of leaving, that the claim was "misleading and undermines trust in official statistics." Among other things, it had ignored the annual rebate that the United Kingdom received from the European Union: 4.52 billion British pounds in 2019 alone. Also omitted were the financial losses due to ending membership in the European Union. Moreover, after Britain formally Brexited in 2021, its conservative government (the same one that had campaigned on Brexit) showed no inclination to invest any of the anticipated savings in the National Health Service.

The European Social Survey, conducted every two years by the University of London, sampled opinion in thirty European nations in late 2022; it found that support for doing the equivalent of Brexit (Italexit, Spainexit, Germexit, etc.) had taken a nose-dive following the British experience. Even taking the pandemic into account, Britain has suffered disproportionately compared to EU members: its GDP shrank by 5.2 percent, investment in the national economy declined by nearly 14 percent. Just as Putin's invasion of Ukraine did wonders for NATO unity, Brexit has, ironically, been a cautionary tale, solidifying support for the European Union among those countries who learned from Cameron's oops. Nigel Farage, one of the loudest pre-Brexit "leavers," had claimed that EU membership was hamstringing UK business. Post-Brexit, the major British business complaint involves the reams of red tape, a problem that had been minor while Britain was in the European Union and that has become stultifying now that it has left.

The 2016 Brexit vote was a harbinger of an international right-wing populist wave that crashed ashore at about that time in the United States (Trump), Brazil (Bolsonaro), Hungary (Orbán), and earlier in India (Modhi), the Philippines (Duterte), and elsewhere, with consistently painful domestic effects.

In finally acknowledging his error, not just by calling the referendum but failing to debunk the leavers' lies, David Cameron added that, "I will, to my dying day, wonder whether there was something more we could have done to secure what I thought was the right outcome — which was to keep Britain in."[12] He might well consider that his personal "right outcome" would have required not committing the bungled Brexit referendum in the first place.

8.5. Misguided Military Muscle-Flexing

In Chapter 3, we looked at some notable military blunders, all of which involved battlefield (*tactical*) decisions. Even more important are *strategic* errors by the "higher ups," those government authorities responsible for going to war in the first place. Since World War II, there have been few formal declarations of war, and none involving the major powers. But there have certainly been lots of major military encounters, some lasting a long time. The labels don't matter to people killed or whose lives are devastated by whatever we choose to call it. Sometimes "wars" are justified. But all too often, they are blunders of the highest order.

Where to begin? There are, alas, too many to discuss here. Because many of these are familiar to modern readers, the recent ones will be described only in barest outline, with the biggest one, ongoing as this book is being written, getting its own special attention. Looking just at the twentieth century, the first clear-cut case of misguided military muscle-flexing led to the Russo-Japanese War (1904–1905). Because it is the twentieth century top-down blunder least known to Americans, we'll review the circumstances of this war in greater detail than the more recent, better known cases in which political leaders screwed up big time.

The big blunderer was undoubtedly Nikolai Alexandrovich Romanov, better known in the West as Nicholas II. Unsurprisingly, the Russo-Japanese War is pretty well known in Japan (the winner) and less so in Russia (the loser). Even with a smart leader in St. Petersburg, it would probably have been difficult at the time to avoid a war between Japan and Russia, given that the imperial ambitions of both countries bumped into each other in North-East Asia. Russia had been seeking to expand eastward into Manchuria and was also in search of a year-round warm water port; Vladivostok was navigable only in summer. At the same time, Japan was committed to moving westward, at least into Korea and then onward to the Chinese mainland. Russia had leased Port Arthur from China and turned it into a major naval base, also intending it for international trade. Japan worried that Russian imperial ambitions would stymie its goals of establishing spheres of influence in Korea and Manchuria, never mind its long-term goal of annexing both outright.

The two countries engaged in tense negotiations, in which Japan proposed that it get effective control of Korea, while Russia gets Manchuria. Nicholas countered with making Korea a neutral buffer between the Russian and Japanese empires. This would have hemmed in Japan while giving Russia free reign throughout much of mainland China. The talks broke down when, following Nicholas's instructions, Russia kept dragging its feet and refusing for months to respond to Japan's proposals (which, to most neutral observers, seemed reasonable—although the opinions of neither Koreans nor Manchurians were ever solicited). Japan's patience was ultimately exhausted and, early in 1904, its navy conducted a successful surprise attack on the Russian Far East fleet anchored at Port Arthur.

Nicholas hadn't been eager for war, but his intransigence—during both the fruitless, drawn-out negotiations and the war that followed—contributed substantially to the dismal outcome for Russia. Moreover, Nicholas was one of the dimmest bulbs in the chandelier of European royalty, and given the generally low wattage in evidence at the time, that intellectual bar was already low. Even as Russia accumulated a consistent string of painful battlefield defeats in the war that followed, the czar stubbornly persisted in his belief that Russia would win. After all, he was God's chosen representative on Earth. He conveniently overlooked Japan's impressive victory over China a decade earlier in the Sino-Japanese War. But, of course, that war merely involved one low grade group of Asian "natives" beating another. Nicholas had no doubt about the inferiority of Chinese, Koreans, and Japanese. He had also been goaded by his cousin, Wilhelm II of Germany, who regularly fulminated against the "yellow peril," and convinced Nicholas that the future of Christianity and of the white race rested on his Slavic shoulders. The deluded czar also assumed that in the event of a prolonged war with Japan (which, remember, was inconceivable because those people were backward, inferior, and hated by God), Wilhelm's Germany would support Russia. It didn't.

There was nonetheless no way those backward Japanese—Nicholas called them "yellow monkeys"—could seriously defeat a major Western power, especially one that enjoyed divine favor. So, it didn't matter that Japan had feverishly and brilliantly modernized its military forces following the Meiji Restoration (1868), that the Far Eastern theater was at the very end of the single-track 5700 mile Trans-Siberian Railway (with no rail available around Lake Baikal), and was half-way around the world from St. Petersburg. He refused to accept that Japanese soldiers had shown themselves highly competent warriors during their successful war with China, and that the Japanese Navy exceeded most European counterparts in quality. It also didn't matter when he received numerous reports that the Russian forces, army as well as navy, were less prepared and less competent than had been advertised. (Does this ring a twenty-first-century bell?) Nor did it matter when it came to Nicholas's decision to pursue the war after a brilliantly executed Japanese naval blockade had prevented the Russian Far East fleet from escaping out to sea, and the Japanese Army took over Korea and captured the high ground behind Port Arthur, from which its artillery demolished the Russian fleet, sinking two destroyers and four battleships, while a fifth had to be scuttled. The commander of the Russian garrison at Port Arthur—showing more wisdom than his boss back home—then surrendered (and was subsequently court-marshalled for doing so and sentenced to death, but later pardoned).

Russia was outclassed and militarily defeated at nearly every turn, which included losing close to eighty thousand troops at the Battle of Mukden in February 1905. Nicholas was nonetheless unwilling or unable to acknowledge what had happened and was ongoing. So, he made the brilliant decision to continue the war—which he remained convinced was a sure-thing victory for Russia—by sending the Russian Baltic fleet half-way around the world, more than eighteen thousand nautical miles, to show the Imperial Japanese Navy who's boss. This was hardly a stealth maneuver: it took seven months because of various intervening complications before the Russian ships arrived in theater, having been forced to go around the southern tip of Africa because the United Kingdom—sympathetic to Japan—refused permission to use the Suez Canal. Early in its epic journey, the hapless Baltic fleet had opened fire on some British fishing boats, mistaking them for Japanese interlopers. This "Dogger Bank Episode" (so named because that's where it took place: off Britian's Dogger Bank) could have precipitated war with the United Kingdom, but was eventually smoothed over.

As the beleaguered Baltic fleet rounded Africa, they received the dispiriting news that Port Arthur had fallen, depriving them of a port and anchorage. But they kept on keeping on, until they were utterly devastated in the extraordinarily one-sided Battle of Tsushima Straits, on May 27–28, 1905. The Russians lost eight battleships, many support ships, and more than five thousand sailors. Japanese losses? Three torpedo boats and 116 men. So much for Japanese racial inferiority. Finally, unable to deny reality any longer, Nicholas agreed to negotiate an end to his embarrassingly one-sided, inept, and tragic war, with US President Theodore Roosevelt as mediator. The Treaty of Portsmouth (New Hampshire) earned Roosevelt a

Nobel Peace Prize, while Russia agreed to abandon Manchuria, to cede the southern part of Sakhalin Island to Japan, and to recognize Korea as within the Japanese orbit. Japan occupied all of Korea five years later.

Nicholas had been deluded in many ways, including his determination that a straight-forward successful war against a weak opponent would inspire national unity in Russia and also improve his sinking reputation with the Russian populace. Fat chance, although in the earliest stages of the war, a predictable rally-round-the-flag effect briefly buoyed his domestic approval. But as one shocking defeat followed another, public opinion turned strongly against the war and against Nicholas. He and the oppressive czarist system came to be seen as partly responsible for the disastrous war and as altogether responsible for directing it incompetently, for its painful outcome, and for prolonging it unnecessarily. The Russo-Japanese War did more than cost Russia its ambitions in the Far East. It contributed mightily to growing dissatisfaction among most Russians. In 1905, that war was a disaster of military over-reach, whose impact went beyond the war itself. It contributed to subsequent naval mutinies in Sevastopol, Vladivostok, and Kronstadt, plus a famous one aboard the battleship *Potemkin*. For many Russians, the belief that the czar was the benevolent, infallible father of his people was shattered. And anger over the war itself contributed greatly to the 1905 Russian Revolution, which came surprisingly close to overthrowing the czar. The Russo-Japanese War and the 1905 Revolution that it sparked showed that the czarist regime was fallible and vulnerable, thereby serving as a prelude to the biggie that followed twelve years later: the 1917 Bolshevik Revolution that changed planetary politics and cost Nicholas and his family their lives.

No one can ever rerun the past, but there's no doubt that Nicholas would have jumped at the opportunity to do so.

Here, in outline, are just a few additional cases of ill-advised twentieth-century military muscle-flexing:

- The Japanese attack on Pearl Harbor, December 7, 1941. The Japanese government felt stymied by the United States when it came to its imperial, expansionist ambitions in Asia and the

Pacific. It also worried that the United States had a strangle-hold on access to such resources as iron and oil. Nonetheless, it was obvious that America exceeded Japan in every dimension: population, natural resources, and economic might. So, the hope, a forlorn one as it turned out, was that a successful surprise attack would shock the United States into seeking a quick peace, giving Japan the freedom of action that it desired. The future turned out rather different. Prime Minister Tojo Hideki, widely seen in the West as a war-monger, said to his colleagues just prior to making that fateful decision, "Occasionally, one must conjure up enough courage, close one's eyes, and jump off the platform of the Kiyomizu."[13] He was talking about a Buddhist temple whose veranda juts out over a cliff and was known as a suicide spot.

Four days after the Japanese attack on Pearl Harbor, Hitler declared war on the United States. He didn't have to and would have been a whole lot better off if he hadn't. Isolationist sentiment was still strong in the United States, including influential closet Nazis and such not-so-closeted Nazi partisans as Henry Ford and Charles Lindbergh. Not only that, but with its newly declared war with Japan, there wasn't much eagerness within the American military or the public for a two-front war. But Hitler forced our hand, to his ultimate detriment.

Just six months earlier, Adolf Hitler had committed another unforced error, one that was even more disastrous: he invaded the Soviet Union. Many Americans don't realize that Germany did not lose World War II because of the Battle of Britain, the Atlantic naval campaign, the Italian or North African theaters, or even D-Day and the ultimately successful Allied advance through Western Europe, but rather on the Eastern Front. The Soviets, while suffering immense casualties, accounted for 76 percent of German troop deaths during the war: an estimated 4.1 million, dwarfing all other German losses in all other theaters. We'll never know what would have happened if Hitler had remained allied with Stalin as briefly occurred following the 1939 Molotov-Ribbentrop Pact. But it is entirely possible that a Russo-German bloc would have been victorious, especially if Adolf had refrained from dragging the United States into that maelstrom.

- The Vietnam War (1964–1973). This was—like Japan's attack on the United States—a war of choice, and a very bad choice at that. (In fairness, there were American officials who seem to have been honestly convinced, at least at the outset, that they were doing the correct and necessary thing.) But the war did huge damage to the Vietnamese people, its countryside, to American military personnel, and to US standing in the world. The Vietnam War resulted in part from obsessive and paranoid anti-communism combined with the "domino theory" rampant at the time, along with a tragic failure to distinguish Vietnamese nationalism from Vietnam as a stalking horse for the Soviet Union and China. The Vietnamese had fought the Japanese for their national sovereignty, then the French, then the Americans. At no time were they part of an international communist conspiracy.

After the North Vietnamese won and Vietnam was unified under communism, no dominoes fell. China and Vietnam (both communist states) actually had a brief war, upsetting the alleged domino board, and the governments of Vietnam and the United States later reconciled—but only after costing the United States more than 58,000 killed along with many more wounded and almost 500,000 afflicted with PTSD. Conservative estimates are that the Vietnamese lost approximately two million persons, to which must be added 200,000 Cambodian and 100,000 Laotian deaths. This doesn't count the innumerable lives lost and devastated by post-war famine and disease, or the millions killed by the Khmer Rouge of Cambodia, who came to power because of the political chaos unleashed by the war that the United States unwisely chose and tragically pursued.

That it should never have happened made the Vietnam War an especially enormous oops. In addition, the means of fighting it often included war crimes. There were episodes of bravery, generosity, and humanity on both sides, but also horrific things done by mostly good people, also on both sides. The Mỹ Lai massacre (in which civilian residents of the village of Mỹ Lai, including women with infants, were herded into a ditch and then machine-gunned) was an especially egregious example. In addition, US forces frequently established "free-fire zones," in which all inhabitants of a designated region—including civilians—were treated as combat targets. Also employed, against the laws of war, was napalm, dropped on entire villages, and Agent Orange, a defoliant that caused long-lasting environmental damage. Each side, namely the Vietcong (South Vietnamese rebels allied with the North) along with North Vietnamese regulars, as well as US operatives, assassinated people known, or believed, or rumored, to favor the other side.

Such murderous brutality made it impossible for the United States to win local "hearts and minds," while atrocities by the Vietcong and North Vietnamese didn't cause as much revulsion on the part of their South Vietnamese counterparts, perhaps because violence perpetrated by foreigners is seen as particularly offensive. Similarly, there was never much popular support for a succession of puppet governments, established by what growing numbers of South Vietnamese came to consider illegitimate foreign forces that had invaded their country (even though they had been invited by the South Vietnamese government and were therefore not technically invaders).

In any event, once the Vietnam War was clearly found to be a losing effort, the Johnson and Nixon Administrations could have and should have levelled with the American people. The Pentagon Papers, courageously made public in 1971 at great personal risk by Daniel Ellsberg, made it clear that the White House and Pentagon knew for many years that the Vietnam War was a lost cause. But until the release of the Pentagon Papers, this damning material was kept under wraps.

The war cost the United States almost $170 billion (just short of $1 trillion in today's money), stalled LBJ's Great Society program, and generated immense fissures in US society. Its impact on Vietnam (North and South) cannot be imagined, never mind calculated. It also became the first war that the United States unequivocally lost. All things considered, the Vietnam War must be judged an immense, tragic error.

- The Soviet-Afghan War (1979–1989). The Soviet military found itself stuck in almost precisely the same trap as the United States in Vietnam. Both superpowers were invited in by the existing national governments, however corrupt and unpopular. Both the United States and the USSR were unable to counter low-tech, highly motivated guerilla fighters whose commitment was deeply ideological and nationalistic, and who were able to blend in with the local population. Like the United States in Vietnam, Soviet forces were unable to win the "hearts and minds" of the Afghan people and were eventually forced to make a humiliating retreat after suffering major losses of men, material, domestic support, and international regard. As with the doomed US incursion into Vietnam, which had to contend with Soviet and Chinese support of the Vietcong and North Vietnamese, the Soviet army—while directly fighting Afghan *mujahedeen*—was also struggling with behind-the-scenes US support for them, organized by the CIA. A dozen years after the *mujahedeen*, with American aid, drove the Soviet army out of their country, they did the same thing to US forces. What went around, came around.
- The US War in Iraq (2003–2011). This was preceded by an extraordinary series of lies, including the trumped-up claim that Saddam Hussein was developing nuclear weapons. He wasn't. Although initially successful, this military misadventure encountered guerilla resistance, and resulted in establishing a puppet Iraqi government that never garnered much popular support. Like the wars in Vietnam and Afghanistan, the Iraq War was conducted with almost no understanding of local

religious, social, and political traditions, which worked strongly against long-term success. The Iraq War also qualifies as a war crime according to the Nuremberg Principles, which were developed in the prosecution of Nazi officials for the crime of "waging aggressive war." It was, like the Russian invasion of Ukraine in 2022, an unjustified military invasion of a sovereign country. In 2003, George W. was Putin.

Why did we do it? Historians will debate this for decades, perhaps centuries, and their answers will almost certainly include the following:

- Oil
- Faulty intelligence, enabled and encouraged by arm-twisting from administration officials, notably Vice President Dick Cheney, who insisted that the CIA and the Defense Intelligence Agency come up with data and analyses that painted Iraq as a threat to US security
- Outright lying by Cheney and other administration officials (notably Paul Wolfowitz, Condoleeza Rice, and Donald Rumsfeld) who manufactured a pretense—weapons of mass destruction—that didn't exist, along with a claimed connection between the Iraqi regime and al-Qaeda (which also didn't exist) to do what they wanted to do anyhow
- Geopolitical hubris, including the delusion that by making Iraq a beacon of Western-style democracy, that tradition would spread to the rest of the Arab Middle East
- The influence of post–Cold War neocons who saw the invasion as an opportunity to flex US muscles and to finally overcome the "Vietnam syndrome" whereby the United States allegedly hesitated to engage itself again, post-Vietnam, in overseas military adventures (notwithstanding Grenada, Bosnia, Kosovo, the earlier Kuwait war, and Libya)

- George W. Bush's rather Freudian desire to exceed his father, who had driven Saddam Hussein out of Kuwait but had refrained from overthrowing him
- Responding to the public's urge to attack somebody—anybody—in retaliation for the terrorist attacks of 9/11 (even though Iraq had nothing to do with 9/11)
- Pressure from a frustrated military-industrial complex in need of a designated enemy

There is doubtless more, including even to some extent a genuine desire to rid Iraq of an oppressive dictator. But definitely not, despite initial claims, do-gooder goals of "liberating" the women of Iraq . . . who, under Saddam's regime, had arguably enjoyed more freedom than in any other Arab state. Whatever the precise constellation of motivations, the impact of the Iraq War included about 4,600 American military deaths, close to 32,000 wounded, and around 300,000 Iraqi deaths directly attributable to the fighting. Among the terrible consequences was ISIS, which almost certainly wouldn't have arisen without this colossal Bushian blunder, perhaps the most egregious error of US foreign policy. Ever.

After occupying Iraq, one of the greatest US missteps—but in no way the only one—was outlawing the Ba'ath Party and disbanding the Iraqi Army, which produced a large number of disaffected and unemployed civilians and military veterans, ripe for incorporation into anti-American resistance warfare. The only real winner of this illegal, ill-advised, terribly costly, and unnecessary war was . . . Iran.

- The US War in Afghanistan (2001–2021). The US invasion of Afghanistan was publicly justified because it struck at the home base of al-Qaeda, which was responsible for the September 11 attacks on the World Trade Centers and the Pentagon. US forces and their allies quickly defeated the Taliban government. Ultimately, though, Americans were unable to win the two-decade fight against underground Taliban networks, which enjoyed growing support throughout the country. As with the Soviets in Afghanistan and the United States in Vietnam and Iraq, foreign military forces ended up alienating much of the countries they occupied, in part because they killed many civilians: sometimes intentionally, but mostly as "collateral damage." In addition, history records that foreign occupiers nearly always evoke nationalist push-back, and Afghanistan was no exception. The Afghan people have a long record of resisting Westerners trying to impose their values on fiercely proud and independent people, whose ancient, complex, and religion-infused cultures were persistently confusing to the muscle-bound occupiers, from ancient times up to the present.

- When, in the 1820s, Greek nationalists were fighting a war of independence against the Ottoman Empire, many Americans lobbied for the United States to support their struggle. Secretary of State John Quincy Adams argued otherwise, announcing that the United States "goes not abroad, in search of monsters to destroy." Would that were true!

8.6. Putin's Pernicious Power Play

In the sad annals of this century's mistaken military muscle-flexing, Putin's invasion of Ukraine deserves a place of its own. More than a year into the war, it's not clear that his heinous action will be ruinous for Putin himself or even for Russia (although we can hope for the former but not necessarily for the latter). Assessing the outcome of such a vast event while it is still going on is like trying to predict the precise path of a horribly destructive category five hurricane. As of this writing, Putin's aggressive war has not gone anything like he had expected or hoped. Aside from the devastating effect it has had on Ukraine and increasingly on Russia, it is also an immense self-inflicted crisis for Putin—a huge oops. How big for him personally, however, remains to be seen. Maybe he will be overthrown in a coup, or killed, or just emerge weaker, or perhaps even stronger. It seems unlikely, in any event, that he will be chastened.

There were many errors involved in planning and carrying out the Ukraine War, and given Putin's authoritarian control of Russia—now magnified into a bona fide dictatorship—there's no doubt that the buck stops with him. He and pretty much he alone would have accepted plaudits if his scheme had worked, and he and he alone bears responsibility if, as has been the case so far, it fails. This doesn't mean that he hasn't already started casting blame elsewhere, on NATO, the collective West, the United States, his own generals. Putin cannot admit being wrong, just as he cannot accept losing. (Does this bring to mind a certain former US president?)

The original plan was for a blitzkrieg assault on Kyiv, to take over the Zelenskyy government, install a pliant coterie of Quislings, and then proclaim victory. None of this happened. In addition to a slew of tactical blunders made by his military, Putin made many strategic errors (with likely more to come). Here is a quick summary:

- He over-estimated the capability of the Russian military, thinking that the conquest of Ukraine would be a walk-over. Many of the early invading tank crews even brought parade uniforms with them, anticipating that they'd soon be part of a celebratory victory parade in downtown Kyiv. (Reminiscent of Hitler's failure to equip his army with winter clothing, under the assumption that his invasion of the USSR in June 1941 would be over before Christmas.)
- He under-estimated the fierce national sentiment of the Ukrainians and their inclination and ability to resist, to innovate, and to adopt tactics adjusted in real time by officers in the field. By contrast, the Russian military style is based on strict hierarchies, in which situational initiative is squelched.
- He hadn't counted on the courage of Volodymyr Zelenskyy and his ability to communicate to his people a sense of national purpose and unity.

- He accepted assurances from his intelligence services that the Ukraine government was filled with fifth-columnists, ready and eager to cooperate with Russian occupiers.

- He was convinced that Europe and the United States were decadent, spent powers, unwilling or unable to support Ukraine in the event of a prolonged war, and, moreover, that they were too divided to put up a united front against his aggression. Instead, the Western allies—especially but not only the United States— promptly provided substantial amounts of lethal, high-tech military aid, which the Ukrainian military quickly and effectively put to devastating use.

- He didn't anticipate the unity of the West, especially Europe's willingness to impose serious economic sanctions against Russia, going far beyond the mostly performative ones that were imposed after Putin's 2014 occupation of Crimea. These sanctions have somewhat hamstrung the Russian economy, notably interfering with its ability to replace high-tech battle-field losses. However, the impact of these financial maneuvers on the Russian economy generally has to some extent been deftly mitigated by its Central Bank.

- As the war dragged on, Putin counted on Europe's dependence on Russian energy (especially oil and natural gas) to continue supplying him with income with which to finance his war. Also, as the war dragged on, he assumed that the threat of inflated energy prices and the pain of dealing with the cold of winter would push the soft European publics to buckle under and accept his aggression in return for domestic comfort. Nonetheless, Russia continues to earn substantial sums via its resource exports, to India, China, and even Europe.

- Putin's two-decade rule had been based on an unspoken social contract with the vast majority of the Russian people: you keep out of politics, don't protest my kleptocracy, cronyism, and suppression of democracy, and in return I'll provide you with social stability and a degree of economic prosperity. The Russian public largely bought in, partly because Putin had stabilized Russian politics and the economy after the chaotic Yeltsin years. When it came to his Ukraine War, Putin had refrained from ordering a general mobilization, to avoid upsetting his implicit deal with the Russian people even as his army failed to achieve its goals and began to suffer major defeats. But as he lost huge numbers of troops, and the morale of those remaining plummeted (not surprisingly!), Putin upset the apple-cart of his unspoken arrangement with the Russian people and, in September 2022, he ordered a "partial mobilization" of 300,000 men.

Insofar as his army needed more soldiers, this was not a mistake, but the result was an unprecedented flow of draft-age men fleeing the country and, among ordinary Russians, the awakening of protests rigorously suppressed but not previously seen. Historically, many people have fled their country when it was invaded, as did literally millions of Ukrainians this time. But it is unusual for such an outflow to happen after one's country has invaded another! In addition, this mobilization has driven home the harsh reality of Putin's war to many citizens who had been previously insulated from it, with many having believed the carefully controlled state propaganda that the war wasn't really a war, but a "special military operation" that was inconsequential, fully justified, and short-lived.

Opposition to the mobilization became so strong that police and military officials adopted indiscriminate press-gang tactics, descending on shopping centers, office buildings, restaurants, and the like, essentially kidnapping all men caught in the dragnet, including many who are elderly or infirm. Such procedures have not endeared the government to its citizens.

- Hand in hand with the war, and becoming more intense in proportion as it has gone badly, Putin initiated a degree of repression last seen at the height of Stalin's iron-fisted dictatorship. Criticizing the war became punishable by up to fifteen years in prison. Even calling it a war, as opposed to a "special military operation," was made a crime punishable by fifteen years in prison.

The gremlins in the Kremlin hadn't conducted a general mobilization or military draft during the failed Crimean War (1853–1856) or the even more disastrous one with Japan (1904–1905)—only during World Wars I and II. Doing so in 2022 cost Putin much of the respect and admiration he had accumulated, while also costing the country a devastating brain drain as the cream of Russian intellectual and scientific society hastened to escape the motherland in a desperate effort to avoid becoming cannon fodder in Ukraine.

- Putin thought that by inflicting atrocities on Ukrainian civilians that their will to resist would be undermined. Instead, the populace has become even more infuriated and united as a result. In addition, rather than frightening the Ukrainian public into submitting, widespread murder, rape, and torture has made Ukrainians more resistant than ever, because such war crimes provide a window into what life under Russian occupation would be like. Putin's forces followed the well-trodden path of "the Russian way of war"—using indiscriminate heavy artillery bombardment to pulverize an opponent, civilian along with military—unconcerned about "collateral damage" and even to some degree counting on it to sap the other side's will to fight. This technique was initially successful in helping his forces gain ground in eastern and southern Ukraine.

    But in addition to outrage over the invasion itself, Putin's green-lighting of terror tactics, along with targeting hospitals, schools, apartment houses, and playgrounds has driven a wedge between Russian designs and even most of those Ukrainians who had been Russia-sympathizers prior to the war.

- Before Putin's War, Russia was the unquestioned Big Brother to the recently independent "stans." Backed by its military, Russia was able to keep the peace among occasionally quarreling members of its pliant Asian bloc. But with Putin and his military pre-occupied with their struggles in Ukraine, with increasing shortages of key military equipment and supplies, and with the Russian armed forces revealed to be something of a paper tiger, these previously subservient allies are increasingly making their own way, separate from the Kremlin.

- Russia is currently more isolated and distrusted internationally than it has ever been, even in the dark days of Stalin's rule. Putinism has become synonymous with severe political repression, in which any criticism of the war—including just calling it a war or holding up a placard (even a blank one!)—leads to arrest and imprisonment. The Russian economy has been subjected to an unprecedented array of sanctions, and although it has temporarily weathered that storm, the medium and long-term prospects are dark indeed. Putin has sought to strong-arm Western Europe into forsaking assistance to Ukraine by cutting off energy exports, especially natural gas. The result has been to kick-start the development of alternative energy sources and to seek new suppliers of fossil fuels. Russia is no longer seen as a reliable energy supplier, which will bedevil any future attempts to resuscitate its long-standing cash cow.

- Largely because of Europe's increasingly successful efforts to wean itself from Russian energy supplies, Putin has mortgaged the Kremlin to Beijing, counting on Chinese purchases and hoping for military assistance as well—which, thus far, has not been forthcoming. China has all the leverage in their relationship, not a pleasant situation for a "strong-man" nationalist.

    (Let's hope that Xi doesn't make an oops re: Taiwan, like Putin did in Ukraine.)

- Yet more bad consequences for Putin and for Russia: In addition to revealing itself as a Potemkin superpower, the Ukraine War has awakened a powerful strain of anti-Russian sentiment in Europe, resulting in increased military budgets throughout the continent. Worse yet, if Putin had really thought that Ukraine was on the verge of joining NATO (it wasn't) he has precipitated an outcome that wouldn't otherwise have occurred: Finland abandoned decades of neutrality ("Finlandization," whereby its government accommodated itself to its gigantic neighbor) and joined NATO on April 4, 2023. Sweden is very likely to follow. Sweden last became part of any international alliance more than two centuries ago, in response to Napoleon. Sweden and Finland each have highly capable military forces, thus providing significant additional strength to NATO. Finland's accession nearly doubles Russia's border with NATO, adding an additional 830 miles that the Kremlin must now worry about. By not only invigorating NATO but also causing an expansion that wouldn't otherwise have happened, Putin made the Western alliance stronger than ever, scoring what in athletics is known as an "own goal" (see Section 6.3).

- As mentioned, following significant Ukrainian gains in late September 2022, Putin announced a "limited mobilization" intended to provide three hundred thousand additional troops. He had refrained from doing this earlier, knowing that it wouldn't go over well with the Russian public, but Russian manpower losses changed his mind. Here's one case in which he was correct: it evoked protests and an exodus of many potential draftees. The situation was so bleak that those inducted included people previously exempted because of age or disability, while also involving a disproportionate number of non-ethnic Russians and less educated inhabitants of poor, rural regions—an apparent strategy of minimizing the pain felt by more influential, urban, and westernized Russians.. Like many dictators, Putin has put his personal stamp on the Ukraine War, lowering the visibility of his military officials. Insofar as this war is seen within Russia as a big-time blunder, it will be difficult for him to suddenly change the narrative and blame failures on his subordinates. There are no valid polls of Putin's popularity, but it couldn't have been helped by the fact that one year into the war, Russia had suffered more military deaths than the United States endured during eight years in Vietnam, and four times more than Soviet losses during a decade in Afghanistan. Vlad the Impaler has impaled himself.

- Before his Ukrainian blunder, Putin's position as Russian leader had been secure and unquestioned. But as his invasion has floundered, something happened that would have been unimaginable prior to February 24, 2022: his position as Russia's undisputed leader has become potentially vulnerable. He is facing his most severe challenge ever to his authority and possibly even to his continuation in office.

Writing in the *New York Times*, Thomas Friedman reviewed some of Putin's errors:

Putin thought that he could capture Kyiv in a few days and thus—at a very low cost—use Russian expansion into Ukraine to forever blunt European Union and NATO expansion. He might have gotten close but for the fact that his isolation and self-delusion resulted in his getting his own army wrong, Ukraine's army wrong, the NATO allies wrong, Joe Biden wrong, the Ukrainian people wrong, Sweden wrong, Finland wrong, Poland wrong, Germany wrong and the European Union wrong. In the process, he's made Russia into an energy colony of China and a beggar for Iran's drones. For someone who has been at the top of the Kremlin since 1999, *that's a whole lot of wrong.*[14]

Vladimir Putin is exceptionally opaque, as befits a former KGB officer. In retrospect, invading Ukraine was extraordinarily reckless, and we'll never know why he did it. But some plausible speculation can be indulged, including why he got so much wrong.

One thing is clear. He didn't expect things to unfold as they did. Putin obviously anticipated that Kyiv would fall immediately and Ukraine would promptly become subservient to Russia, with everything happening so quickly that the West would have no chance to respond. After all, he had made short shrift of Georgia without any serious international repercussions, and although snatching Crimea (2014) took longer, the outcome was never seriously in doubt, and Western responses were minor compared to the prestige within Russia and the personal satisfaction it brought him. With twenty/twenty hindsight, Putin's miscalculations are plain, but the question remains: what might have been going on to bring about such an immense blunder?

After all, the truth is that for all his soullessness and brutality, Vladimir Putin is highly intelligent, able to run rings around a certain "very stable genius"—which he did, over and over. This makes it all the more mysterious that he stumbled into what certainly seems to be such a major oops. The previous bullet point list summarized some of the mistakes Putin made while planning the invasion and while carrying it out. Let's look now at the underlying basis for the whole misbegotten enterprise: what led to the strategic mistake of initiating this unprovoked act of aggression in the first place.

Among the precipitating factors is an earlier mistake made by NATO and the United States in particular. Shortly after the USSR disbanded itself, there arose the question of NATO membership for the former satellite states of Eastern Europe. Then Secretary of State James Baker told Gorbachev, conversationally but not by formal commitment, that these newly autonomous countries would not join NATO. Almost immediately afterward, however, they applied and were admitted, with the full support of the United States. Soon, NATO was therefore expanded right up to the Russian border. There seems little doubt that by misleading the Soviet leader and then backtracking on the verbal commitment, the United States blundered, contributing to Russian insecurity and outright paranoia. Under this interpretation, Putin's assault on Ukraine was driven by personal pique and a desire for revenge, as well as, perhaps, a need to preclude Ukraine from joining NATO.

In any event, Putin has used this NATO expansion and the supposed threat of Ukraine joining the alliance as a way of justifying his Ukraine War. He has even claimed that the West pressured Estonia, Latvia, Lithuania, Poland, Romania, and the like to join NATO, which is simply absurd. In fact, the pressure was in the opposite direction, as these states were desperate to join the alliance so as to guarantee that they would not be re-incorporated into the Russian sphere of influence or even gobbled up by Russia itself. Insofar as it was a mistake to extend NATO right up to the Russian border, this was less because it agitated the Russian bear than because it provided Putin with a subsequent *casus belli* to be used for public consumption. Moreover, early in the war, the Kyiv government made it clear that if an enforceable mechanism could be established that guaranteed Ukraine's independence as part of a negotiated settlement, they would agree to an arrangement whereby Ukraine would not join NATO and would become formally neutral between Russia and the West.

If Putin had really thought that Ukraine might join NATO so that he attacked to prevent it, his unprovoked aggression—actually, self-provoked—would have been an even bigger oops, because Ukrainian membership in NATO was never in the cards. New members require unanimous approval and France and Germany had already made it clear that they wouldn't agree, because of the simmering conflict with Russia already underway, as well as a further NATO requirement that new members have peaceful borders. Putin surely knew this.

When it comes to borders, the reality is that Russia's west had never been as secure from possible attack as it was prior to the Ukraine War, and this for a country with a traumatic history of being invaded from the East (the Mongols) as well as the West (the Teutonic Knights in the thirteenth century, Sweden in the early eighteenth century, Napoleon in the nineteenth, Germany in World War I and then again in World War II). This is not to say that as a result of the Ukraine War, Russia is now liable to be invaded, as he has claimed; nor is Russia at war with NATO. Rather, Putin's blunder has united, further militarized, and expanded NATO, thereby undermining what had been a degree of geopolitical stability previously unknown before his adventurism.

For a coldly calculating, ostensibly cerebral guy, Putin was and still is captive to a romantic, mystical sense of Russia's global destiny, combined with his personal horror at the USSR's earlier dissolution. Putin sees himself as a student of history, but his view is remarkably blinkered, a kind of imperial nostalgia linked to expansionist fantasies. He maintains that Ukrainians and Russians are "one people" and that the former isn't even a "real country." Rather, it was torn from the flesh of Mother Russia in 1922 by the Bolsheviks, around the time that the USSR was officially formed and the various Soviet republics were established. Its subsequent emergence as a fully independent, sovereign state in 1991 was yet another geostrategic abomination that resulted from that greater catastrophe: the dissolution of the USSR under Gorbachev. Conquering Ukraine would be, for Putin, the beginning of a long-overdue process of undoing that injustice and a necessary part of fulfilling Russia's global destiny as leader of "Rus mir"—Russian world—destined to be the hegemon bestriding Europe and Asia, just as he is destined to be a twenty-first-century incarnation of eighteenth-century czar Peter the Great, with whom he has long been obsessed.

Incorporating Ukraine into Mother Russia has become a necessary first step because, in Putin's deluded mind, Ukrainians are Russians who simply don't realize it. Those "Nazis" that control the government in Kyiv are actually self-proclaimed Ukrainians who misperceive themselves as Ukrainians rather than what they really are: Russians. He even expected that the Russian invaders would be welcomed as liberators—shades of Dick Cheney's fantasy, when he was George W. Bush's vice president, of a similar reception of US troops by Iraqis. In both cases, reality intervened. Like Cheney and George W., Putin has been taken hostage by his own ideas. His denial of Ukraine's nationhood and identity (especially post-2014) has only increased it, just as the Vietnam War enhanced Vietnamese nationalism and the Iraq War awakened similar feelings among Iraqis.

Early in the invasion, Putin also proclaimed that his goal was to liberate Russian Ukrainians who were allegedly being persecuted by their central government and to cleanse Ukraine from its supposed control by Nazis, gangsters, and drug dealers. Also child-abusers, gay activists, and other threats to the traditional (i.e., Russian Orthodox) conception of marriage and the family. Later, as things went badly for the invaders, Putin changed his tune, claiming that his war was in defense of Mother Russia, which was under attack by NATO. (Analogously, when it was acknowledged that Iraq had no weapons of mass destruction, the Bush Administration justification shifted to promoting Middle East democracy and liberating Iraqi women.)

Putin's worldview is obsessively centered on his version of the Trumpian trope, to Make Russia Great Again, with the proviso that Russia has always been great, but its essential, underlying glory had been resented and repressed by outside forces—notably the Swedes, Poles, and Lithuanians a few centuries ago, before that, by the Mongols, and now by the immoral, irreligious, and rapacious West. Along with the arch-conservative Bishop Kirill, "Patriarch of Moscow and all Rus' and Primate of the Russian Orthodox Church"—who provides loyal theological endorsement of his war—Putin has also railed against same-sex marriage and transgender rights, claiming that they represent the epitome of godless decadence, paradoxically combined with immense strength. One can understand why Putin has become a favorite of far-right groups in the United States.

Peter the Great, Putin's fever-dream idol, ruled the Russian Empire from 1682 until 1725, and is, ironically, especially renowned for establishing his namesake city, St. Petersburg, as Russia's "window on the West." Putin is desperate to close that window, while also regaining Russian lands, as his predecessor had done. While visiting an exhibit honoring his predecessor, Putin speechified that "Peter the Great waged the great northern war for twenty-one years. It would seem that he was at war with Sweden, that he took something from them. He did not, he returned [what was Russia's]."[15]

Although Putin's worldview superficially seems consistent, because it posits a thousand-year continuity of Russian greatness ever hobbled by its enemies, internal as well as external, it is in fact contradictory, perceiving Russia as imbued with greatness but also backward and needing spiritual modernization. Similarly, he sees the West as, on the one hand, effete and degenerate, and yet on the other, fiendishly powerful.

In a rambling two-hour speech in February 2023, Putin claimed that the United States and its NATO allies had treated Russia with a "contemptuous and disdainful attitude" and behaved "rudely and unceremoniously from year to year." The collective West has lorded it over Russia in a "state of euphoria created by the feeling of absolute superiority, a kind of modern absolutism." Especially painful was that after the fall of the Soviet Union, the West hadn't treated Russia "professionally, smoothly, patiently."[16] It appears that much of his goal in invading Ukraine has been to assuage his own hurt feelings. And, equally bizarre, he expected that his actions would generate greater respect for Russia and for himself.

Previously, Putin had expressed much of his distorted view of history in a grievance-infused essay published in July 2021, titled "On the Historical Unity of Russians and Ukrainians." In it, he went back to the ninth century, claiming that since then, Ukrainians have been either Russians duped into thinking that they possess a phony identity called "Ukrainian" or are part of an endless stream of traitors to Mother Russia. In the aftermath of stunning Ukrainian battlefield advances in the late summer of 2022, he sounded increasingly unbalanced and paranoid, ranting that the West and the United States have long sought to dismember Russia and turn the remnants into subservient colonies. Moreover, his opponents are practicing "outright Satanism." "They do not want us to be free; they want us to be a colony," he proclaimed in September 2022. "They do not want equal cooperation; they want to loot. They do not want to see us a free society, but a mass of soulless slaves."[17] In his February 2023 speech, he claimed that "they were the ones who started this war,"[18] even as the world had seen films of miles-long columns of Russian armor invading Ukraine twelve months earlier—reminiscent of the quip attributed to Groucho Marx: "Who you gonna believe, me or your own lying eyes"?[i]

We'll never know all of what went on in Putin's mind when he decided to attack Ukraine and when he continued to justify it afterward. Maybe he has simply been lying, or perhaps pretending to believe his own lies while simultaneously knowing their falsity. It is also possible that he has been genuinely deluded. It doesn't really matter, however, because in the real world, beyond each person's psychology, consequences are what counts. And the consequences of the Ukraine War have been nothing less than catastrophic, the biggest blunder of the twenty-first century.

We've looked in turn at Putin's initial errors as well as his likely motivation for invading Ukraine, and some of the consequences of this reckless action. Next, I will try to explain the forces behind those initial errors and what led a seemingly intelligent man (admittedly, a thoroughly immoral one) to go so far astray.

"Confirmation bias" is the widespread tendency to absorb only information that confirms what we already think is true or that we want to be true. Putin's commitment to Making Russia Great Again (MRGA, but with the Russian Orthodox cross instead of red baseball caps) has been so strong that he doubtless wanted to think that most Ukrainians would jump at the chance to be reunited with their fellow Russians. And even if they resisted, that resistance was guaranteed to be weak and half-hearted. Wrong on both counts. He also wanted to believe that the West was so flabby, feeble, and disunited that, if push came to shove and for some reason those benighted Ukrainians resisted his benevolent efforts, they wouldn't receive any effective outside aid. Wrong again.

He is too cagey, however, to have based these conclusions on his opinions alone, without confirmation from outside his own psyche. And here he fell victim to the autocrat's dilemma: the more despotic and single-handed a ruler's reign, the less willing are colleagues and especially subordinates to

---

[i] This is from the Marx Brothers movie *Duck Soup* and was uttered by Chico, disguised as Groucho, when he was discovered in bed with another man's wife.

provide honest information that goes against the boss's preconceptions. Stalin had been caught flat-footed when Hitler invaded the Soviet Union in 1940, just one year after the two despotisms had signed the Molotov-Ribbentrop non-aggression pact, despite the fact that the Soviet dictator had received numerous warnings from independent sources that Operation Barbarossa was about to happen. It has even been reported that Stalin had one of his own spies executed when the spook informed his boss of the imminent attack. For years, the Brits had been working to win Stalin to their side, so he assumed that his loyal, honest subordinate must have been suborned by those sneaky Brits.

Before Putin's invasion of Ukraine, Russian operatives within Ukraine had unlimited opportunities to assess the extent of Ukrainian military preparedness, the mood of the population, and the likely response of the West. Russia has an enormous and mostly effective intelligence service, so it boggles the mind to think that the boss in the Kremlin was as blind-sided as his predecessor, sixty-two years earlier. But he was, and likely for the same reason: confirmation bias on his part combined with reluctance or fear preventing his sycophants from telling Putin the truth. "Sycophancy is the curse of authoritarians," wrote the *Washington Post*'s David van Drehle. He continued:

> Vladimir Putin has wielded so much power for so long that all streams of information have become polluted. The inner circle draws its comforts and privileges from its skill at telling the leader what he wants to hear; the outer circle—wishing to move inward— observes, and learns to lie. Sooner or later, the leader makes a truly bad decision that springs reality from the prison of lies. For Putin, that bad decision is the invasion of Ukraine. All of Russia is not as stupid as this decision would suggest—but the Russians who correctly perceived the patriotism of the Ukrainian people had no way to warn Putin. The Russians who knew about the weakness of their army had no avenue to inform Putin. The Russians who understood the latent strength of the West weren't welcome

around Putin. The Russians familiar with the unpreparedness of the civilian reserves weren't consulted by Putin. All the leader heard was the groveling echo of his own misconceptions.[19]

Stalin refused to believe the truth: that he was about to be invaded. The result was more than twenty million Soviets dead. Putin almost certainly wasn't told the truth: about the country he was about to invade and about the poor state of Russian military preparedness. And insofar as anyone levelled with him, he likely didn't believe what he was told. The outcome of Putin's war is impossible to predict. It has already been terrible for innumerable Ukrainians and Russians. Many in the West—and likely in Russia, too—are hoping that it will be terrible for Mr. Putin as well. (Although Kremlin observers have warned that if he is replaced, the new leader could be even worse.)

It is possible that because he has backed himself into a corner and seems to be constitutionally unable to accept defeat, something hitherto unimaginable might happen, namely, resort to nuclear weapons. In this regard it is especially worrisome that Putin seems to have embraced something of a death cult. In November 2022, he addressed a carefully assembled audience supposedly consisting of mothers of mobilized soldiers, but mostly pro-Putin activists and relatives of government officials. "One day we will all leave this world," he said. "The question is how we lived. With some people, it is unclear whether they live or not. It is unclear why they die, because of vodka or something else. When they are gone, it is hard to say whether they lived or not. Their lives passed without notice. But a man who died in war did not leave his life for nothing. His life was important."[20] It was the Roman gladiators' announcement, "We who are about to die salute you," modified to the "Putin mir" command version: "You who are about to die, salute me!" (And be willing to die for me and my war.)

Historically, the Russian people have shown an extraordinary ability—and, it appears, willingness—to do precisely this, enduring great loss in order to prevail. During World War II, which they call the Great Patriotic War, more Soviets died during a single battle, the siege of Leningrad, than were lost by the United States, United Kingdom, and France combined during the entire war. It has been reliably estimated that during the battle of Stalingrad, for every *one* German, Romanian, Hungarian, and Italian invader who died, the Soviets lost more than *ten*. And yet, the USSR won those battles and the war. Given this and the brute fact that Russia is many times larger than Ukraine in population, land area, military strength, and that it retains—despite sanctions—a potent economy, it is difficult to see Russia losing a drawn-out war of attrition, despite the immensity of Putin's blunder.

Moreover, in addition to its strategic arsenal, Russia has the world's largest stockpile of comparatively low yield battlefield bombs and warheads. If he uses even one in a desperate effort to stave off defeat, it would be disastrous in many ways, including the possibility that one mistake will lead to another, ending—quite literally—in all-out nuclear war. There is also no scenario in which "going nuclear" would help Putin win his war, but if he is sufficiently desperate or detached from reality, it is at least possible that he might try. Thus far, Russian failures and Ukrainian successes have only induced him to double down, adding one mistake upon another. On September 21, 2022, in a national address announcing his increased military mobilization, Putin said, "When the territorial integrity of our country is threatened, we will certainly use all the means at our disposal to protect Russia and our people. This is not a bluff."[21] There is no doubt that among these "means" are nuclear weapons. When someone says, "This is not a bluff," it's likely a bluff. But we can't know for sure.

In his collection, "Dramatis Personae," the poet Robert Browning wrote that "a man's reach should exceed his grasp, Or what's a heaven for?" It is clear that when Putin reached for Ukraine, it was beyond his grasp. Never mind heaven: we'll all be fortunate if his over-reaching doesn't lead us all to hell.

Epilogue

"**W**e learn from experience," wrote George Bernard Shaw, "that no one ever learns from experience." Make that *from their own experience.* But from *someone else's?* There is much to learn from the experience of others, particularly their blunders. What then can a reader learn from this book? Start with the fact that everyone makes mistakes, even some of the most renowned among us: so, be kind to yourself. Because mistakes are universal, you'll make some, too. Go ahead and blame yourself if you deserve it. But learn from your oops, instead of hating yourself for them or bitching and moaning that whatever has gone wrong is someone else's fault, or the result of malign fate.

It has become popular to replace automobile "accident" with "crash" or "collision," and for good reason. To be sure, accidents happen and always will, but the word obscures the reality that in most cases, a car crash is the result of someone going too fast, being inattentive, driving in unsafe conditions, or the like. But whatever the cause, a crash is the result, and using that word removes any suggestion that no one or no thing is responsible.

The oops recounted in this book were not accidents; they were errors that could have and should have been avoided. Direct lessons from these blunders? Some are easy. "Don't go the wrong way on a football field" (Jim Marshall's run). And don't do it in any other context. Also "Don't fly blind into heavy clouds" (as Wrong-Way Corrigan claimed). Others are a bit more subtle. "Don't hesitate to quit while you're ahead—or at least, not too far behind" (Napoleon's rejection of Metternich's Frankfurt Proposal), "Don't over-reach" (Napoleon again, when he invaded Egypt, then Portugal, and, most of all, Russia), as well as when Hitler made a comparable oops, invading the Soviet Union. "Don't let yourself be carried away by a charismatic, fast-talking jerk" (Alcibiades and Athens' Sicilian silliness). "Beware of wishful thinking" (the Spanish Armada, and the Japanese attack on Pearl Harbor). "It's good to be trusting, but not to be a sucker" (Varus and the Battle of Teutoburg Forest). "If it seems too good—or too bizarre—to be true, it probably is" (the Trojan Horse). "When planning something big, dangerous, and difficult, make sure that your compatriots are competent" (the assassination of Archduke Ferdinand). "Comfort is good, luxury is even better—but only if you can afford it, and if it doesn't bog you down and leave you helpless in the middle of a screaming wilderness, constantly ambushed by those who hate you" (Gentleman Johnny in the run-up to the Battle of Saratoga). "Interrogate your own assumptions, and don't trust sycophants" (Putin). "Don't start throwing your weight around until you have a good estimate of how much weight you really have" (Putin again, and George W. Bush in Iraq and Afghanistan). "Refrain from adultery, or if you can't, don't get caught" (Bill Clinton, Newt Gingrich, Gary Hart, Mark Sanford et al.). "Don't believe everything you hear or read" (except for this book!).

In conclusion, take seriously the prospect of failure, of blundering, of oopsing, and try to identify what could possibly go wrong, while not letting those possibilities lead to paralysis. One way to avoid making a mistake is to do nothing. Sometimes, that's best. Other times, a decision or an action is called for. Either way, and whenever possible, try to cultivate what we might call a sense of imaginative realism. And be open to the unexpected.

Stephen Crane is best known for his novel *The Red Badge of Courage*. He also wrote short stories, essays, and some dark, strange, and compelling poems. Here's a good one to end on:

God fashioned the ship of the world carefully.
With the infinite skill of an All-Master
Made He the hull and the sails,
Held He the rudder
Ready for adjustment.
Erect stood He, scanning His work proudly.
Then—at fateful time—a wrong called,
And God turned, heeding.
Lo, the ship, at this opportunity, slipped slyly,
Making cunning noiseless travel down the ways.
So that, forever rudderless, it went upon the seas
Going ridiculous voyages,
Making quaint progress,
Turning as with serious purpose
Before stupid winds.
And there were many in the sky
Who laughed at this thing.

Acknowledgments

Nearly always, many people contribute to the writing of a book. Not in this case: I pretty much wrote it by myself, which seems appropriate because nearly every mistake examined in this book was largely due to one person. So, insofar as *OOPS!* is a mistake, I have continued that one-person tradition.

There are a few exceptions, however, so please blame them for any especially egregious oops. Judith Lipton first suggested that a book about blunders would be a good idea; in a moment of credulousness and weakness, I agreed. Eli Altman made several suggestions about material to add (I followed two of them, probably the wrong ones). Eric Myers agreed to waste his time by representing the project and did so, I admit, most ably. Caroline Russomanno at Skyhorse Publishing agreed, for some reason, to publish it. She also did the line-editing whereupon her eagle-eye caught many of my errors . . . but probably not all of them. (Any that remain are entirely her fault. Certainly not mine.) Tony Lyons, Skyhorse's publisher, tried to dissuade me from the title; he failed, so we'll never know how wrong I was in sticking with it. My grandchildren did their best to keep me from writing this book, but alas, they also failed.

Notes

Chapter 1

1   Nietzsche, Fredrich. *Human, All Too Human*. transl: Alexander Harvey, Chicago: Charles H. Kerr and Co. 1878.
2   Ovid. *Metamorphoses*. transl. David Raeburn and. Denis Feaney. New York: Penguin. 2004.

Chapter 2

1   This and other quotations from *Frankenstein* are from the 1818 edition, reprinted by Penguin, New York, 2018.
2   Ibid.
3   Ibid.
4   Ibid.
5   Ibid.

Chapter 3

1 Thucydides. *The Peloponnesian War*, (Book 2.34-46).

2 Hanson, Neil. *The Confident Hope of a Miracle: The True History of the Spanish Armada*. New York: Knopf, 2005.

3 Williams, T. Harry. *Lincoln and His Generals*. Bexley, OH: Gramercy Books, 2001.

4 Williams, T. Harry. *2001*.

5 Williams, T. Harry. *2001*.

6 Sears, Steven W. *Controversies and Commanders: Dispatches from the Army of the Potomac*. New York: Mariner Books, 2000.

7 Boritt, Gabor S. *Why the Confederacy Lost*. New York: Oxford University Press, 1992 .

8 Quoted in Fuller, J. F. C. *Grant and Lee: A Study in Personality and Generalship*. Bloomington: Indiana University Press, 1957.

9 Service, Robert. *The Last of the Tsars: Nicholas II and the Russia Revolution*. Oakland, Ca.: Pegasus Books. 2018.

10 Dimbleby, Jonathan. *Operation Barbarossa: The History of a Cataclysm*. New York: Oxford University Press, 2021.

11 Gordon, Elaine Sciolino, with Michael R.; Times, Special to The New York Times (1990). "U.S. Gave Iraq Little Reason Not to Mount Kuwait Assault." *The New York Times*. ISSN 0362-4331. Retrieved 8 May 2021.

12 Hastings, Max. *The Korean War*. New York: Simon & Schuster, 1988.

Chapter 4

1 Quoted in Nevins, Michael. *Meanderings in New Jersey's Medical History*. Bloomington, IND: iUniverse, Inc., 2011.

2 Quoted in Gordon, Richard. *The Alarming History of Medicine: Amusing Anecdotes from Hippocrates to Heart Transplants*. New York: St. Martin's Press, 1997.

3 Quoted in Blum, Deborah. *The Poisoner's Handbook: Murder and the Birth of Forensic Medicine in Jazz Age New York*. New York: Penguin, 2010.

4 H M Connolly, J L Crary, M D McGoon, D D Hensrud, B S Edwards, W D Edwards, H V Schaff. "Valvular heart disease associated with fenfluramine-phentermine." *New England Journal of Medicine.* 1997. 337(9):581-8.

5 Weiner, Norbert. *Cybernetics or Control and Communication in the Animal and the Machine.* Cambridge, Mass: MIT Press, 1948.

6 Moniz, Ernest. "Prefrontal Leucotomy in the Treatment of Mental Disorders." *American Journal of Psychiatry.* 1937. Retrieved August 21, 2020 from https://books.google.com/books?id=tXd98Ify7WgC&pg=PA237%7Cchapter&hl=en#v=onepage&q&f=false.

7 Cronkite, Walter. *Eye on the World.* New York: Cowles Book Company. 1971.

8 Hanage, W.P., Testa, C., Chen, J.T. *et al.* "COVID-19: US federal accountability for entry, spread, and inequities—lessons for the future." *Eur J Epidemiol* 35, 995–1006 (2020). https://doi.org/10.1007/s10654 -020-00689-2.

9 Anonymous. "The Federal Governments Coronavirus Actions and Failures. The Brookings Institution. 2020. https://www.brookings.edu /research/the-federal-governments-coronavirus-actions-and-failures -timeline-and-themes/.

10 Wood, Daniel and Geoff Brumfiel. "Pro-Trump counties now have far higher COVID death rates. Misinformation is to blame." 2021 https:// www.npr.org/sections/health-shots/2021/12/05/1059828993/data -vaccine-misinformation-trump-counties-covid-death-rate.

11 Lahut, Jake. "His People are Going to Suffer and That's Their Problem," Business Insider, 2020 https://africa.businessinsider.com/politics /his-people-are-going-to-suffer-and-thats-their-problem-jared -kushner-said-new-york/k56kz0y.

12 Colvin, Jeff. "The biggest errors the Trump administration made in response to COVID," 2020, https://fortune.com/2020/11/13/covid -trump-administration-mishandling-mistakes-coronavirus/.

13 Ibid.

14 Hope Yen, Lauran Neergaard and Candice Choi. "AP FACT CHECK: Trump distorts on vaccine, state distribution" 2020 AP News, https://apnews.com/article/ap-fact-check-joe-biden-donald-trump-politics-coronavirus-pandemic-76d1580f82b1586b207990396c1e3b5f.

15 Anderson, Stuart. "Trump Takes Credit For Vaccine Created By Others, Including Immigrants." 2020, *Forbes* https://www.forbes.com/sites/stuartanderson/2020/12/01/trump-takes-credit-for-vaccine-created-by-others-including-immigrants/?sh=4c551c7b374c.

16 Ibid.

17 Holtgrave, Dave. "12 ways the Trump administration botched America's response to Covid-19," CNN. 2020. https://www.cnn.com/2020/10/29/opinions/ways-trump-botched-covid-response-holtgrave/index.htm.

18 Ibid.

19 Singh, Maanvi. "Trump's case of coronavirus was far worse than he admitted, report says," *The Guardian* 2021 https://www.theguardian.com/us-news/2021/feb/11/trump-coronavirus-ventilator-covid-illness.

20 Solender, Andrew. "All The Times Trump Has Promoted Hydroxychloroquine" *Forbes*. 2020. https://www.forbes.com/sites/andrewsolender/2020/05/22/all-the-times-trump-promoted-hydroxychloroquine/?sh=4fb907d24643.

21 Ibid.

22 Ibid.

23 David Holtgrave, 2020.

24 Ibid.

25 Michael D. Shear and Maggie Haberman. "Health Dept. Official Says Doubts on Hydroxychloroquine Led to His Ouster" *New York Times*, 2021, https://www.nytimes.com/2020/04/22/us/politics/rick-bright-trump-hydroxychloroquine-coronavirus.html.

26 Stolberg, Sheryl Gay. "A Mad Scramble to Stock Millions of Malaria Pills, Likely for Nothing" *New York Times*, 2020. https://www.nytimes.com/2020/06/16/us/politics/trump-hydroxychloroquine-coronavirus.html.

27 Cathay, Libby. "Timeline: Tracking Trump alongside scientific developments on hydroxychloroquine" ABC NEWS. 2020 https://abcnews.go.com/Health/timeline-tracking-trump-alongside-scientific-developments-hydroxychloroquine/story?id=72170553.

28 Holtgrave, 2020.

29 Ruper, Aaron. "Trump just mused about whether disinfectant injections could treat the coronavirus. Really" *Vox.* 2020. https://www.vox.com/2020/4/23/21233628/trump-disinfectant-injections-sunlight-coronavirus-briefing.

30 Sapolsky, Robert. personal communication.

31 Reverby, Susan. *Examining Tuskegee: The Infamous Syphilis Study and its Legacy.* 2009. Chapel Hill, North Carolina: The University of North Carolina Press.

Chapter 5

1 "Summary of the Final Report on Hwang's Research Allegation". Seoul National University Investigation Committee. January 10, 2006.

2 Kai Bird and Martin J. Sherwin. *American Prometheus: The Triumph and Tragedy of J. Robert Oppenheimer* 2006. New York: Vintage Books.

3 Ibid.

4 I thank Martin Hellman for pointing out the nuclear relevance of the Concorde disaster.

5 Constable, Pamela. "Kashmir: High Stakes at High Altitudes" *Washington Post.* 1999 https://www.washingtonpost.com/archive/politics/1999/06/25/kashmir-high-stakes-at-high-altitudes/fb4a6712-e14b-454c-b2b4-6cfe6ea66cc3/.

6 Davis, Nicola. "Soviet submarine officer who averted nuclear war honoured with prize" *The Guardian.* 2017 https://www.theguardian.com/science/2017/oct/27/vasili-arkhipov-soviet-submarine-captain-who-averted-nuclear-war-awarded-future-of-life-prize.

7 Barash, David P. *Threats: Intimidation and its Discontents.* New York: Oxford University Press, 2020.

8 Ibid.

9 Jones, Nate. *Able Archer 83: The Secret History of the NATO Exercise That Almost Triggered Nuclear War*. New York: The New Press. 2016.

10 Stern, Fritz; Charles, Daniel; Nasser, Latif; Kaufman, Fred (2012). "How Do You Solve a Problem Like Fritz Haber?". *Radiolab* (Interview). Interviewed by Jad Abumrad, Robert Krulwich. New York, NY: WNYC.

11 Charles, Daniel. *Master mind : the rise and fall of Fritz Haber, the Nobel laureate who launched the age of chemical warfare* New York, NY: Ecco. 2005.

12 Friedrich, Bretislav; Hoffmann, Dieter; Renn, Jürgen; Schmaltz, Florian (eds.), Clara Immerwahr: *A Life in the Shadow of Fritz Haber, One Hundred Years of Chemical Warfare: Research, Deployment, Consequences*, New York: Springer International Publishing, 2017.

13 Ibid.

14 Grossman, Lisa. "Metric Math Mistake Muffed Mars Meteorology Mission". *Wired*. 2010. https://www.wired.com/2010/11/1110mars -climate-observer-report/.

15 Siddiqi, Asif A. *Beyond Earth: A Chronicle of Deep Space Exploration, 1958-2016*. Washington, DC: NASA History Program Office, 2018.

16 Squire, J. C. *Collected Poems*. London: Macmillan 1959.

17 Dennett, Daniel. *Darwin's Dangerous Idea*. New York: Simon & Schuster. 1996.

18 "Kelvin On Science." *The Newark Advocate*, 1902, https://zapatopi.net /kelvin/papers/interview_aeronautics_and_wireless.html.

19 Goldschmidt, Richard. *The Material Basis of Evolution*. New Haven, Conn: Yale University Press. 1940.

20 Gregory, Jane. *Fred Hoyle's Universe*. Oxford, UK: Oxford University Press. 2005.

Chapter 6

1 Creamer, Robert W. *Babe: The Legend Comes to Life* (First Fireside ed.). New York: Simon & Schuster. 1974.

2   Lieb, Fred. *Baseball As I Have Known It*. New York: Coward, McCann and Geoghagen. 1977.

3   Stout, Glenn. *The Selling of the Babe: The Deal That Changed Baseball and Created a Legend*. Thomas Dunne Books. 2016.

4   Smelser, Marshall. *The Life That Ruth Built*. New York: Quadrangle/ New York Times Book Co. 1975.

5   Corrigan, Douglas. *That's My Story* New York: E.P. Dutton, 1938.

6   Knickerbocker, H.R. *Is Tomorrow Hitler's? 200 Questions On the Battle of Mankind*. New York: Reynal & Hitchcock. 1941.

7   Goldstein, Richard. "Revisiting Wrong Way Riegels" *The New York Times*. 2003. *https://www.nytimes.com/2003/12/25/sports/college-football -revisiting-wrong-way-riegels.html*.

8   Shoemaker, Willie. *Shoemaker*. Arlington, VA: Andrea/Brian Press. 1984.

9   https://www.youtube.com/watch?v=7ujwjqIldwU.

Chapter 7

1   McFadden, Christopher. "From DVDs to streaming, here's the incredible history of Netflix" 2020. https://interestingengineering.com/culture /the-fascinating-history-of-netflix.

2   Morris, Chris. "12 corporate blunders that could have been avoided" CNBC Leadership Insights. 2015. https://www.cnbc.com /2015/04/03/12-corporate-blunders-that-could-have-been-avoided .html#:~:text=Toys%20'R'%20Us&text=The%20petition%20 yielded%209%2C000%20signatures,%E2%80%9CI'm%20so%20mad.

3   Ibid.

4   Bonsall, Thomas E. *Disaster in Dearborn: The Story of the Edsel*. Stanford, CA: Stanford University Press. 2002.

5   Ibid.

6   Ibid.

7   Bausells, Marta. "JK Rowling's life advice: ten quotes on the lessons of failure" The Guardian. 2015. https://www.theguardian.com/books /booksblog/2015/mar/30/jk-rowling-very-good-lives-advice-10 -quotes-lessons-of-failure.

8   Ferri, Jessica. "15 Famous Books That Were Initially Rejected" *Early Bird Books*. 2015. https://earlybirdbooks.com/15-famous-books-that-were-initially-rejected.

9   Verillo, Erica. "Publishers Say the Darndest Things" Medium. 2016. https://curiosityneverkilledthewriter.com/publishers-say-the-darndest-things-dff9838090aa.

10 Carter, Alex. "17 Famous Authors and Their Rejections" Mental Floss 2017. https://www.mentalfloss.com/article/91169/16-famous-authors-and-their-rejections.

Chapter 8

1   van Brugen, Isabel. "Liz Cheney Fires Warning to Pro-Trump Republicans During Jan. 6 Hearing". *Newsweek*. 2022. https://www.newsweek.com/liz-cheney-warning-pro-trump-republicans-january-6-hearing-panel-1714615.

2   Coleman, Ken. "On this day in 1967: Gov. George Romney says he was 'brainwashed' on Vietnam War" Michigan Advance. 2021. https://michiganadvance.com/blog/on-this-day-in-1967-gov-george-romney-says-he-was-brainwashed-on-vietnam-war/.

3   Gwertzman, Bernard. *"Ford Denies Moscow Dominates East Europe" The New York Times. 1976. https://www.nytimes.com/1976/10/07/archives/ford-denies-moscow-dominates-east-europe-carter-rebuts-him-ford.html*.

4   Bai, Matt. "How Gary Hart's Downfall Forever Changed American Politics" *New York Times Magazine*. https://www.nytimes.com/2014/09/21/magazine/how-gary-harts-downfall-forever-changed-american-politics.html.

5   Hammer, Mike. "Sex Charges End Hart's Campaign" *The Oklahoman* https://www.oklahoman.com/story/news/1987/05/09/sex-charges-end-harts-campaign/62690669007/.

6   Simon, Roger. 2007. "Questions that kill candidates' careers". Politico https://www.politico.com/story/2007/04/questions-that-kill-candidates-careers-003617.

NOTES

7 Marlow, Shirley. "Dukakis Was Upset His Reply on Death Had No Life" Los Angeles Times. 1989. https://www.latimes.com/archives/la-xpm -1989-07-26-mn-10-story.html.

8 King, Josh. "Dukakis and the Tank". *Politico*. 2013. https://www.politico .com/magazine/story/2013/11/dukakis-and-the-tank-099119/.

9 Anonymous Russia: Excerpts From Putin's State-Of-The-Nation Speech Radio Free Europe/Radio Liberty. 2005. https://www.rferl .org/a/1058630.html.

10 Lyall, Sarah, and Mark Landler. "David Cameron Is Sorry. Really, Really Sorry" *New York Times*. 2021. *https://www.nytimes .com/2019/09/20/world/europe/david-cameron-brexit-sorry.html*.

11 Martin, Michelle, and Emma Bowman. "David Cameron Talks Brexit And His 'Greatest Regret' In New Book 'For The Record'" npr. 2019. https://www.npr.org/2019/09/29/764199387/david-cameron-calls -the-brexit-referendum-his-greatest-regret.

12 Ibid.

13 Freedman, Lawrence. *The Future of War. A History*. New York: Publi-cAffairs 2017.

14 Friedman, Thomas. "Putin and Netanyahu Show Why Bad Things Happen to Bad Leaders" *New York Times*. 2023. https://www .nytimes.com/2023/03/14/opinion/benjamin-netanyahu-israel-putin -russia.html.

15 Roth, Andrew. "Putin compares himself to Peter the Great in quest to take back Russian lands" *The Guardian*. 2022. https://www.theguardian .com/world/2022/jun/10/putin-compares-himself-to-peter-the-great -in-quest-to-take-back-russian-lands.

16 Ignatius, Peter. "What a year of war has revealed of three leaders" *The Washington Post*. 2023. https://www.washingtonpost.com/opinions /2023/02/21/ukraine-war-anniversary-zelensky-biden-putin/.

17 Dixon, Robyn, and Catherine Belton. "Putin, czar with no empire, needs military victory for his own survival" *The Washington Post*. 2023. https://www.washingtonpost.com/world/2023/02/20/putin-czar -with-no-empire-needs-military-victory-his-own-survival/.

18 Ignatius, 2023.

19 van Drehle, David. "Putin is limping toward an endgame in Ukraine. Should the West go along?" *The Washington Post*. 2022. https://www .washingtonpost.com/opinions/2022/09/27/ukraine-putin-annexation -should-west-agree/.

20 Dixon and Belton, 2023.

21 Roche, Darragh. "Vladimir Putin Issues Nuclear Threat Over Ukraine— 'This Is Not a Bluff'" *Newsweek*. 2022. https://www.newsweek .com/vladimir-putin-threatens-nuclear-strikes-over-ukraine-this-not -bluff-1744758.

Index

NOTES

NOTES

NOTES

NOTES

NOTES

NOTES

NOTES

NOTES

NOTES

NOTES

NOTES

NOTES

NOTES